Quantitative Research for the Qualitative Researcher

Quantitative Research for the Qualitative Researcher

Laura M. O'Dwyer
Boston College

James A. Bernauer
Robert Morris University

Los Angeles | London | New Delhi
Singapore | Washington DC

Los Angeles | London | New Delhi
Singapore | Washington DC

FOR INFORMATION:

SAGE Publications, Inc.

2455 Teller Road

Thousand Oaks, California 91320

E-mail: order@sagepub.com

SAGE Publications Ltd.

1 Oliver's Yard

55 City Road

London EC1Y 1SP

United Kingdom

SAGE Publications India Pvt. Ltd.

B 1/I 1 Mohan Cooperative Industrial Area

Mathura Road, New Delhi 110 044

India

SAGE Publications Asia-Pacific Pte. Ltd.

3 Church Street

#10-04 Samsung Hub

Singapore 049483

Copyright © 2014 by SAGE Publications, Inc.

Library of Congress Cataloging-in-Publication Data

A catalog record of this book is available from the Library of Congress.

9781412997799

Acquisitions Editor: Reid Hester

Editorial Assistant: Sarita Sarak

Production Editor: Brittany Bauhaus

Copy Editor: QuADS Prepress (P) Ltd.

Typesetter: C&M Digitals (P) Ltd.

Proofreader: Laura Webb

Indexer: Diggs Publication Services, Inc.

Cover Designer: Scott Van Atta

Marketing Manager: Terra Schultz

Permissions Editor: Karen Ehrmann

13 14 15 16 17 10 9 8 7 6 5 4 3 2 1

Brief Contents

Detailed Contents

Chapter 5: Measurement and Instrumentation in Quantitative Research 98

Chapter 6: Minimizing Alternative Explanations for Research Findings: Internal Validity 135

Preface

Thank you for choosing to read *Quantitative Research for the Qualitative Researcher!* Our intention is to provide an introduction to quantitative research methods in the social sciences and education especially for those who have been trained in, or are currently learning, qualitative methods. This book might also be a useful supplement for courses in quantitative methods at the upper undergraduate or graduate levels. There are two important features of this book worth noting. The "Guidelines for Evaluating Research Reports" found in the Appendix can be used to extend understanding of any quantitative article by providing an organized way to examine essential features that are described in this book. In addition, we reference several quantitative articles on a companion website in appropriate sections of the book and allow readers to make immediate connections to the ideas being discussed. Using these articles in conjunction with the *Guidelines* and relevant sections of the text can provide an even deeper understanding of important ideas and concepts.

❖ PURPOSE OF THIS BOOK

Why should qualitative researchers want to learn more about the quantitative tradition? This question has been foremost in our minds as we developed the original idea for this book and as we formulated each chapter. We came to the realization early on that we view research in the social sciences as an exciting quest for discovery using disciplined inquiry, regardless of whether this inquiry is located in the qualitative or quantitative tradition. Our primary goal therefore in writing this book is to promote understanding and appreciation of the quantitative tradition in the social sciences especially for those who are most familiar with the qualitative tradition. By expanding their knowledge, skills, and appreciation of the quantitative tradition, we hope that our readers will acquire an enhanced repertoire of tools for reading, evaluating, and conducting research. In addition, we hope that our readers will develop an appetite for collaborating with colleagues who pose interesting research questions that can be addressed across traditions.

While an increasing number of books present a balanced approach to quantitative, qualitative, and mixed methods (e.g., Gay, Mills, & Airasian, 2009; Johnson & Christensen, 2000; Springer, 2010), we think that our contribution is a digestible book that concisely conveys the fundamental concepts and skills underlying quantitative methods by identifying the commonalities that exist between the quantitative and qualitative traditions. These concepts, skills, and commonalities can then be used as a springboard for further learning in both traditions.

While this book is intended primarily for those practicing or aspiring researchers who are predisposed to use qualitative methods, it is intended neither to try to convert qualitative researchers to the quantitative tradition nor to make "mixed methods" researchers out of them. Rather, its central aim is to promote understanding and appreciation of the two traditions based on the fact that the complexity inherent in both people and phenomena are consistent with possessing such understanding and appreciation. It is with complete agreement with the sentiment attributed to Albert Einstein "many of the things you can count, don't count. Many of the things you can't count really count" that we undertook this book.

This book grew out of our experience in teaching research design, analysis, and statistics to undergraduate and graduate students in the fields of social science and education. Whereas James teaches qualitative research methods at Robert Morris University in Pittsburgh, Laura teaches quantitative methods at Boston College. Many of our doctoral students gravitate toward qualitative dissertations, and while this may reflect their true aspirations and predispositions, we think that this choice may sometimes be based on a sense of foreboding toward anything connected to that dreaded 10-letter word—statistics!

While this book is *not* intended to convince individuals to switch to a quantitative mind-set, it *is* intended to demonstrate that all research traditions (quantitative, qualitative, mixed) share the common goal of trying to discover new knowledge by using a systematic approach. By providing a clear description of concepts underlying quantitative methodology, we hope to promote openness to this tradition and the recognition that the appropriateness of using a particular method depends on the questions asked and not a "posture" that has come to characterize practitioners in each tradition (Guba, 1981). While some of us tend to ask questions that can best be answered by "crunching numbers," others ask questions that require "crunching words." However, no matter what kind of crunching one may do, it is first necessary to have quality data that have been collected in a systematic and reflective manner. To put it another way, we hope that readers come to recognize that qualitative and quantitative approaches are not intrinsically antagonistic; in fact, we hope that by the time you have read this book that you understand why the two traditions are complementary.

We also want to demonstrate that good quantitative research is not primarily about statistics but rather about *problem quality, design quality, evidence quality,* and *procedural quality.* These criteria apply equally to qualitative research. Unfortunately, we have found that while most faculty consider the "paradigm wars" a thing of the past, mistrust or at least misunderstanding still exists in the ranks. Thus, another goal of this book is to promote a greater willingness to integrate quantitative and qualitative approaches in teaching, learning, and research.

❖ THE AUTHORS

A little bit about ourselves: James's background is rather eclectic; he taught in secondary education, special education, and, for a time, worked in banking and non-profit administration. Though initially trained in quantitative methods, James transitioned to the qualitative tradition several years ago and now considers himself primarily a qualitative researcher. At Robert Morris University, James teaches research methodology and educational psychology and his research interests include both K–12 education and higher education. Laura has spent most of her career in the academy. Although originally trained in applied physics, electronics, and geophysics, she made the switch to educational research more than 15 years ago. At Boston College, Laura teaches quantitative research methods and statistics, and her research focuses on the impact of school-based interventions on student and teacher outcomes, often technology based. We think that this strange admixture of backgrounds has helped us produce a book that will engage readers of a qualitative bent who are nonetheless open to make an overture to the "other side". While this openness may be driven by a variety of motives, such as to fulfill a university requirement, supplement a qualitative course, increase self-efficacy, or simply satisfy curiosity, we have tried to write a book that readers will come to consider well worth their investment in time and treasure.

❖ INTENDED AUDIENCE

We would now like to be a little more explicit in regard to the content and intended audience for this book. As described earlier, our aim is to promote an appreciation and increased understanding of the fundamental structure and aims of quantitative methods primarily for readers who may have little or dated background in this area. Although "appreciation" is attitudinal and "understanding" is cognitive, we think that these two desired outcomes are intrinsically connected. If one learns a bit more about quantitative methods but still considers its practice akin to voodoo, then what have we gained? Rather, we hope that qualitative readers leave this sojourn feeling even better about their own preferred methodological leanings, with an appreciation that some problems of interest are more amenable to quantitative methods and that quantitative methods can complement qualitative perspectives in ways that they may not have envisioned previously.

Like most authors, we would like to think that people the world over will find this book so intriguing that they may take it to remote idyllic beaches to find pearls of wisdom; however, we have reluctantly accepted the fact that perhaps this vision may be a bit grand. We do think, however, that graduate students and upper-level undergraduate students will find that this book reinforces and perhaps expands what they are learning while offering additional insights. In addition, although this book could be used as a stand-alone text for an introductory course in quantitative research methods, it would probably be more useful as a complementary text to help build a bridge between the qualitative and quantitative traditions.

❖ ORGANIZATION OF THIS BOOK

This text is divided into 11 chapters, divided over four sections. We have interspersed definitions of key terms and concepts in all chapters and include a glossary at the end of each chapter. Starting in Chapter 3, we include a section at the end of each chapter that refers to published articles as examples of how quantitative research is conducted, described, and interpreted. In total, six published articles are described, two or three at the end of each chapter. We hope that these real-world research examples will help readers break down the components of quantitative research and galvanize their understanding of the concepts and methods covered in this text. An overview of the six articles is provided in Table P.1, and the complete published versions are available at **www.sagepub.com/odwyer**. Also, to complement the text, we provide an appendix that contains guidelines for evaluating research reports (e.g., journal articles, dissertations, etc.). Although these guidelines are "slanted" toward quantitative research, we show parallels with qualitative research that are consistent with the theme of this book. At the end of each chapter, we have included discussion questions that have been designed not so much to arrive at precise answers but rather to promote creative thinking about the linkages between quantitative and qualitative research traditions.

Section I, titled "Research in the Social Sciences: Qualitative Meets Quantitative," comprises Chapters 1 to 3. In these chapters, we provide an advance organizer in the form of a description of research in general—including its aims and methods. Our intent here is to first provide information about what constitutes "quality research." Because it is our contention that there is a fundamental unity underlying all research, we next discuss the unifying concepts of research that apply regardless of whether one is examining problems through a quantitative

Table P.1   Summary of the Research Articles Referred to in This Text

Article No.	Reference	Research Design	Sample and Data
Article 1	Yang, Y., Cho, Y., Mathew, S., & Worth, S. (2011). College student effort expenditure in online versus face-to-face courses: The role of gender, team learning orientation, and sense of classroom community. *Journal of Advanced Academics*, 22(4), 619–638.	Non-experimental, cross-sectional study with descriptive and predictive objectives	Convenience sample of 799 college students at a midwestern university
Article 2	Clayton, J. K. (2011). Changing diversity in U.S. schools: The impact on elementary student performance and achievement. *Education and Urban Society*, 43(6), 671–695.	Non-experimental, longitudinal trend study with descriptive and predictive objectives	Purposive sample of 24 school districts with 56,056 fifth graders in Virginia

Article No.	Reference	Research Design	Sample and Data
Article 3	Porfeli, E., Wang, C., Audette, R., McColl, A., & Algozzine, B. (2009). Influence of social and community capital on student achievement in a large urban school district. *Education and Urban Society, 42*(1), 72–95.	Non-experimental, cross-sectional study with descriptive and predictive objectives	Purposive sample of 80 elementary schools from an urban school district in the southeast
Article 4	Núñez, A, Sparks, P. J., & Hernández, E. A. (2011). Latino access to community colleges and Hispanic-serving institutions: A national study. *Journal of Hispanic Higher Education, 10*(1), 18–40.	Non-experimental, cross-sectional study with descriptive and predictive objectives	Stratified random sample of first time, first year college students available in a nationally representative BPS:04 data set
Article 5	Van Voorhis, F. L. (2011). Adding families to the homework equation: A longitudinal study of mathematics achievement. *Education and Urban Society, 43*(3), 313–338.	Quasi-experimental, longitudinal panel study with non-random assignment to treatment and control conditions	Convenience sample of 135 third-grade students in four elementary schools in a southeastern urban school district, followed over 2 years.
Article 6	Booksh, R. L., Pella, R. D., Singh, A. N., & Gouvier, W. D. (2010). Ability of college students to simulate ADHD on objective measures of attention. *Journal of Attention Disorders, 13*(4), 325–338.	True experimental cross-sectional study with random assignment to treatment and control conditions	Convenience sample of 110 undergraduates enrolled in a psychology course at a southern university.

Note: BPS:04, Beginning Postsecondary Students Longitudinal Study 2004.

or qualitative lens. We also try to explicate the difference between "problem finding" and "problem solving" and how these differences also help traverse the qualitative–quantitative continuum. However, we also give some background about the "paradigm wars," highlighting that while there is a fundamental unity between the traditions, differences remain, some of which are significant. We conclude Section

I by explicating the purposes, philosophical assumptions, methods, and further conceptions of the "quality" of qualitative research, followed by a similar treatment of quantitative research. The sequence of qualitative followed by quantitative discussion is not accidental, but rather, it is based on the assumption that most of our readers are qualitatively inclined. Our sequencing of the content is designed to help those readers transition from thinking qualitatively to thinking quantitatively. In Chapter 3, we begin to include sections called "Connections to Qualitative Research." These sections are designed to help our readers gain a better understanding of the quantitative tradition by pointing out salient concepts, terminology, and perspectives that "connect" to the qualitative tradition.

In Section II, titled "The Sine Qua Non for Conducting Research in the Quantitative Tradition," we engage readers with the essentials of conducting research in the quantitative tradition. In Chapters 4 through 6, we provide an overview of the sampling and external validity, instrumentation and measurement, and internal validity, respectively. Our coverage of these topics is purposefully presented prior to our coverage of the most common quantitative research designs and data analysis procedures. We organized the text this way because we believe that our readers will be able to develop a more complete understanding of quantitative research designs if they understand the common principles that underlie all quantitative research. By continuing to make connections in Section II between the terms used in both traditions, we hope to prompt readers to recognize that they may already have a solid platform for understanding quantitative methods. The "Connections to Qualitative Research" found in each of these chapters were sometimes easy to formulate, but at other times, it made us realize that, while the two traditions are complementary and in pursuit of the same common goal, there are indeed important differences. In these sections, we pull together and reaffirm the complementary nature of quantitative and qualitative research by stressing their shared empirical and systematic components, as well as by celebrating their differences. In the end, we hope that readers will come to agree with our conclusion that these differences provide the basis for an even more powerful methodology.

Section III, titled "Research Design and Data Analysis in the Quantitative Tradition," comprises Chapters 7 through 10. Chapters 7 and 8 introduce readers to the most common non-experimental and experimental research designs used in the social sciences, respectively. In each chapter, we describe the essential characteristics of the design, the steps undertaken during implementation, the strengths and limitations of the design, as well as common threats to external and internal validity. In addition, we point readers to the pertinent sections of Chapter 9 that describe associated data analysis procedures and continue to include our "Connections to Qualitative Research" sections. Chapters 9 and 10 round out Section III and focus on descriptive and inferential analyses as the basic data analysis procedures used to analyze the data generated by quantitative research designs. As readers will see, the methods used to analyze qualitative and quantitative data are quite different. However, despite the differences, analyses in both traditions seek to make sense of the collected data using tried-and-tested analysis approaches. We hope that these chapters will encourage readers to develop an appreciation for the fact that the unifying goal of qualitative and quantitative research is to discover new knowledge that can help describe, explain, and predict the world around us.

Section IV, the final section of this text, includes only Chapter 11. The purpose of this chapter is to provide readers with some final advice as to how to use a multiple mind-set to appreciate problems from both quantitative and qualitative perspectives.

In an appendix at the end of the text, we provide readers with "Guidelines for Evaluating Research Summaries." The purpose of this appendix is to provide our readers with step-by-step guidelines for evaluating research summaries (e.g., journal articles, dissertations, etc.). These guidelines have been "field tested" for several years in graduate research classes and are consistent with the terms and concepts we introduce in the preceding chapters.

❖ WHAT THIS TEXT IS NOT!

Now that we have told you what this book is about, we need to also tell you what it is *not* about. It is not a book that seeks to provide a comprehensive treatment of either quantitative or qualitative methods; rather, it is meant to provide a unifying framework for understanding and appreciating both the underlying commonalities as well as the differences. As such, we refer readers to more specialized research design, measurement, and data analysis texts for additional coverage of some topics. For coverage of research methods in general, we recommend texts such as Creswell (2008), Mertler and Charles (2010), Gay, Mills, and Airasian (2009), McMillan and Schumacher (2006), Gall, Borg, and Gall (2003), and Fraenkel and Wallen (2011). For additional information about specialized research designs (e.g., survey research designs, true and quasi-experimental designs, etc.), we recommend texts such as Dillman, Smyth, and Christian (2008), Rea and Parker (2005), Fowler (2008), Groves, Fowler, Couper, and Lepkowski (2009), Fink (2012), Wright and Marsden (2010), Fowler (2008), Shadish, Cook, and Campbell (2002), Kirk (2012), and Keppel and Wickens (2004). For additional coverage of measurement issues, we recommend DeVellis (2011) and Netemeyer, Bearden, and Sharma (2003), and for additional coverage of statistics and data analysis, we recommend texts such as Privitera (2012), Howell (2010), Glass and Hopkins (1996), and Shavelson (1996).

Because we are in agreement with a constructivist approach to learning, we do not see this text as the final destination but rather as a steppingstone toward developing a more advanced and nuanced understanding of quantitative research methods. Our ultimate hope is that, as a consequence of this book, readers develop a greater appreciation of both traditions and that this appreciation will spur increased understanding as well as collaboration.

SECTION I

Research in the Social Sciences: Qualitative Meets Quantitative

T he intention of the Preface was to serve as a gentle introduction to what we are trying to accomplish in this book. With the Preface fresh in your minds, we hope that you understand that we are proponents of *both* the qualitative and quantitative traditions! Therefore, the purpose of Section I is to first provide a general but unifying discussion of research in the social sciences (Chapter 1) followed by an overview of research in the qualitative tradition (Chapter 2) and finally leading to an introduction to research in the quantitative tradition (Chapter 3).

What readers will find in these first three chapters is something we think is unique—a firm foundation on which to build an appreciation of both the qualitative *and* quantitative traditions. You see, we find learning about the world to be so exciting that we felt we had to do something to show that the demarcations we have erected that define "legitimate" ways of knowing must not stand in the way of trying to empower individuals to appreciate the insights available to those who think of themselves as behavioral scientists, educators, musicians, novelists, physical scientists, playwrights, poets, or social scientists.

The first three chapters invite readers to enter into the world of research with eyes wide open to the possibilities of what we can discover if we use all of the capacities given to us rather than settle for "half a loaf." The purpose of Chapter 1 is to show that "problems" come in multiple shapes, colors, and sizes and that all of them present opportunities for both self-fulfillment and to contribute to the welfare of others. Ten questions directed toward the definition of quality research will hopefully lead readers to see the underlying unity of efforts to understand phenomena more fully. Chapter 2 narrows the focus to qualitative research, where we assume many of our readers (though certainly not all) find themselves. Here, we lay what we perceive as the most fundamental aspects of the qualitative approach to inquiry in order to provide a familiar welcome to those who are grounded in this tradition as well as to those who want to learn more about it.

In Chapter 3, we begin our quest to examine the quantitative tradition and, through our "Connections to Qualitative Research," hope to continually remind you that reality is of one cloth—but of an intricate weave. For those who are new to the quantitative tradition, we hope that you come to trust us enough to lead you through this approach and to emerge with a greater appreciation of how this tradition can contribute to your understanding of phenomena.

1

Understanding the Purpose of Research in the Qualitative and Quantitative Traditions

I n this chapter, we begin our journey with a discussion of research per se as well as some of the fundamental philosophical assumptions that underlie the qualitative tradition. We then offer 10 questions that we think get at the heart of what constitutes quality research. Subsequently, we set the stage for introducing research in the quantitative tradition by introducing some of the differences between qualitative and quantitative research and discuss the paradigm wars that characterize the historical differences of the research traditions.

❖ WHAT IS RESEARCH?

Why should those individuals who are qualitatively inclined want to learn about the quantitative tradition and its associated methods? Just as a variety of physical tools enable us to enlarge on what we can do, so too does having facility with the distinct research tools offered by the quantitative and qualitative traditions enable us to explore phenomena in ways that embrace multiple ways of knowing (Gardner, 1983). In addition, conceptualizing the quantitative and qualitative traditions by using different primary symbol systems (numbers vs. words) in pursuit of the same goal of discovering new knowledge promotes both cognitive and creative outcomes as noted by Vygotsky (Karpov & Haywood, 1998).

So what exactly is research? While the prefix "re" means "again" or "anew" and the verb "search" means "to examine," the entire word "research" is usually defined as "scientific inquiry." Although neither of us (the authors) are etymologists, one of our preferred definitions is "research is a systematic process to make things known that are currently unknown by examining phenomena multiple times and in multiple ways." That is, we see research as an open invitation to use multiple perspectives, data sources, replications, and methods to investigate phenomena. While there is nothing especially original or earth shattering about this definition, we respectfully ask our readers to adopt it at least temporarily so that we can begin and end our journey together while enjoying the experience along the way.

If one focuses only on differences *within* the qualitative tradition, Creswell (2007) indicates that while qualitative research in general espouses the philosophical assumptions reproduced in Chapter 2, Figure 2.1, there are differences among researchers in relation to paradigmatic and interpretive perspectives, including the role of postpositivism, constructivism, advocacy, feminism, and critical theory. There are also differences regarding the purposes and methods associated with specific designs, such as ethnographic, phenomenological, and grounded theory. While the quantitative tradition does not encompass the same degree of philosophical and paradigmatic diversity as the qualitative tradition, it includes a variety of designs, depending on whether the purpose is to explore, describe, or explain.

If one contrasts quantitative and qualitative traditions, there are obvious identifiable differences. However, we argue that there is no fundamental conflict in terms of our definition of research as described above. As Guba (1981) pointed out early on, "There is no inherent reason why either paradigm cannot accommodate, and be contributed to, by either methodology" (p. 78). There is, however, one more consideration regarding differences across traditions that should be noted; namely, *what is desired to be known.* Some researchers may want to know what makes a clock tick faster, while others want to know why the clock ticks instead of squeaks, or perhaps even why clocks are necessary in the first place. What is considered interesting and pivotal to a problem thus becomes the specific focus of each researcher. While all researchers try "to make things known that are currently unknown," the particular aspect of the unknown that is investigated depends on the interests, paradigmatic perspectives, and predispositions of each researcher. Everybody is on the same team, it just may not be obvious at times—so let's move on and examine some of the characteristics that indicate team membership.

❖ WHAT CONSTITUTES QUALITY RESEARCH?

To develop a common base of understanding, we now briefly define what we mean by qualitative and quantitative research. In a nutshell, *qualitative research seeks to discover new knowledge by retaining* **complexities** *as they exist in* **natural settings***, whereas quantitative research seeks to discover new knowledge by simplifying complexities in settings that tend to be more contrived.* Of course, when one tries to provide a pithy one-sentence definition for something that has commandeered thousands of advocates, millions of opposing words, and decades of work, an unintended consequence may be the alienation of some readers. However, since we (the authors) have managed to coexist in relative harmony and have appreciated what each has had to say, we offer ourselves as living proof that numbers and words need not collide!

Now that we have presented definitions of research and the two major types of research, we move forward and define "quality" in research by proposing 10 guiding questions that we find relevant for conducting sound research in both quantitative *and* qualitative traditions:

1. Do the research questions have practical or theoretical significance?

2. Are the terms used in the research questions clearly defined?

3. Have the research questions been adequately positioned within the literature?

4. Were appropriate participants selected to answer the research questions?

5. Is the research design appropriate for investigating the research questions?

6. Are the instrument(s) appropriate for generating the data needed to answer these questions?

7. Have procedures been ethically and rigorously followed?

8. Were appropriate methods used to analyze data?

9. Were results appropriately presented, interpreted, and synthesized with the literature to answer the research questions and draw conclusions?

10. Has the report of the research been written clearly, aesthetically, and unambiguously?

Question 1: Do the Research Questions Have Practical or Theoretical Significance?

Creativity and questions that excite the mind are the incubators of quality research and provide the necessary foundation for quality studies in both traditions. On the other hand, questions that are mundane, uninteresting, or trivial are not typically endorsed by journal editors or doctoral committees, regardless of the brilliance of the design or analysis. A research study is organic with its components having a necessary interdependence, so while doing things right is important, it is first necessary to ask the right questions. Rigor without direction usually results in ending up in an unknown or undesirable place. If answers to proposed research questions are not thought to be potentially helpful for understanding important phenomena or to perform important work in a better way, then conducting research based on such questions is generally a waste of time and resources. Asking the right questions in the right way is an essential element of quality research, whereas triviality and lack of clarity are twin enemies that can doom a study before it has begun. Being in a position to answer "yes" to Question 1, while not sufficient to ensure quality, trumps the other criteria.

It should be noted, however, that while clearly specifying all research questions *prior to* collecting data is the accepted protocol for quantitative studies, the qualitative tradition allows for the addition, deletion, or modification of research questions *concomitant with* data collection. The rationale for this latter approach is that as a deeper understanding of participants and contexts unfolds as the study progresses, richer questions sometimes evolve. Clandinin and Connelly (2000) express perhaps a more fundamental issue when they say that research questions generally "carry with them qualities of clear definability and the expectation of solutions, but narrative inquiry carries more of a sense of a search, a 're-search,' a searching again" (p. 124). With respect to this difference between the quantitative and qualitative traditions, we see it as related more to *process* rather than an underlying common *intent*. The goal of both traditions is to formulate important questions that spring from human creativity and insight and possess the potential for going beyond what is already known to add to the existing body of knowledge—regardless if these questions are formulated prior to conducting a study or emerge as the study progresses.

Question 2: Are the Terms Used in the Research Questions Clearly Defined?

Closely allied with asking the right questions is making sure that both writers and readers understand the questions in the same way. As Floden points out using an example related to teacher certification, unless central terms are clarified, there are myriad definitions that may be attached to them by myriad readers (Moss et al., 2009, p. 505). Because of this potential ambiguity, we believe that quality studies should include a definition of terms and variables in the introduction that further clarify the research questions. Not only will such definitions clarify the study for readers, they will also help researchers to stay on the right path as they plan and conduct their studies.

Question 3: Have the Research Questions Been Adequately Positioned Within the Literature?

While research can be thought of as discovery learning that draws on individual creativity and insights, it can reach its full potential only when it also draws on the insights and ideas of others; that is, as researchers exclaim, "we discovered," they should also proclaim, "the following individuals helped us to discover." The value of any discovery is contextually dependent on what others have previously found or theorized, especially since it provides a framework for interpreting findings. Engagement with the literature over long periods of time also provides an "advance organizer" to help generate creative sparks that can later ignite into questions of significance. A quality study does not materialize or exist in a vacuum; rather, it needs to incubate as ideas arise and as connections are made through reading and listening to what others have said. This is why a review of the relevant literature (whether done prior to or concurrently with a study) is so important—it helps us formulate questions that, while "original," spring from or fit with the work of others.

Quality work does not recognize the artificial dichotomy that we have built between quantitative and qualitative research; it depends on one's long-term commitment to learn about a specific phenomenon. Quality research depends on quality questions, and quality questions depend on making connections to what others have previously discovered. However, to bring the argument back to the essential criterion of researcher creativity noted in Question 1, the Nobel prize winner Albert Szent-Gyorgyi (1893–1986) once said, "Discovery consists of seeing what everybody has seen and thinking what nobody has thought." While we can benefit tremendously from what others have said, each of us has the potential to unearth our own insights and thereby make unique contributions to the literature, thus paying back the debt owed to those from whom we borrowed.

Question 4: Were Appropriate Participants Selected to Answer the Research Questions?

One must not only ask the right questions in the right way, but these questions must be directed toward those who are in a good position to answer them. Whether conducting an experimental or an ethnographic study, there must be a clear rationale for how and why particular participants and settings have been included in the study, even if a participant materializes almost by happenstance. While quantitative research often requires a relatively large representative sample using a type of random selection so the findings can be generalized to a larger population, qualitative research focuses on rich or **thick description** based on a limited number of participants and settings that enable readers to determine to what extent findings may be transferable to their own settings. As Wolcott (1988) so aptly expresses it by citing Margaret Mead, the question in qualitative research is *not* "Is this case representative?" but rather "What is this case representative of?" (p. 203). Nonetheless, the key consideration is that under both traditions, participants are central to the study and need to be selected in a way that is consistent with the research questions that are asked and the degree of control that is possible or desired.

Question 5: Is the Research Design Appropriate for Investigating the Research Questions?

The purpose of a research design is to provide a framework for conducting the study and to minimize "alternative explanations," while also supporting claims for generalizability or transferability to other participants and settings. In quantitative studies, the features of designs related to generalizability and causal understanding are referred to, respectively, as external validity and internal validity (Chapters 4 and 6). Qualitative research also strives to arrive at a valid and accurate understanding of phenomena, as well as a type of generalizability, although as we will see in Chapter 2, with a reduced emphasis on the a priori need for transferability of findings, as well as a different approach for doing so.

There are various kinds of research designs within both research traditions. For example, within the qualitative tradition, typical designs include ethnographic, case study, phenomenological, grounded theory, and narrative (see Chapter 2). Typical designs in the quantitative tradition will be introduced in Chapter 3 and described in detail in Chapters 7 and 8. Each of these designs suggests the type of data to be collected, methods of data collection, and methods of analysis that are "designed" to lead to valid and trustworthy answers to research questions.

Question 6: Are the Instrument(s) Appropriate for Generating the Data Needed to Answer the Research Questions?

In both quantitative and qualitative traditions, the evidence (data) that we collect provide the basis for answering research questions, and the quality of this evidence depends on the quality of the instruments that are used to generate it. In quantitative studies, **validity** and reliability are essential attributes of instruments (e.g., tests or questionnaires). Whereas validity is generally defined as the degree to which an instrument measures what it is supposed to measure (Creswell, 2008; Kerlinger, 1973), reliability is described as the consistency of measurement. Of these two criteria, validity is considered the more important, since measuring what is intended is the crux of the matter, and if an instrument is valid, then by definition, it is also reliable (Gay, Mills, & Airasian, 2009). There are various types of validity and reliability that are considered important for a particular quantitative study depending on its purpose (see Chapters 5 and 6).

Regarding qualitative studies, the researcher is the primary instrument because qualitative researchers are more intimately involved with participants compared with their quantitative colleagues (see Chapter 2) to capture the complexities of human feelings, intentions, experiences, and context. This intimacy includes not only the data collection phase (using interviews, observation, or artifacts) but also the results and interpretation stages, where **member checking** and **peer checking** are often used to promote the overall **trustworthiness** of a study. However, in both qualitative and quantitative studies, the quality of instrumentation leads directly to the quality of evidence that, in turn, leads directly to the quality of results and interpretation.

In addition, Floden addresses the desirability of "sharing instruments across studies" within a research community based on a common understanding of what constitutes valid and quality data in a particular scholarly field (Moss et al., 2009, p. 505). This component of quality contrasts with the notion of developing and using instruments only for a single study. While this advice can be easily applied to quantitative research, its transition and application to qualitative research may not be as straightforward. However, one could argue that trying to make connections among qualitative studies would be easier if questions asked of informants in related studies were at least partially based on a common understanding of the most important underlying concepts and phenomena. Of course, the contextually related and participant-related idiosyncrasies central to rich description in qualitative studies preclude a rigid interpretation of commonalities among "instruments," since this could be construed as unnecessarily reductionist. Nonetheless, the need to collect data that are judged by peers to be trustworthy is a major component of quality of both quantitative and qualitative studies.

Question 7: Have Procedures Been Ethically and Rigorously Followed?

Conducting a study *ethically* demands that researchers obtain the informed consent of participants, protect them from harm (physical and emotional), preserve their privacy and anonymity, and strictly maintain confidentiality of data (Lichtman, 2013). Contrary to popular opinion, the purpose of **institutional review boards** (IRBs) is *not* to frustrate researchers! Their actual mission, beginning with the establishment of the National Commission for the Protection of Human Subjects in 1974 and the issuance of the Belmont Report in 1979, has been to protect participants from harm by adding a layer of protection at the proposal stage. An additional criterion sometimes incorporated into IRB protocols is an evaluation of the reasonable success of a study so that participants will not be asked to spend their time and energy on something that will contribute little or nothing to the knowledge base. This is where the role of the IRB connects with the criteria of the quality of questions (Question 1). In summary, under *no* circumstances should a study be conducted if the procedures pose material harm to participants.

A second aspect of procedures to consider is the rigor with which they are conducted. While creativity is the wellspring for generating ideas for quality research questions (Question 1), conducting a study *rigorously* means that well-thought-out processes are followed during implementation and that critical steps are not skipped for the sake of expediency. Without such rigor, opportunities not only are wasted for discovering significant new knowledge, research may produce knowledge of dubious value. While conducting a quality study is certainly not a "cookie cutter" enterprise, there is something to be learned from following a recipe. For example, although master chefs may judiciously "pepper" their creations with an array of seasonings based on insights nurtured through experience, they generally do so based on the processes described in a recipe that has been found to produce a quality offering. Likewise, researchers (both quantitative and qualitative) need to thoughtfully develop and then rigorously follow processes that have been developed to arrive at trustworthy answers to research questions. At this stage of the research process, researchers almost need to assume alternating personas—while creativity is present throughout, they must periodically step back and look dispassionately at the process to ask self-directed questions regarding whether proper protocols and precautions are being followed.

This "stepping back" is often manifested in quantitative studies by making sure that arrangements, settings, and equipment are properly in place and that measurement instruments are properly administered. On the other hand, qualitative researchers often resort to employing **reflexivity**, where they exercise a conscious awareness of their cognitive and emotional filters comprising their experiences, worldviews, and biases that may influence their interpretation of participants' perceptions. In both cases, however, rigor is served because there is recognition that quality outcomes rarely result from shoddy processes. Additionally, it is critical for researchers to be aware *as the study is being conducted* of whether strands connecting procedures to the goal of discovering new knowledge are being properly woven. Results can then be deemed meaningful not only because they are based on meaningful questions but also because the procedures used to investigate these questions are as transparent as possible, providing assurance to readers that results are credible.

Question 8: Were Appropriate Methods Used to Analyze Data?

All too often, statistics is thought of as the central element in quantitative research and also the major hurdle that stands between success and failure for aspiring researchers. We have also found that statistics is a major reason why many graduate students gravitate toward qualitative research. There are probably many underlying factors for this preference, but it may also be the case that the role of statistics in the design–measurement–statistics triumvirate is often perceived as the *most* important.

When you stop and think about it regarding quantitative studies, if you have interesting research questions, a good plan for conducting a study (design), adhere to rigorous procedures, and take the necessary steps to collect quality evidence (measurement), then the only thing left is to "run the numbers" in a user-friendly computer program (e.g., SPSS), so it can provide the answers. OK, maybe this is a bit simplistic, but the point is that if one wants to do a quantitative study or to embed a quantitative component in a qualitative study, it is not necessary to be adept at statistical derivations. What is needed, however, is an understanding of which statistical methods are appropriate to use based on the research question, design, and data (specifically the type and "level' of data), and this book has been designed to help you with this decision. Naturally, in any activity there are degrees of expertise, whether we are talking about carpentry, baking, or statistics, and such expertise is largely determined by the amount of time one devotes to a pursuit. For those who desire to learn more about statistics, we provide a background of fundamental concepts in Chapters 9 and 10.

Analysis in qualitative research has the same purpose as in quantitative studies—to make sense of data in relation to research questions. However, whereas data in quantitative studies comprise numbers, data in qualitative studies comprise primarily words, pictures, and artifacts. Given this discrepancy, it is not surprising that the methods used to analyze these data differ. However, making sense of data (whether numbers or words) requires a systematic and thoughtful approach. Although there are additional nuances in quantitative data analysis methods that will be covered in Chapters 9 and 10, there is an overarching shared commonality of purpose and goals, whether one is trying to answer questions based on numerical versus linguistic or artistic evidence.

Question 9: Were the Results Appropriately Presented, Interpreted, and Synthesized With the Literature to Answer Research Questions and Draw Conclusions?

Readers are generally most interested in what was found and what these findings mean. While Chapter IV in dissertations typically reports results and Chapter V focuses on interpretation, this is not always the case. In fact, for those of us who work primarily within the qualitative tradition, analysis and results are often intermixed with interpretation in pursuit of trying to accurately present our informants' perceptions while recognizing that our interpretation of these perceptions could add additional meaning to findings based on our own self-awareness (Wolcott, 1994, p. 422). No matter where and how results are presented, there needs to be a clear connection from questions to results and conclusions whether these questions were posed prior to or concurrent with data collection.

Just as a research study begins with creative research questions, it ends with interpreting and integrating empirical results with the literature in a creative and insightful manner to answer these questions. Typically in quantitative studies, the conclusions or discussion section presents the first opportunity for the researcher to "speak"; that is, up to this point, the results are expected to speak for themselves, although in a muted voice. Why "muted"? Because neither facts nor results alone are equipped to impart meaning to readers, and "meaning" is what it's all about!

Let's first take a simple example: the old saying about whether a glass is half empty or half full—the proverbial pessimist and optimist. The point is that both the pessimist and the optimist are looking at the same "facts"—first, agreement that there is indeed water in a glass, and second, agreement that the glass is filled halfway with water. Similarly, if the results of a study indicate that a certain instructional procedure results in significant differences in achievement between an experimental and control group, the researcher still needs to interpret these findings in relation to the nature of the participants and setting, sample size, environmental conditions, costs, needed equipment and materials, as well as the related literature. Even if the conscientious quantitative researcher cites practical significance and effect size (Chapter 10), results still need to be interpreted in terms of *meaning* and *implications*, or else the results are essentially meaning*less*.

The same holds true for qualitative studies. Even though data consist of words, pictures, and artifacts, these data also need to be interpreted in order to extract meaning. Although interpretation can begin during data collection and analysis, allowing researchers to reveal themselves at an earlier point in the write-up compared with the quantitative tradition, it is important to recognize that results are essentially vacuous in the absence of the act of interpretation, which transforms findings into something understandable, useful, and, hopefully, even thought provoking.

It should also be noted that the act of interpretation involves making comparisons. The human mind seems to need to compare in order to make sense out of just about anything in life—chocolate, cars, schools, or governments. Our preferences and choices regarding a particular type of car or government require that we exercise informed judgment regarding the relative worth of one choice over another based on internalized criteria. For example, when we decide to buy a new car, we usually have an idea about what type of car we want, how much we can afford to pay, desired accessories, and so on. We then shop around with these criteria serving as ready-made interpreters of relative worth. We make the choice of buying a particular car by comparing the features of each car in relation to these underlying standards or criteria. In research, the proper criteria for comparison to interpret findings requires that we compare empirical results to our research questions as well as to what others have found as codified in the literature. Interpretation also requires a creative leap based on our own experience, ingenuity, creativity, and critical thinking that represents our "take" on what we have found. The combination of grounding in the literature, alignment with research questions, and creativity and insight is essential to drawing quality conclusions for both quantitative and qualitative studies.

Question 10: Has the Report of the Research Been Written Clearly, Aesthetically, and Unambiguously?

While satisfactory answers to Questions 1 to 9 should add up to a quality study, there is no way for others to endorse or even know about it if it is not reported clearly. Communicating in a clear and pleasing manner is both an art and a science and demands as much effort as conducting the study. Quality writing demands a willingness to edit and rewrite until the kernel of what we are trying to convey becomes clear. Good writing also entails a willingness to allow critics to inspect your work and suggest where you still need to revise content or structure or both. It is also important to adhere to accepted style conventions such as American Psychological Association style or whatever style is required by a particular journal. Although it may sometimes appear to be just another hoop to jump through (e.g., IRBs), the rationale for writing standards is to help define and solidify a community of scholars who voluntarily adhere to a particular writing protocol so that meaning can remain at the forefront of a study due to the transparency afforded by accepted writing conventions.

While we stand by these 10 questions as definers of quality, we will see later that the old adage "the devil is in the details" is certainly applicable when we discuss the characteristic of *rigor*. This saying is especially true of the complexities and terms inherent both within and across research traditions that leave many of us scratching our heads as we try to figure out what it all means. Floden argues that too often we classify research as simply good or bad because we fail to recognize the "gradations of quality" (Moss et al., 2009, p. 505) that actually exist. These "gradations" can include studies that use research designs that guard against threats to internal validity (Chapter 6) and, hence, are considered "rigorous," yet the study may actually be of lower quality because the questions it seeks to answer are relatively trivial.

Some qualitative researchers may object to these questions as criteria of quality in part because of the linearity conveyed by such a numbered list. In terms of paradigmatic terminology, some may object because they see this list as a product of postpositive thought. Our actual intent here is quite pragmatic. We simply want to identify markers of quality that can be used to conduct and evaluate research in education and the social sciences. These markers should not be considered iconoclastic, nor are they intended to be applied as a strict recipe, but rather should be used in conjunction with thoughtful reflection as researchers go about designing and conducting a study as well as evaluating studies done by others. We would also be quite surprised if readers did not find some aspects of these criteria deficient and have better questions in mind. We welcome this stance since positive criticism is a key component of learning from others!

❖ QUALITY QUESTIONS IN RELATION TO THE FINAL RESEARCH SUMMARY

Although conducting research and reporting it are intimately connected, the written report itself can also convey an exaggerated sense of linearity. Research is above all a creative endeavor that allows us to think about and search for new meanings, and this thinking and searching is usually not a linear process; rather, it often becomes circular as the researcher experiences an insight that affects a section of the report that has already been written, which may then suggest a modification in another section, and so it goes. Nevertheless, because the written report is the accepted way to share findings, we thought it might be of value to relate the 10 questions delineated above to the sections of a prototypical dissertation (or other major research study).

Questions 1 (*Significance*) and 2 (*Terms*) are usually included in Chapter I (Introduction), because it indicates whether the proposed study addresses problems that are thought to be important. It should also be noted that practicality is also an important consideration—biting off more than one is ready, willing, or able to chew is not an uncommon problem among both novice and seasoned researchers.

Question 3 (*Literature*) defines Chapter II (Review of the Related Literature), where relevant literature is searched and integrated to provide a context for research questions. Although the literature search typically is a distinct section of the written report, it is sometimes integrated with other parts of a qualitative report, and can be conducted following or during data collection, which is consistent with the inductive nature of qualitative research (see Chapter 2).

Questions 4 to 8 (*Participants, Design, Instruments, Procedures, Analysis*) relate to Chapter III (**Methodology**) describing the technical aspects of a study (participant selection, procedures, design, instrumentation, and data analysis) and together with Chapter I (Introduction) and Chapter II (Literature Review) constitute the typical research proposal. Satisfactory answers to Questions 4 to 8 provide the link or *process* that justifies the connection between the *content* components at each end of the study—research questions and literature on one end and results and conclusions on the other. While it is true that luck and happenstance sometime play a role in producing worthwhile products, it is generally accepted that quality processes are directly related to quality outcomes. While it is sometimes thought that processes used in qualitative studies are "looser" than in quantitative studies, this is simply not the case. While numbers, tables, and statistical formulae may lend an air of precision to a study, they are of value only if the problem and research questions admit of such precision. One interesting example of this for those of us who fly is the specificity used to indicate departure and landing times (e.g., 3:12 p.m.) when factors such as wind, weather, and the availability of gates are often beyond the control of anybody. The critical consideration is whether methodological processes are aligned to the purpose for doing the study. Much of the remainder of this book addresses this very issue. Questions 4 to 8 can be partially evaluated in light of the planning process but can only be *fully* judged for quality after the study has been completed. That is, while we can say that we are going to do things in an ethical and rigorous manner, the real question is whether we have in fact, done so—if you have a good plan but fail to follow it, you may end up with something completely different than expected—or nothing at all!

Question 9 (*Results and Conclusions*) refers to Chapters IV and V of the typical dissertation and represents the prize that has been sought beginning at Question 1. If the researcher has identified research questions that are interesting (Questions 1 and 2), positioned these questions in the literature (Question 3), and established and followed rigorous methods (Questions 4 to 9), then the stage has been set for discovering new knowledge based on empirical findings and for interpreting these findings in light of the extant literature. The job is now done—almost!

Question 10 (*Writing It Up*) can properly be thought of as the act of sharing the research journey with a wider audience. It is only when key hits screen that you can begin a conversation with those who may only get to know you from your work. By publishing your study, you have now entered into a discussion with those whom you "listened to" during your literature review as well as with those who will now listen to what you have to say . . . and so the conversation continues!

❖ PROBLEM FINDING VERSUS PROBLEM SOLVING

Another characteristic that applies equally to quantitative and qualitative approaches is that the "process for making known what was formerly unknown" focuses primarily on solving problems rather than *finding* problems to solve. In fact, let us modify this assertion by preceding *problems* with the adjective *good* to create an even starker contrast. If one looks at textbooks on social science research, most of them say little regarding how we should go about identifying the object of our research efforts (**problem finding**) versus the process for doing so (**problem solving**). As Wolcott (1994) admits, "The idea that research can be viewed as problem 'setting' rather than problem solving did not set too well when I first encountered it" (p. 401).

Those of you who have already completed or are currently going through the rite of passage of a masters or doctoral thesis are undoubtedly aware of the "significance of the problem" component and therefore might rightly argue that this assertion is not new or novel (see Question 1 in our list above). However, based on our own observations, we think that we often spend so much time teaching separate quantitative and qualitative methods in graduate school that these methods become disembodied from efforts to creatively identify problems that are ripe with potential. As a consequence, graduate students (and faculty) sometime tend to focus first on a method for conducting research (perhaps based on an initial comfort level with a specific instructor or on a particular methodology) rather than reflecting on a broad range of possible topics and then gradually narrowing this topic into a researchable problem. It is our hope that this book can help put Humpty Dumpty back together again by demystifying quantitative and qualitative approaches and to put them both at the service of conducting meaningful research studies.

❖ QUALITATIVE AND QUANTITATIVE TRADITIONS AND THE "PARADIGM WARS"

There is nothing like a disagreement to get folks engaged, so why not start by talking about a war that fortunately has been fought with words rather than other weapons. Most of what has been said thus far has focused on the commonalities of quantitative and qualitative research in terms of their purposes and the characteristics of quality research, and that will remain our enduring theme. However, to provide a more complete description, the time has come when we must begin to use the connective term *versus* when discussing these two research traditions. Since Jim is primarily a qualitative researcher and Laura is primarily a quantitative researcher, you can imagine the rich sources of data that we have related to the "versus" theme!

The story of "versus" is discussed in an article by N. L. Gage in the *Educational Researcher* in 1989. This retrospective piece related the "war" between the **objectivist–quantitative theory** and the **naturalist–interpretivist–critical theory** research **paradigms** and identified the following three possible versions of what might transpire by 2009: (1) demise of "objective quantitative" research, (2) rapprochement among the paradigms, or (3) continuation of the paradigm wars. Gage went on to say that whatever version came to pass would be a direct result of the efforts of the "philosophers, scientists, scholars, research workers, in short, the members of AERA [American Educational Research Association] and their counterparts around the world" (p. 10).

Due to the efforts and desires of the groups cited by Gage, we like to think that the second version, in fact, "won" by the apocalyptic year of 2009. There is now an increased acceptance across the qualitative–quantitative wall. In fact, with the growing acceptance and promulgation of mixed methods, we think that the wall itself has begun to crumble. That is the good news. On the other hand, some sections of the wall remain intact. Since Gage referred to the American Educational Research Association, we would like to give our thoughts on its annual meeting, where thousands of researchers and educators convene to deliver and attend sessions where research findings are disseminated. At the 2010 meeting in Denver, Colorado, Jim, because of his background in both methodologies, attended back-to-back sessions one day in which the first session dealt with quantification in school assessment and the second session focused on narrative inquiry. This sequential experience can probably be best visualized by evoking the image of Dorothy leaving her house and stepping into a strange new world where the famous line "Toto, I don't think we are in Kansas anymore" was first uttered. Not only were the language and terms used at these sessions different, so too were the unspoken assumptions as to what knowledge was supposed to look like and how it should be discovered. Afterward, it seemed like one could almost see the parallel worlds that folks inhabited as they navigated to either a numbers or a words session.

Our understanding of the paradigm wars is rooted in our experiences as doctoral students where our training focused on quantitative methodology. Although we attended different graduate schools, we were both quite happy with our chosen fields, since it seemed to both of us that qualitative researchers eschewed numerical data and instead used something else that was obviously a poor substitute! While we were both somewhat aware of the chasm between quantitative and qualitative approaches, neither of us were aware of the historical context that resulted in establishing education as a field of study, or the establishment of quantitative methodology as the sine qua non for educational research in the early 20th century (Lageman, 2000).

Regarding quantitative research, while it posits the existence of "intervening variables," once they are stated, they are usually not of much continuing concern (except for perhaps procedures such as path analysis where further explanation is sought). An example of an intervening variable is "learning" that is assumed to occur between the introduction of an intervention and the resulting outcome that is usually measured by a test. However, qualitative researchers would also like to know a little bit more about these intervening variables, such as why they occur, how they occur, and in what contexts they occur. While they may be interested in the same topic as quantitative researchers, their "take" on the topic can be quite different—much like a crystal looks different to observers depending on where they are standing in relation to it. This brings us to this watershed—the problem *as perceived* should drive method, and every researcher has the right and the obligation to frame the problem in a way that is consistent with her or his particular creative insight. By valuing and respecting idiosyncratic ways of thinking about and examining phenomena, we set the stage for new ways of learning that we may have previously ignored or even disdained. In the following chapters, we try to help with this process.

❖ CONCLUDING REMARKS

The purpose of this first chapter was to define research in a more inclusive manner in order to reflect the common aim of both the quantitative and qualitative traditions—to make things known that are currently unknown using a systematic process. However, the term *systematic* should not be construed in a rigid sense as is usually associated with the factory model of education and scientific management (Taylor, 1947) but rather with the notion of an awareness and constancy of purpose as one engages in a research study, whether that purpose is to provide rich description or to identify causal relationships. This chapter also stresses that no matter whether a study is quantitative or qualitative, there are markers of quality that should permeate the endeavor, and that without these markers, contributions to increased understanding are severely limited. We also touched on another critical consideration: Problem finding is at least as important as problem solving—perhaps more so. It is no use trying to discover how to make schools more efficient when the real problems are much deeper and the solutions much harder to find. Finally, there was a brief description of the "paradigm wars." Although these wars are said to be basically finished (probably more from attrition and plain exhaustion than any decisive victory), researchers still have their preferred ways of looking at problems, and we argue that each of our unique perspectives on these problems should be respected and viewed as opportunities to learn from each other, as well as to discover more complete pictures of phenomena.

DISCUSSION QUESTIONS

1. If you were asked to explain the differences and similarities between research in social science fields such as education and anthropology with research in the physical sciences such as chemistry and physics, how might you respond?

2. What are some areas or problems in your field where quantitative and qualitative traditions might both be helpful?

3. Which one of the 10 "quality questions" do you find most essential? Why?

4. Do you find any of the 10 "quality questions" confusing or relatively unimportant? Explain.

KEY TERMS

Complexities: those characteristics of phenomena that have not been reduced or simplified.

Institutional review board (IRB): official bodies established by organizations to evaluate whether adequate ethical standards are incorporated into research plans and proposals.

Member checking: under the qualitative tradition—enlisting the collaboration of participants to substantiate data analysis and interpretation.

Methodology: systematic procedures that are recognized to help answer questions.

Natural settings: the context surrounding phenomena that is left undisturbed by the researcher.

Naturalist–interpretivist–critical theory: sees the world as context dependent and where meaning and perceptions of phenomena and reality vary among individuals.

Objectivist–quantitative theory: sees the world and reality as stable, predictable, and generalizable where phenomena can be measured accurately.

Paradigms: possible ways to "see" the world and to make sense of the phenomena that inhabit it.

Peer checking: under the qualitative tradition—enlisting the collaboration of colleagues to review how a researcher went about collecting, analyzing, and interpreting data in order top promote trustworthiness.

Problem finding: identifying problems that are worth finding answers to.

Problem solving: processes and procedures to find answers to problems.

Reflexivity: the act of reflecting on your own perspectives and values during data collection, analysis, and interpretation.

Thick description: detailed and sensory language that captures the essence of people, phenomena, and contexts.

Trustworthiness: generally defined as the degree to which findings in a qualitative study can be "trusted"; this term conveys and integrates aspects that are formally separated under the quantitative tradition (see Chapters 4 to 6).

Validity: refers to the accuracy of the inferences made. Several forms of validity are discussed—external validity (Chapter 4), instrument validity (Chapter 5), internal validity (Chapter 6).

2

Research in the Qualitative Tradition and Connections to the Quantitative Tradition

B ecause the primary (though not exclusive) audience of this book is assumed to be qualitative researchers, Chapter 2 is not intended to be a comprehensive treatment of qualitative inquiry; rather, it is intended to be a brief overview of the fundamental concepts underlying the qualitative tradition peppered with additional ideas for our readers' consideration. Because we will begin specific methodological discussions related to quantitative methodology in Chapter 3, we view this current chapter as a launching pad to the chapters that follow. Our hope is that this approach will help our readers construct their own personal framework that is large and inclusive enough to accommodate both traditions. In addition to the references at the end of this book, we have listed several additional sources at the end of this chapter for those readers who desire to learn more about qualitative research.

As noted in the Preface, we have found that students sometimes gravitate toward qualitative research because of anxiety about statistics that they mistakenly believe is the cornerstone of research in the quantitative tradition. What they often find, however, is that while qualitative research does not use statistical tests, it presents challenges of a different nature; namely, a complexity that demands large doses of time, effort, and analysis. While we could use the phrase "going from the frying pan to the fire," we think it more productive to simply reinforce the notion outlined in Chapter 1 that quality research demands both creativity and rigor regardless of which tradition is used—first comes the passion and then the method.

❖ PURPOSE AND CHARACTERISTICS OF QUALITATIVE RESEARCH

In Chapter 1, we said "qualitative research seeks to discover new knowledge by retaining complexities as they exist in natural settings." The three key terms in this definition are *discover, retaining complexities*, and *natural settings*. While complexities and natural settings were introduced and defined in Chapter 1, it is worth emphasizing that coupled with discovery, these three terms convey the essence of what researchers do, whether conducting an ethnographic study of a motorcycle gang or a grounded theory study related to the attributes of genius. Stake (1995) begins his introduction to case study research by saying, "A case study is expected to catch the complexity of a single case. A single leaf, even a single toothpick, has unique complexities" (p. xi). While Stake goes on to say that rarely would a leaf or a toothpick merit conducting a case study, the fundamental point remains that qualitative research (whether a case study or another qualitative approach) is all about *not* rushing to unwind the inherent complexities of phenomena or participants but rather to first celebrate and appreciate their uniqueness. When we integrate the three key terms noted previously (discover, retaining complexities, and natural settings) with our Chapter 1 definition of research as "a systematic process to make things known that are currently unknown by examining phenomena multiple times and in multiple ways," we arrive at a conception of qualitative research that combines the appreciation and sensitivities of the artist with the rigors of science—not a small achievement!

The 10 questions that we advanced in Chapter 1 for defining quality research may strike some qualitative researchers as being too "scientific." However, we think that this perception may be the result of the presentation medium itself—a numbered list. Lists by their very nature convey order, linearity, and simplification, so it is quite natural to link a list of quality questions with the quantitative tradition. As an antidote to this perception, we now amplify what we said previously in relation to Questions 1 to 3 (Research Questions) and Question 9 (Results and Conclusions) as follows: Creativity is the beginning and the end, the alpha and the omega of quality research, and it is only as a consequence of creative problem finding *and* solving that the other questions of quality make sense. To amplify this assertion even further, qualitative researchers value their unique approaches for understanding and appreciating phenomena, and these understandings and appreciations more than likely were not achieved by slavishly following sequential steps. Rather, qualitative research offers the opportunity to capture the "thick description" (Geertz, 2003) and diversity in our world much like the artist or the filmmaker.

Qualitative researchers also recognize that they must periodically step outside of the picture they are painting or the film they are producing that describe the "what" and the "why" and cast a critical eye toward the "how" that defines quality processes and procedures. Sometimes, qualitative researchers find that they must add, delete, or modify research questions and approaches as a study progresses due to incremental understanding or "progressive focusing" (Parlett & Hamilton, 1976) of the phenomena under study. Consequently, they must be ever aware of the necessity to provide readers with a clear and focused account of not only what they have found but also how the focus of their inquiry may have changed as participants and contexts reveal themselves more fully. For example, in a study that one of the authors is currently conducting, the initial focus was on the lives of high school graduates in general, a combination of available participants, context, and serendipity resulted in a new focus on school career guidance. As a result, the research questions changed in midstream.

❖ PHILOSOPHICAL ASSUMPTIONS OF QUALITATIVE RESEARCH

We wish we could bypass terminology related to philosophy and just jump into the excitement of actually doing research! The problem with this approach is that without a lexicon that defines important attributes of anything (cars, houses, computers, pets, or individuals), it is not only difficult to communicate with others, but it also restricts our own thinking and growing understanding of phenomena. For example, if researchers did not understand the terms *reflexivity* and **positionality**, how would they know that it was acceptable to creatively intertwine their experiences, values, and acknowledged "biases" into their accounts? If researchers lack a grasp of the fundamental philosophical assumptions underlying qualitative research, they would be rudderless as they conducted their study or tried to describe it to others.

One of the most important philosophical underpinnings of qualitative research is ontological—that is, related to the nature of reality or being. Qualitative research assumes that there are multiple "realities" as perceived through the unique lenses of each individual. Phrases such as "beauty is in the eyes of the beholder" and "one person's weeds are another man's flowers" reflect the fact that perceptions constitute each person's reality, and these perceptions (and hence reality as perceived) change as a function of time, experience, circumstances, and learning. What becomes a bit tricky is how to reconcile this shifting view of reality with enduring convictions that are related to things such as theology, loyalty, patriotism, and love. Suffice it to say that consistent with the premise of this book, we see no essential conflict that precludes the practical and *pragmatic application* of both qualitative and quantitative research methods to problems to obtain an enriched appreciation and understanding of phenomena. Consistent with our definition of research as "examining phenomena multiple times and in multiple ways," complementary contributions can be made either in the same study (mixed methods) or in studies conducted at different times that focus on different aspects of the same phenomenon. For example, findings from an ethnographic study of an urban school district can be enhanced by findings from a quantitative study that examines the relationships among expenditures, student completion rates, and test scores across school districts. While qualitative researchers certainly need not don the mantle of "mixed methods researcher," quantitative and qualitative researchers can benefit from openness to the contributions that each of the traditions can make for understanding people and phenomena.

Table 2.1 reproduced from Creswell (2007) defines five different philosophical assumptions related to the ontological, epistemological, axiological, rhetorical, and methodological aspects of qualitative research. As noted earlier, multiple realities relate to **ontology** or beliefs about the nature of being, whereas **epistemology** describes beliefs underlying knowledge claims. Qualitative research assumes that learning about multiple realities and multiple perspectives implies that the researcher and the participant co-construct knowledge; that is, knowledge is not seen as a static objective truth but rather as the result of efforts to carve out an ever widening, richer, and more comprehensive understanding of reality via empathetic observing, listening, and discussion. Conversely, the quantitative tradition is based on an underlying assumption of a single reality that is independent of the perceptions of individuals. While these two opposing assumptions seem to present irreconcilable differences, Lichtman (2013) points out that qualitative researchers do not accept any and all versions of reality but rather only those with enough support that warrant reasoned consideration. Lichtman also notes that while quantitative researchers try to limit their influence on outcomes, many acknowledge that these efforts are not always completely successful (p. 14). In fact, as we review the remaining three assumptions, please keep in mind that while there are indeed philosophical differences between the traditions (much like Democrats and Republicans), when it comes to actually solving complex problems, competent researchers are first and foremost critical thinkers and recognize that they may not possess the most accurate and complete understanding of a problem. In most cases, each of us has only a piece of the truth that suggests that listening and learning from others (while perhaps not completely agreeing with them) seems like a reasonable attitude to cultivate. We include in this list our predisposition toward research traditions that may not be our first choice.

When we speak about **axiology**, we refer specifically to the values that we bring to a study while conducting and interpreting it. While "objectivity" is seen as a desired attribute when we are trying to make decisions, qualitative researchers posit that even when we try to be objective, our values color judgments and evaluations. In fact, as we will see when we discuss quantitative research, even supposedly "objective" approaches and tests carry with them a great deal of human intentionality and values. Rather than pretend that they are colorless and valueless, qualitative researchers seek "transparency" or a willingness to expose their values and biases to public scrutiny as they relate to the phenomena and the people that they study. They also utilize both reflexivity and positionality to make clear that they cannot pretend to be "objective" even

Table 2.1   Creswell's Philosophical Assumptions in Qualitative Research

Assumption	Question	Characteristics	Implications for Practice (Examples)
Ontological	What is the nature of reality?	Reality is subjective and multiple, as seen by participants in the study	Researcher uses quotes and themes in words of participants and provides evidence of different perspectives
Epistemological	What is the relationship between the researcher and that being researched?	Researcher attempts to lessen distance between himself or herself and that being researched	Researcher collaborates, spends time in field with participants, and becomes an "insider"
Axiological	What is the role of values?	Researcher acknowledges that research is value-laden and that biases are present	Researcher openly discusses values that shape the narrative and includes his or her own interpretation in conjunction with the
Rhetorical	What is the language of research?	Researcher writes in a literary, informal style using the personal voice and uses qualitative terms and limited definitions	Researcher uses an engaging style of narrative, may use first-person pronoun, and employs the language of qualitative research
Methodological	What is the process of research?	Researcher uses inductive logic, studies the topic within its context, and uses an emerging design	Researcher works with particulars (details) before generalizations, describes in detail the context of the study, and continually revises questions from experiences in the field

Source: Creswell (2007, Table 2.1, p. 17).

though they try to represent reality from the perspective of participants as clearly as possible. The reason for this transparency is not to offer themselves as a public sacrifice but rather to allow readers to discern the extent to which the written report may reflect personal values and worldviews. The disclosure of values and biases and the use of the first person are seen as supportive rather than antithetical for achieving trustworthiness primarily because of the transparency afforded to readers who can then weigh the evidence and judge truth value for themselves.

The assumption underlying the **rhetorical** assumption is that by speaking in the first person, the researcher closes the gap within the researcher–informant–reader triumvirate and, thereby, achieves conversational access to a richer understanding of the phenomena, context, and informant and a more natural expressive relationship with readers. This assumption is also consistent with the epistemological assumption that knowledge claims are strengthened rather than diminished when there is closeness rather than scientific detachment between the researcher and the informant.

Finally, regarding the *methodological* assumption, since reality is thought of as co-constructed and idiosyncratic rather than "out there," the role of the researcher is to try to learn about phenomena and informants by observing, listening, and empathizing inductively rather than deductively. Simultaneous with this approach and disposition is the researcher's cultivation of self-awareness of her or his feelings and beliefs that should properly be viewed as complementary to the understanding of phenomena rather than as an unwanted "bias." The positive impact of self-disclosure is especially useful when brought periodically to the foreground of the written account so that readers are afforded the opportunity to view multiple angles of the phenomenon on which to base their own interpretations.

If you review these assumptions, you will see overlap among them; in fact, a fairly dense entanglement of ideas define the essential underpinnings of qualitative research. As we will see in Chapter 3, the philosophical underpinnings associated with quantitative research differ in important and even critical ways from qualitative research. However, if you accept the contention that there can be complementary contributions from each tradition, it is our belief that the paradigm wars will finally become a distant memory. This does not mean that we qualitative and quantitative researchers need to sing Kumbaya around the campfire but rather that for the sake of our profession and our students, we need to recognize once and for all that both traditions are valid and of intrinsic value. As Donald Campbell (certainly not known as a qualitative researcher) argues in the preface to Yin's (2012) book on case study research, Yin's prior experience in psychology and subsequent development of case study research was facilitated by his focus "on that most hard-to-specify stimulus, the human face, and that this experience provided awareness of the crucial role of pattern and context in achieving knowledge" (p. viii), while Saldana (2009) describes the role of coding in qualitative research as trying to "organize and group similarly coded data into categories or 'families' because they share some characteristics—the beginning of a pattern" (p. 8). Similarly, while Tukey (1977) advocated exploratory data analysis of numerical data to discover patterns and thereby build inductively from data to theory, so too did Glaser and Strauss (1967) with the development of grounded theory. While this overlap and congruence of terms and intentions between qualitative and quantitative researchers does not signify a complete rapprochement between the paradigms, it does create a transitional space where boundaries begin to blur and where proponents of each tradition can begin a conversation based on what is common and unites and not what is different and divides. At the same time, differences between the traditions may spur new insights among researchers based on these very differences and may yield new insights that were not possible with an either/or worldview.

❖ TECHNICAL COMPONENTS OF EMPIRICAL INQUIRY IN QUALITATIVE RESEARCH

In the spirit of this book, we focus primarily on the complementary nature of quantitative and qualitative inquiry, including analogous terms that are used to identify the "technical" components of these two research traditions. We also point out a few "rough spots."

As we will see in Chapter 3, quantitative empirical inquiry consists of three major components—design, measurement, and statistics—where "design" serves as the overall plan for the study, "measurement" refers to the instruments used for data collection, and "statistics" is the set of procedures used to describe and make inferences about these data. The three components of qualitative empirical inquiry are design, data collection, and analysis, respectively, and these terms are defined by the same basic functions as indicated for quantitative research. As pointed out in Chapter 1, while differences do exist between the two traditions, we think that these very differences supplement rather than detract from their complementary relationship because they jointly help us understand and appreciate phenomena. Before we discuss these however, we will discuss the roles of **variables, research problems** and **research questions,** and research hypotheses in the qualitative tradition.

Variables, Research Problems and Questions, and Research Hypotheses

Chapter 3 points out that the quantitative tradition is very much concerned with identifying different types of variables to ascertain how they might influence each other. *Independent* and *dependent variables* are probably the most well-known, where the former is examined to discover their effect on the latter after controlling for other "extraneous variables." Variables are also important in qualitative research but are usually (though not always) identified inductively where "coding" or "categorizing" is used to name or label these emerging variables. In addition, while it may be of interest to discover what factors influence phenomena, research designs under the qualitative tradition are not meant to "control" for extraneous influences; rather, the identification of possible causes and effects is more contextually based.

In both traditions, research problems are related to topics that interest us and that we may want to investigate. Possible qualitative topics and problems in the social sciences are vast and can be subsumed under fields such as anthropology, sociology, history, and education. For example, some researchers may be interested in the influence of education on career choices, while others might be interested in how graduates now view the value of their past secondary school experiences. The range of possible combinations of topics, fields, and problems is almost infinite under both the qualitative and quantitative traditions!

Finally, Chapter 3 discusses research questions and hypotheses in relation to the quantitative tradition and the "Ten Guiding Questions" enumerated in Chapter 1. As we indicated in Chapter 1, these guiding questions apply to both traditions but not in exactly the same way. For example, while qualitative researchers pose research questions, some may emerge during the study rather than being entirely specified in advance of data collection. Also, while some qualitative researchers pose hypotheses, these are more flexible than those under the quantitative tradition and serve to guide rather than direct data collection and analysis.

The Design–Measurement–Analysis Triad

Research Design

Table 2.2 briefly describes seven well-known qualitative designs (sometimes referred to as *approaches* (Creswell, 2007; Lichtman, 2013)).

Table 2.2   Overview of Qualitative Research Designs

Research Design	Purpose
Case Study	Describe the attributes of a "bounded" system (person, entity)
Ethnomethodology	Discover how participants make sense of their everyday lives
Ethnography	Identify the cultural characteristics of a group
Grounded Theory	Inductively construct theory that is grounded in data
Historical	Understand and interpret the past
Narrative	Learn about a participant via storytelling and re-storying
Phenomenology	Learn how participants experience a particular phenomenon

We use the metaphor of the crystal to convey that these designs enable researchers to observe and interpret its facets based on the unique angles afforded to each observer. Creswell (2007) also metaphorically describes qualitative research by referring to it as an "intricate fabric" and those who weave this fabric on their looms as "creative artists" (p. 35). While these designs seek to discover a different or unique "reality," they are all based on interpreting this reality from the perspective of participants instead of trying to attain an "objective" standpoint. However, qualitative researchers also acknowledge that the lens through which they see and try to interpret reality as perceived by others is not entirely precise; rather, they recognize that they themselves color what they see and hear, and hence, their interpretations of reality are not completely isomorphic to that of the participant. An analogy is the phrase "believing is seeing" versus its antithesis "seeing is believing." The latter assumes that what one sees is the only reality, whereas the former assumes that we construct and impose our own perception of reality to some extent on phenomena based on our values and experiences. Qualitative researchers are more of the "believing is seeing" type; rather than decry this state of affairs, they celebrate it because they do not deem idiosyncratic conceptions as "threats to validity" but as a process that offers a richer understanding and appreciation of phenomena. However, qualitative researchers also recognize the attendant responsibility to try to be explicit about their take on things (reflexivity), or to put it in more negative terms, to make their "biases" explicit. In a sense, qualitative researchers take on the dual responsibility of not only trying to interpret reality from participants' perspectives but also to come to grips with their own views and values. They must also try to understand, regardless of the particular design selected, to try to understand how these views and values intersect and intertwine with those of participants during the process of creatively interpreting and writing up findings.

It should also be noted that oftentimes in qualitative research, a more generic approach is used from both a design and analysis standpoint. While there are some designs (e.g., grounded theory and phenomenology) with attendant specific methods of analysis, the underlying essence of all qualitative research is to understand participant perceptions and how phenomena are lived and experienced by them. Some studies therefore focus on extracting the essence of participant meaning through the collection of data via observation, interview, and artifacts without explicitly using or citing a specific design or **data analysis** approach (see, e.g., Thomas, 2006).

Measurement and Data Collection

We would like to stress the pivotal role that data collection (sometimes subsumed under "measurement" in the qualitative tradition) plays in empirical inquiry under both traditions since it serves as a kind of fulcrum between design and analysis. In fact, once we decide on the instruments and the data to collect based on considerations of trustworthiness (termed *validity* in the quantitative tradition), we have made a tacit agreement that these instruments and the data generated from them will no longer be subject to further scrutiny; therefore, the focus shifts to the tools of data analysis to seek answers and conclusions. This state of affairs is somewhat similar to a court of law where evidence is admitted according to the rules governing its acceptance; thereafter, it is analyzed and debated by protagonists and antagonists and then brought to a proper conclusion (verdict) by a jury. Once the evidence is admitted, all decisions and conclusions are based on it. Hence, we are bound under both traditions to produce the right kind of data and in the right way so that our results and conclusions can be trusted as described in Question 6 (Chapter 1) regarding quality research.

On a less harmonic note, we must simply accept the fact that numbers and words (while complementary) still embrace different inherent characteristics. For example, while it is clear that adding and dividing numbers is a legitimate way to find out the average score on a test, this is not the way that words are manipulated to ascertain the meaning that participants attach to phenomena. When qualitative research and naturalistic inquiry began to grow as a field in education in the 1970s and 1980s, qualitative researchers had an understandable sense of defensiveness vis-à-vis the "rationalistic" paradigm (Lageman, 2000). While that paradigm held sway for decades, the structure of qualitative research was (and still is) being built with new materials that sometimes result in unforeseen products. When qualitative researchers tried to describe the nature of data and findings, they conceptualized and communicated their new understandings in terms of what was already accepted and understood both by themselves and by their readers based on the quantitative tradition. In our opinion, these initial attempts to fit "a round peg into a square hole" while noble have had continuing impacts on clarity and understanding within and across traditions.

For example, the terms *trustworthiness* and **credibility** are often seen as a surrogate for the term *validity* as used in quantitative research. However, *within* the quantitative tradition, there are two distinct ways that the term *validity* is used—either in reference to the robustness of designs for controlling threats to internal and external validity or in reference to the validity of measuring instruments and the subsequent data that are generated by these instruments. To make matters worse, there are different types of validity in the quantitative tradition related to measurement that are usually discussed in tandem with the concept of **reliability**, which also has several variations (see Chapter 5). The same term conveying different meanings has resulted in confusion among quantitative researchers that we think has extended to the qualitative area. The question is whether an important term such as *credibility*, that is seen as a component of *trustworthiness* and then is juxtaposed with the term *validity* in the quantitative literature, can actually convey the intended meaning as conceptualized and advanced by qualitative researchers (see Guba, 1981; Maxwell, 1992; Wolcott, 1994). This may indeed be a case (and we are sure there are others) where each tradition must respectfully stand back and say something like, "By Jove, you've got something there that does not quite fit our paradigm, but we will do our best to understand what you are doing." As Lichtman (2013) puts it in the Preface to her book on qualitative research, "I do not believe we need to find parallel criteria to those used in quantitative research. At the same time, however, the field needs to stake a legitimate place in the scholarly community" (p. xx).

Finally, while trying to use similar terms and meanings for the two traditions may not always work as well as we would like, we reiterate that the unique insights that can be garnered from each tradition far outweigh concerns about terminology. Put another way, we contend that while each tradition has its own unique way of portraying reality, this very uniqueness results in making these portrayals more complete, accurate, and illuminating even if they use different tools to paint these portraits. We liken this to a cooperative learning setting where students bring their own unique insights to bear on the way a phenomenon is perceived, *what* problems need to be addressed, and *how* these problems might be addressed; in the process, students come to view both the methods used and even the problem itself in ways that they had not previously envisioned. Could this description be analogous to one where a melding of the quantitative and qualitative traditions results in researchers looking at problems in novel ways that may yield solutions to hitherto unresolved societal problems?

Data Analysis

Unless you use an appropriate means for making sense of data, you cannot adequately answer research questions or promote further understanding of a topic. While the primary processes for analyzing quantitative data are descriptive and inferential **statistics** (Chapters 9 and 10), processes used for analyzing qualitative data generally rely either on some type of **coding** or narrative or a combination of both of these methods. The essential point is that whether one is analyzing numbers or words, researchers need to use the appropriate processes and tools to "make meaning" from these data, and this usually involves employing some type of **data reduction** using either statistics in the quantitative case or coding in the qualitative case.

Unfortunately, statistical analysis in the quantitative tradition sometimes assumes a role larger than the design and measurement components, perhaps because of its image of mathematical rigor and precision—it certainly seems to cast a visible pallor on students at times! While statistics serves an important role in quantitative research, we argue that design and measurement play an equal (or perhaps even more important) role since they determine to a large extent what statistical tests or procedures are appropriate. In fact, once the design is established and the type of data is identified, it can be fairly straightforward to select a statistical procedure to analyze these data.

Much has been written about the various ways that qualitative data can be analyzed (Gibbs, 2007; Miles & Huberman, 1994; Saldana, 2009; Strauss, 1987), but there is still confusion and uncertainty among both students and researchers regarding how to actually go about this task. This confusion is due primarily to the fact that qualitative research is essentially *interpretive.* Unlike quantitative research, where results can be evaluated by their degree of "statistical significance" and "effect size" (Chapter 10), there is no comparable single criterion for evaluating findings in qualitative research. Researchers are the primary data collection instrument in qualitative studies and, consequently, must find ways to interpret and make sense of their data. Lichtman (2013) succinctly summarizes the primary processes for analyzing qualitative data as "coding, categorizing, and conceptualizing" (p. 251), a characterization that we think captures the essence of making sense of qualitative data. Whether researchers use a generic coding strategy (Thomas, 2006) or a specific strategy such as the constant-comparison method associated with grounded theory (Charmaz, 2006; Strauss & Corbin, 1990), Lichtman (2013) argues that the key is to use a systematic approach since "a systematic approach to analysis and interpretation brings order and understanding to your qualitative research project" (p. 246). The same can be said for quantitative research—systematic rigor is the leitmotif of both traditions.

Interpretation

Finally, whether using quantitative or qualitative methods, facts and findings must be *interpreted* to make sense of them, since they simply cannot speak for themselves. Just as in a jury trial, facts and evidence are interpreted in different ways by opposing lawyers in pursuit of the "truth." Some cynics may refer to the interpretation of data or evidence as the work of spin doctors who put forward what they want others to see while camouflaging negative evidence by placing it in the background rather than the foreground of their arguments. We take another position: that "truth" can be a slippery commodity (at least when trying to capture the complexities of human behavior) and that a willingness to at least consider conflicting evidence and points of view can get us closer to truth and not further from it. Just as different types of voices and instruments contribute to performing a complex piece of music, so too do different voices and instruments contribute to our growing understanding of complex phenomena.

❖ STRENGTHS AND LIMITATIONS OF QUALITATIVE RESEARCH

Due to its focus on the "why" and the meaning attributed by participants to events and circumstances, qualitative research can provide a rich and deep understanding of complex phenomena. Rather than try to immediately simplify data through reduction or modeling, qualitative researchers try to preserve complexity as long as possible in order to understand the meaning that participants themselves attribute to phenomena.

Although phenomenology is but one of several approaches or designs typically used in qualitative research (see Table 2.2), its general premise of empathizing with the "lived experiences" of participants by "bracketing out" one's own viewpoints seems to resonate throughout all qualitative designs. However, qualitative researchers also recognize, try as they might, that they themselves are a living and viable component of any research endeavor that cannot be "bracketed" completely and that reflexivity forms an essential part of the "intricate fabric" (Creswell, 2007, p. 35) that is being woven. Qualitative research can also be thought of metaphorically as a conversation (as opposed to a monologue); where the conversation takes unpredictable twists and turns and everybody engaged in it is changed in some way by the process. At its best, this dynamic is a win–win where all parties (participants, researcher, and readers) are enriched. Qualitative research offers us the possibility of learning about our world in ways that embrace poetry, music, art, narrative, nuance, context, and human intention; therefore, it can play a major part in helping educators and social scientists better understand our world and the humans who inhabit it.

Even though what follows is somewhat of a "straw man" (since by this time readers should recognize that we are proponents of *both* traditions), we think that by pointing out some "gaps" in qualitative inquiry, perhaps the quantitative tradition can be more readily positioned as a complement to it—devious but hopefully effective! As described earlier, qualitative research seeks to make known what was formerly unknown by appreciating the complexity of phenomena and participants in their natural settings. To achieve this purpose, rich and thick data are collected, analyzed, and interpreted in an artistic yet systematic manner. However, as a corollary to the desire to understand complex phenomena, it is often the case that there are things to be learned that are not amenable to the type of data and analysis typically utilized in the qualitative tradition. A metaphoric example may help here. While we learn to appreciate the beauty of a flower by looking at it rather than dissecting it, it is also helpful to know something about the chemical composition of the soil in terms of potassium and other attributes (that are often expressed in quantitative terms) in order to make sure that we provide an ideal environment for the flower to thrive. In the same way, we sometimes need to know some things about our participants and phenomena that provide us with the kind of additional information that allows us to appreciate them more fully, and this information may be quantitative rather than qualitative in nature—numbers not words.

To extend the argument further, if you want to find out about the remembrances of graduates of Catholic schools using a phenomeno-logical approach, while the most important data can most likely be obtained by interviewing informants, it might also be desirable to know something about the number of Catholic schools compared with public schools. It might also be helpful to know something about enrollment trends and achievement data from these schools to promote a better understanding of the environmental context. This quantitative information can be thought of as complementary to the primary phe-nomenological aim. However, let us hastily add that this exhortation should not be construed as our promoting "mixed method" studies to the exclusion of "pedigree" approaches; rather, we simply want to point out that using both types of information sometimes helps us paint a more accurate and interesting picture. While mixed methods are sometimes appropriate for answering a particular research ques-tion, there are still many situations where either a specific qualitative or quantitative approach is best. Designing a study in such a way just to be able to dub it "mixed methods" because this approach may be in vogue is more likely to result in a mediocre study rather than one that illuminates and contributes to genuine understanding.

We support the notion that there are inherent limitations to a strictly qualitative (or quantitative) approach *in relation to* particular problems and research questions, and in such cases, a mixed methods approach makes eminent sense. Alternatively, the inherent aesthetic qualities and effectiveness of a solo design (whether qualitative or quantitative) often argue for a pedigree approach. However, even when a pedigree approach is used, we hope that it is recognized that there is still much that could be learned using other approaches both within and across traditions—multiple methods, sources, and replications provide a much firmer basis for claiming that we understand phenomena.

❖ CONCLUDING REMARKS

In this chapter, we presented an overview of qualitative research, including its purpose, assumptions, strengths, and limitations. While this treatment was not comprehensive, the intent was to serve as a refresher for those who are already active in the field of qualitative inquiry as well as to suggest an initial framework for learning for those who may be new to the field. Another purpose of this chapter was to serve as a bridge from the qualitative to the quantitative tradition in the chapters that follow. Specifically, we have tried to assure readers schooled in the qualitative tradition that the quantitative tradition can contribute to their understanding of phenomena. While not sufficient to transform readers into accomplished quantitative researchers, the following chapters are meant to provide an approachable way to understand and appreciate the fundamental ideas underlying the quantitative tradition and to serve as a springboard for further learning. Additional "springboards" include both the "Guidelines for Evaluating Research Summaries" found in the Appendix as well as several articles that can be found on the companion website. Readers will be encouraged to use these resources in concert with the text in order to extend their understanding. Finally, the "Connections to Qualitative Research" that appear in the following chapters have been designed to help readers stay grounded in the qualitative tradition while seeking to more fully understand the quantitative tradition.

DISCUSSION QUESTIONS

1. Qualitative research is sometimes referred to as "interpretive research". Do you think this characterization is accurate? Why or why not?

2. Which philosophical assumptions underlying the qualitative tradition do you think quantitative researchers might find most difficult to accept? Why?

3. What kind of data do you like to collect, analyze, and interpret? Why?

4. If you were a journalist and had to write a column about the impacts of unemployment, what are some quantitative sources of data you might use? What qualitative sources?

KEY TERMS

Axiology: based on the values that undergird decisions and perspectives.

Coding: techniques used to analyze qualitative data (see Saldana, 2009).

Credibility: based on the answer to the question, "are the findings believable?" Under the qualitative tradition, a critical element of "trust-worthiness"; sometimes seen as analogous to the term *validity* under the quantitative tradition (see Chapter 5).

Data analysis: procedures used to make sense of data in order to answer the research questions.

Data reduction: the process of simplifying data so that it can be inter-preted; usually achieved by either *statistics* under the quantitative tra-dition or *coding* under the qualitative tradition.

Epistemology: examines the essence of knowledge and how it is obtained.

Ontology: concerned with the nature of existence, being, and how real-ity is perceived.

Positionality: informing readers of your perspective in relation to data collection, analysis, and interpretation so that they are aware of how your "position" may affect findings.

Reliability: generally defined as the *consistency* of data produced by instruments under the quantitative tradition (see Chapter 5). Under the qualitative tradition, this is sometimes referred to as "dependability," where the researcher is considered the primary instrument.

Research hypothesis: a tentative statement that predicts the specific relationships, similarities or differences, or causal mechanisms that the researcher expects to observe among the attributes being investigated (Chapter 3).

Research problem: any topic, issue, or phenomenon that the researcher is interested in studying.

Research question: distinct from, but arising from the research prob-lem, the research question(s) is an actual question that indicates to the audience exactly what the researcher aims to study (Chapter 3).

Rhetorical: focusing on oral and written communication and its rela-tionship to knowledge.

Statistics: data analysis techniques used to analyze quantitative data and categorized as either descriptive or inferential (see Chapters 9 and 10).

Variable: an attribute or characteristic that *varies* among individuals or groups (Chapter 3).

ADDITIONAL READINGS IN QUALITATIVE RESEARCH

In addition to the sources cited in the References, here is a list of other books that we think readers may find useful for understanding, designing, and analyzing qualitative studies.

Bernard, H. R., & Ryan, G. W. (2010). *Analyzing qualitative data: Systematic approaches*. Thousand Oaks, CA: Sage.

Bogdan, R. C., & Biklen, S. K. (2007). *Qualitative research for education: An introduction to theories and methods* (5th ed.). Boston, MA: Pearson.

Marshall, C., & Rossman, G. B. (2011). *Designing qualitative research* (5th ed.). Thousand Oaks, CA: Sage.

Sokolowski, R. (2000). *Introduction to phenomenology*. New York, NY: Cambridge University Press.

Yin, R. K. (2012). *Qualitative research from start to finish*. New York, NY: Guilford Press.

3

Research in the Quantitative Tradition

I n this chapter, we provide an overview of the quantitative research paradigm not just as an alternative methodological approach but as one requiring researchers to at least temporarily assume a different worldview or schema. Our purpose is not to appraise the value of qualitative in comparison with quantitative research; our aim instead is to help readers create and maintain an inclusive understanding of both research traditions. As you go through this chapter, remember that the researcher's qualitative or quantitative training (or bias!) should not dictate the research methodology; instead, the type of research question posed should guide how the researcher proceeds.

Our "Connections to Qualitative Research" sections also begin in this chapter. The goal of these sections is to construct bridges between the two traditions that will promote readers' appreciation and understanding of the complementary nature of the two traditions and to show that both research traditions are fundamentally connected by their underlying purpose of discovering new knowledge. Although we think that you will find our "Connections" helpful, it is primarily through self-reflection as you proceed through the chapters that you will be able to forge personal links between the traditions.

❖ PURPOSE AND CHARACTERISTICS OF QUANTITATIVE RESEARCH

Some of the questions that researchers are interested in addressing require an approach that differs from the qualitative one described in Chapter 2. For instance, a researcher may be interested in describing the attributes or behaviors of a large group of individuals; in examining the relationships among the behaviors of the individuals in that group; or in some cases, may be interested in knowing whether a particular treatment or intervention changes the attributes or behaviors of individuals or groups. In these situations, the researcher may find that quantitative methods are more appropriate than qualitative methods.

Looking back to the list of quality indicators, we first introduced in Chapter 1, you will notice that the following question "Is the research design appropriate for investigating the research questions?" (Question 5) comes *after* the questions related to formulating the research questions (Questions 1–3). Our ordering in this case was intentional: The research design that a researcher adopts should be aligned with the purpose of the research. Stated more explicitly, it is our position that a researcher is not a qualitative *or* quantitative researcher. Rather, there are research questions that are best addressed with a qualitative design, and there are research questions that are best addressed with a quantitative design. Moreover, there are researchers who address research questions suitable for qualitative designs and researchers who address research questions suitable for quantitative designs. And many times, these researchers are the same individuals!

Clearly, being able to address only one type of research question is limiting not only for the researcher as an individual who strives to develop and evolve as a scholar but also for the field of which you are a member. Creative research questions generate new and exciting knowledge; therefore, if we are hamstrung by the type of questions we can ask, our contribution to the field will be diminished. Likewise, researchers who embrace both the research traditions are likely to be better prepared to collaborate with colleagues by asking and seeking to answer interesting questions that do not fit neatly into one tradition or the other. As such, we ask our readers who consider themselves to be "qualitative researchers" to rethink the nomenclature they use to describe themselves—at least temporarily.

In Chapter 1, we started off by stating that "quantitative research seeks to discover new knowledge by simplifying complexities in settings that tend to be more contrived." If we deconstruct this sentence, we already see a major difference between the quantitative and qualitative approaches. While research in both traditions attempts to discover new knowledge, qualitative research attempts to discover that new knowledge by retaining the complexities that exist in natural settings, and quantitative research aims to do so by distilling complex phenomena into simpler representations (in some cases, into mathematical functions or equations).

Individuals who are new to the quantitative tradition often believe that the most important difference between the qualitative and quantitative traditions is the type of data collected. They believe that the primary distinguishing characteristic is that qualitative research relies on the collection of rich description of phenomena (usually in the form of words), while quantitative research requires the collection of numbers. However, this is not entirely true. While it is often the case that the approaches warrant the collection of different forms of data, each tradition has a different epistemology and axiology about how data will be used.

In Chapter 2, we said that qualitative research assumes that there are multiple "realities" as perceived through the unique lenses of individuals. Perceptions constitute each person's reality, and these perceptions (and hence reality as perceived) change as a function of time, experience, circumstances, and learning. Therefore, research in the qualitative tradition can be characterized as providing an *emic* account of reality that is unique to the individuals under study and is meaningful and value laden for the researcher (Creswell, 1998). Conversely, the attributes that characterize research methods in the quantitative tradition include the following: objectivity, precision, empiricism, logical reasoning, generalizability, replication and verification, parsimonious explanation, and conditional conclusions in the interpretation of empirical results (Creswell, 1998; McMillan & Schumacher, 2006; Mertler & Charles, 2010). Quite the opposite of the emic account, this culturally neutral *etic* account of reality is not value laden for the researcher.

Although the 10 guiding questions laid out in Chapter 1 may remind some of you of the steps in the scientific method, these particular questions were developed from a broader perspective to capture the commonalities that exist in the quantitative and qualitative approaches. For those of you unfamiliar with the **scientific method**, it is an approach that involves the formulation, testing, and refinement of hypotheses; the systematic collection of empirical evidence through measurement; and in specific situations, conducting experiments. In the following section, we expand on the philosophical assumptions of research in the quantitative tradition in the hope that it helps readers appreciate the multidimensionality of quantitative research and embrace both traditions as equally valid and complementary for understanding the complex world in which we live.

> It is our position that a researcher is not a qualitative or quantitative researcher. Rather, there are research questions that are best addressed with a qualitative design, and there are research questions that are best addressed with a quantitative design.

❖ PHILOSOPHICAL ASSUMPTIONS OF QUANTITATIVE RESEARCH

The scientific method, on which research in the quantitative tradition is predicated, is derived from the philosophical and epistemological system known as *positivism*. Under the positivist schema, the scientific method is the best approach for understanding phenomena in the world around us, and in addition, claims about the world are only meaningful when they can be verified through observation (Gall, Borg, & Gall, 1996). One of the essential differences between qualitative and quantitative research is that the former relies on an **inductive reasoning** approach, while the latter relies on a **deductive reasoning** approach. That is, qualitative methods tend to generate theories (inductive), while quantitative methods tend to test theories or hypotheses (deductive). Just to be clear, all research, regardless of whether it is qualitative or quantitative, involves stages that are both inductive and deductive and one does not preclude the other. For example, we can think of many situations, even when conducting controlled experiments, where the researcher might notice patterns in the data that lead them to develop new theories and hypotheses. Rather, we are saying that the *purpose and intention of the inductive and deductive approaches are different*. In addition, the deductive approach tends to work from the general to the specific. In this way, deductive reasoning is often thought of as a top-down approach, whereby one starts with a theory and then narrows that theory down to a more specific hypothesis that can be tested empirically using data that have been collected. The question here is whether the data confirm or refute the original theory and hypothesis that were developed from it. As readers will notice, this is quite a bit narrower and less exploratory than the inductive approach described for qualitative research in Chapter 2.

As first introduced in Chapter 2, the quantitative tradition embodies three primary components—design, measurement, and statistics. If we return to Creswell's (2007) schema of the philosophical assumptions related to ontological, epistemological, axiological, rhetorical, and methodological aspects of qualitative research, we can draw distinctions and parallels between the qualitative and quantitative approaches.

The ontological assumption in the quantitative tradition assumes that phenomena in our world can be measured and understood. To extend this idea further, we are not interested in the measurements we take on an individual per se; rather, we are interested in generalizing from a group of individuals to a larger population. As such, the ontology of research in the quantitative tradition is different from that in the qualitative tradition. In fact, we can draw a parallel between this way of thinking and the physical sciences. In high school, you may have learned about Newton's Laws of Motion, the "physical laws" that govern how forces act on an object that is at rest and in motion. Newton's Second Law of Motion states that when a force acts on a mass, it will accelerate: The larger the mass, the greater the force needed to accelerate it. The key point here is that the "law" that describes the amount of force needed to accelerate a particular mass will be approximately the same regardless of where on Earth you take measurements. The relationship can in fact be distilled into a simpler representation described by a simple mathematical formula: Force = Mass × Acceleration. In this way, the physical laws that govern motion are stable on our planet, stand up to scientific examination, and can be replicated by others. To take this one step further, we state that theories or hypotheses are not meaningful unless they can be tested empirically, and findings must be replicable to be credible. We recognize that there are many important differences between research in the social sciences and research in physics; however, a reliance on empirical evidence to test theories or hypotheses is at the core of the positivist approach that emerged in the early 20th century.

The qualitative and quantitative research traditions also differ in terms of their epistemology and axiology. Individuals conducting qualitative research operate under the assumption that, while they try not to disturb the context, their presence affects the situation, context, or individual being studied and that even when they try to be objective, their judgments and evaluations are colored by their values. Conversely, individuals conducting quantitative research aim for scientific independence, detachment, and objectivity when they state their research questions and hypotheses, select the participants for their studies, collect data to address the research questions, conduct their analyses, and, finally, draw their conclusions. As we acknowledged in Chapter 2, this is easier said than done—even supposedly "objective" approaches and tests carry with them a great deal of human intentionality and value. Nevertheless, quantitative research aims to minimize the attachment between the investigator and participants and to quarantine the values of the researcher as much as possible.

In general (although this isn't always the case), the scientific detachment of the researcher is evident in the way that the findings from quantitative research are summarized and interpreted. Unlike the rhetorical assumption in the qualitative tradition, researchers describing their theories, hypotheses, methods, analyses, and conclusions from a quantitative study will rarely write in the first person. This approach is consistent with the epistemological assumption of quantitative research that knowledge claims are based on objective empirical evidence and that there is scientific detachment between the researcher and the phenomena being investigated; in this way, the quantitative researcher writes from the perspective of the "disinterested" scientist.

Instructors of quantitative research methods, often hear students say, "I hope my research will support my hypothesis that . . . ." Since objectivity is one of the cornerstones of quantitative research, we need to continuously remind ourselves that we do not *hope* when conducting quantitative research! Rather, armed with the goal of making our research as detached and objective as possible, we aim to take a hands-off, "white gloves" approach—an intentional scientific detachment between the researcher and the individuals or groups participating in a study.

❖ TECHNICAL COMPONENTS OF EMPIRICAL INQUIRY IN QUANTITATIVE RESEARCH

Quantitative inquiry comprises three major components—design, measurement, and statistics. In this case, "design" serves as the overall plan for the study, "measurement" refers to the instruments used for data collection, and "statistics" is the set of analysis procedures that quantitative researchers use to describe their data and to make inferences (generalizations) about the larger population. Thus far, we focused on the complementary and supplementary nature of qualitative and quantitative research. Now that we are getting more to the heart of the matter—quantitative research methods for qualitatively trained researchers—we will focus less on comparing the two approaches. Instead, we will go headlong into quantitative research as a paradigm for understanding the world around us. In the remainder of this text, we will use the following axiom to guide our coverage of research in the quantitative tradition:

> Researchers should choose research designs, procedures, data collection instruments, and data analysis methods that: are appropriate for addressing the question(s) posed; allow generalizations to be made to other participants and settings beyond their study; and that minimize all feasible alternative explanations for the results observed.

In subsequent chapters, we will attempt to unpack each part of the axiom. In this chapter, we will begin with a discussion about variables, research questions, and research hypotheses. We begin with these because they are central to any discussion about research in the quantitative tradition. Also in this chapter, we provide an introduction to the design–measurement–analysis triad as it is interpreted in the quantitative tradition. In later chapters, we discuss the design–measurement–analysis triad in more detail.

Variables, Research Problems and Questions, and Research Hypotheses

Variables

When conducting research in the quantitative tradition, researchers use the term *variable* to describe the characteristics or behaviors that they are investigating. For example, researchers might collect data about the mathematics performance of a group of high school students. In this case, the variable of interest would be "mathematics performance." A researcher might also be interested in non-cognitive variables such as attitudes, beliefs, or behaviors. Technically, a **variable** is an attribute that varies among individuals or groups. For example, you and your colleague have different colored eyes or are different genders—in this case—eye color and gender are attributes on which you vary from each other; these are variables. Similarly, you and your colleague may have different heights or if you were to take a mathematics test, you may have different test scores—here, height and performance on a mathematics test are variables. By definition then, a variable is the opposite of an attribute that is **constant** among individuals or group. For example, among a group of females, gender is constant.

Readers will notice that there are differences between the types of variables we used as examples in the previous paragraph. For example, the variable "eye color" is different from the "height" variable; this is because differences in eye color indicate a qualitative difference among individuals, while differences in height indicate quantitative differences in the "amount" of height. To further illustrate this point, the data in Table 3.1 shows the observed height, eye color, and school name for five high school students. Readers will notice two columns for the eye color variable; one that indicates the actual color and another that is a numerical representation where 1 = *brown*, 2 = *blue*, and 3 = *green*. Likewise, there are two columns under the high school name heading; one that shows that all students are enrolled in Johnson High School, and a numerical representation of that constant. In this case, all five students are assigned the same number for high school membership, 1. While both the numerically coded eye color variable and the height variable are numbers, they are quite different from each other. Specifically, the numbers assigned to the eye color variable are arbitrary and do not represent quantitative differences among the five individuals, whereas the different height values represent actual quantitative differences among the observed attributes. In addition, the difference between the two types of variables limits how they can be used; for example, while it is appropriate to conclude that the average height among these five individuals is approximately 67.2 inches, it is not appropriate to conclude that the average eye color is 1.6!

In this example, the eye color variable and the school name constant are *categorical* variables, whereas the height variable is a *continuous* variable. Stated more formally, a **categorical variable** is one that varies only in type but not amount. Conversely, *a* **continuous variable** is one that

Table 3.1   Hypothetical Example of Categorical and Continuous Variables

Subject	Eye Color		Height (inches)	High School Name	
Jane	Brown	1	66	Johnson HS	1
Mark	Green	3	69	Johnson HS	1
Susan	Brown	1	64	Johnson HS	1
John	Brown	1	73	Johnson HS	1
Ann	Blue	2	64	Johnson HS	1

varies in amount or degree along a continuum from low to high. While continuous variables can be mathematically manipulated (i.e., an average can be computed, the values can be summed, etc.), categorical variables cannot be mathematically manipulated. Examples of categorical variables include gender, race, and career type, and examples of continuous variables include weight and distance. Even unobservable attributes such as attitude, anxiety, or depression can be classified as continuous; for example, individuals differ on the "amount" of anxiety or depression they feel. In sum, there are different types of variables used to represent different attributes, and the types of variables we use will dictate how we use them. Additional information about how we measure different attributes and characteristics will be provided in Chapter 5.

Besides classifying variables as categorical or continuous, we can also classify variables according to how they are going to be considered as part of the research study. This practice allows researchers to indicate to their audience which variables are central to the research study and which are secondary or even nuisance variables; *independent* and *dependent* variables are essential attributes for addressing the research questions posed, and extraneous variables are nuisance variables that need to be controlled during a study.

An **independent variable** is one that is hypothesized to lead to changes in some other variable being studied. And, *the* **dependent variable** is hypothesized to change in response to changes in the independent variable. We use the phrase "lead to changes in" loosely at this point because, as we expect will become evident in later chapters (Chapters 7 and 8), isolating cause and effect relationships is not possible with every type of research design. For now, we will proceed with this definition in which the dependent variable "depends on" changes in the independent variable.

In many research studies, the independent and dependent variables will be logically distinct from each other. However, in other cases, which variable is the independent variable and which is the dependent variable is not so clear. The classic example of this point occurs in studies that examine the effects of smoking; it is safe to assume that in a study examining the relationship between the number of cigarettes smoked and pulmonary function, the independent variable is the number of cigarettes smoked, and the measure of pulmonary function is the dependent variable. Logically, this implies that the number of cigarettes smoked is hypothesized to lead to changes in pulmonary function. It is unlikely to be the other way around.

In other research studies, the distinction is not so clear-cut. For example, in a study examining the relationship between students' performance in mathematics and science, the distinction is not as straightforward—changes in science performance could be hypothesized to lead to changes in mathematics performance, or changes in mathematics performance could be hypothesized to lead to changes in science performance. Ultimately, designating the variables as independent and dependent will depend on the purpose of the research and the research questions posed.

In the example examining the relationship between students' performance in mathematics and science, the independent and dependent variables are both naturally occurring. That is, the researcher simply measures science and mathematics performance and examines the relationship between the two. However, in some cases, the researcher creates an independent variable by manipulating some condition. In these situations, the independent variable is referred to as a *manipulated independent variable*. For example, if the researcher is interested in examining the effect of a new teaching method on science performance, he or she would assign some students to receive the new method of instruction and others to receive the traditional method. The method of instruction is a manipulated independent variable where the levels of this independent variable might be 0 = *traditional instructional method* and 1 = *new instructional method*, and the independent variable is hypothesized to lead to changes in performance on a science test (dependent variable).

In social science research, *extraneous variables* can create problems for researchers. In our guiding axiom at the outset of this chapter, we said that researchers must choose designs, data collection instruments, and data analysis methods that "minimize all feasible alternative explanations for the results observed." Extraneous variables are the source of these alternative explanations for the results observed;

extraneous variables are nuisance variables that are peripheral to the research study but because they are associated with the dependent variable, can provide alternative explanations for the results observed when uncontrolled. For example, in the study examining the effect of a new teaching method on students' performance in science, teachers' experience in the classroom might be considered an extraneous variable. Specifically, teachers' experience is not central to the study in which students' science performance (the dependent variable) is compared for the groups that received the new and traditional instructional methods (instructional method is the manipulated independent variable), but if left uncontrolled, it could provide a plausible explanation for any differences observed between the two groups. In this way, extraneous variables confound the results. Note that the process of classifying an attribute as an extraneous variable always depends on the research purpose and the research questions; a variable that is classified as extraneous in one study might be classified as a central independent or dependent variable in another study. The process of minimizing or controlling for the effects of extraneous variables is central to conducting research in the quantitative tradition, and so these points will be revisited in Chapter 6 when we discuss internal validity.

Research Problems and Research Questions

The **research problem** is any topic, issue, or phenomenon that the researcher is interested in studying, and a researcher's capacity to conduct rigorous research that contributes to the field is predicated on his or her understanding of the literature related to that problem. Researchers should have a deep understanding of the problem and how it is positioned within the field. Understanding the literature and its place in the research planning process will help ensure that the research being conducted is addressing an interesting and important topic in an appropriate way such that the results can contribute to society's understanding of the research problem.

Prior research should be used to

- ✓ Guide the formulation of the research questions and hypotheses
- ✓ Guide the choice of research design and sampling plan
- ✓ Identify possible extraneous or nuisance variables and conditions that may need to be controlled for or minimized through design elements

✓ Identify new populations or subpopulations to which their planned study could generalize

✓ Identify the most appropriate data collection tools for providing valid and reliable data to address the research questions

In Chapter 1, we outlined 10 guiding questions for conducting research in both the qualitative and quantitative traditions. It was no coincidence that our first three questions on that list relate to the research questions; rigorous research is predicated on asking significant and clear questions that are grounded in and guided by prior research (although the sequencing of this "grounding" may occur later in qualitative studies). Readers should note that the research problem is distinct from the research question; the research problem is any topic, issue, phenomenon, attribute or characteristic that the researcher is interested in studying, whereas *the* **research question** is an actual question that indicates to the audience exactly what the researcher aims to study. As a reminder, the first three guiding questions are as follows:

1. Do the research questions have practical or theoretical significance?

2. Are the terms used in the research questions clearly defined?

3. Have the research questions been adequately positioned within the literature?

The researcher's understanding of the research problem circumscribes his or her ability to formulate significant, researchable questions. Gaps or weaknesses in the researcher's understanding can lead to vague or unimpressive research questions that do not contribute to the field. Under the qualitative tradition, however, deeper understanding of the problem evolves as a function of increased time "in the field," and initial research questions are sometimes modified rather than being held constant.

Effective research questions have particular characteristics. Specifically, they are based on a sound theoretical framework and a deep understanding of prior research and evidence, address a relevant and interesting problem in an unbiased manner, and aim to investigate new dimensions of that problem. Effective research questions are also practical given the researcher's resources, expertise, availability, and so on and should be able to be addressed in an ethical way. In addition, they are clear and succinct and delineate the specific relationships, similarities or differences, or causal mechanisms that the research is going to study.

Finally, effective research questions provide explicit definitions of the attributes being measured to address the research questions. In technical terms, this last point is referred to as providing an **operational definition** of the attributes. When we *operationalize an attribute, we define the attribute according to the actual steps that will be taken to measure it.* Operational definitions are essential in research because they indicate what observable behaviors will be used to define the attribute; they provide the specificity that is needed in conducting rigorous research; and by indicating to other researchers exactly *how* the attribute is being defined in the study, operational definitions allow for replication. This specialized way of defining attributes when conducting research in the quantitative tradition is distinct from using a dictionary or constitutive definition of the attribute (i.e., using other words to describe the attribute) or defining the attribute by using examples of how it manifests. In most cases, these types of definitions cannot provide the specificity needed to indicate the observable behaviors that will define the attribute in such a way that will allow other researchers to replicate the research. Table 3.2 outlines the characteristics of effective research questions and hypotheses.

Research Hypotheses

As noted previously, research in the quantitative tradition is aligned with the scientific method and the philosophical system known as *positivism. This is distinct from the postmodernism or poststructuralism* philosophical system *aligned with the qualitative tradition.* As such, quantitative methods are *deductive;* they test theories and hypotheses by examining whether the observed data support or refute the original theory and hypothesis. This, of course, differs from the inductive approach we described in Chapter 2 as being central to qualitative research. Research hypotheses, therefore, are typically stated when conducting research in the quantitative tradition. Readers should note that we do not prove or disprove research hypotheses; rather, empirical evidence is used to decide whether the hypothesis is tenable or untenable. More formally, *a* **research hypothesis** is a tentative statement that predicts the specific relationships, similarities or differences, or causal mechanisms that the researcher expects to observe among the attributes being investigated. Implicit in this definition is the following: the evidence provided by the study *must be able to either support or refute the research hypothesis.* This

Table 3.2   Characteristics of Effective Research Questions and Hypotheses

Effective Research Questions:	Effective Research Hypotheses:
✓ Are based on a sound theoretical framework and a solid understanding of prior research and evidence	✓ Are based on a sound theoretical framework and a solid understanding of prior research and evidence
✓ Address a relevant and interesting problem in an unbiased manner	✓ Address a relevant and interesting problem in an unbiased manner
✓ Aim to investigate new dimensions of a research problem	✓ Aim to investigate new dimensions of a research problem
✓ Are practical given the researcher's resources, expertise, availability, etc.	✓ Are testable given the researcher's resources, expertise, availability, etc.
✓ Can be asked in an ethical way	✓ Can be tested in an ethical way
✓ Are clear and succinct	✓ Are clear and succinct
✓ Delineate the specific relationships, similarities/ differences, or causal mechanisms being studied	✓ Delineate the specific relationships, similarities/ differences, or causal mechanisms that are expected
✓ Provide explicit operational definitions of the attributes being measured to address the research questions	✓ Provide explicit operational definitions of the attributes being measured to support or refute the hypothesis

reaffirms the need for the theoretical and operational alignment of the research problem, the research questions, the research hypotheses, and the empirical evidence that is collected as part of the study.

While research hypotheses are stipulated as part of the deductive process and can ensure that the researcher is focused on the evidence needed to answer the research questions, there are drawbacks to stating research hypotheses at the outset of a study. In particular, a pre-stated hypothesis may lead the researcher to miss phenomena that might be important to the study or may lead to intentional or unintentional bias on the part of the researcher. In addition, not all research designs require the statement of hypotheses; for example, research hypotheses are generally not useful in purely descriptive research, such as survey research designs.

Effective research hypotheses share the same characteristics as effective research questions. Effective research hypotheses address a relevant and interesting problem in an unbiased manner and aim to investigate new dimensions of that problem; are clear and succinct; delineate the relationships, similarities or differences, or causal mechanisms that are expected; and provide operational definitions of the attributes that will be measured. In addition, effective research hypotheses are testable given the researcher's resources, expertise, availability, and so on, and they are based on sound logic, an understanding of prior research and evidence, and a solid theoretical framework. Table 3.2 summarizes the characteristics of effective research questions and hypotheses.

The Design–Measurement–Analysis Triad

Research Design

When researchers decide that their research problem and research questions are best addressed using quantitative methods, there are many different types of research designs that the researcher can use. There are two primary approaches to conducting research in the quantitative tradition, and they differ from each other in their purpose—*non-experimental research* and *experimental research*. **Non-experimental research designs** are adopted when the goal of the research is to examine naturally occurring attributes, behaviors, or phenomena. Conversely, **experimental research designs** are used when the goal of the research is to examine the effect of a treatment or intervention on some attributes or phenomena. It is important to notice here that the contrasting goals of non-experimental and experimental research imply different functions for the researcher. When engaging in non-experimental research, researchers observe and measure naturally occurring attributes, behaviors, or phenomena and aim to avoid influencing the context in which the research is being conducted. In contrast, researchers engaging in experimental research aim to directly control the context by creating different conditions for groups of participants.

Non-Experimental Research Designs. Many seminal textbooks describe non-experimental research designs as a set of discrete approaches for examining naturally occurring phenomena. For example, Fraenkel and Wallen (2011) differentiate between survey, correlational, and causal comparative research designs. Likewise, Wiersma and Jurs (2009), Mertler and Charles (2010), McMillan and Schumacher (2006), and several other seminal research methods textbooks describe a variety of non-experimental research designs. We think that these texts are each excellent, and in fact, both of us have used every one of them at one point or another in teaching our courses. However, in reflecting how best to introduce and describe non-experimental research designs to readers who may be qualitatively inclined, we have opted to simplify our discussion.

Specifically, we find that some of the distinctions are confusing. For example, some authors differentiate between causal comparative research designs and ex post facto research designs, while others use the terms interchangeably. Both these designs are non-experimental in nature, but it is our understanding that the term *ex post facto* designs refer to studies in which data are gathered retrospectively, while causal comparative is used to describe studies in which data are gathered from pre-formed groups and the independent variable is not manipulated as in an experiment.

After many years of teaching research methods, we have also noticed that students who are new to the tradition become confused by the vast number of technical terms. As an example, consider the term *causal comparative research design*. Someone coming across this term for the first time could easily assume that because the word *causal* is used in the label, this design would invariably allow causal inferences to be made from non-experimental data. In fact, this is not the case—only in very exceptional cases will causal comparative studies allow causal inferences to be made.

In addition, while guiding our own students through the quantitative research design process, we have often noticed that because the designs are presented as discrete entities in many textbooks, students fail to see that more than one research design can be used in a single study. For example, a survey research design may be used to collect data, but the types of questions posed require students to examine relationships (i.e., correlational-type question) or examine differences among pre-existing groups (i.e., causal comparative-type question). In sum, the presentation of common quantitative research designs often imply that the approaches are entirely distinct from each other, and most important, they often fail to reflect what real researchers do in the field.

In an effort to avoid confusing our readers, we will refrain from describing non-experimental research designs as survey, causal comparative, correlational, or ex post facto. Instead, we describe non-experimental research designs according to two characteristics: (1) the primary objective of the research and (2) the role of time in the data collection process. We are certainly not the first to adopt this schema for organizing descriptions of quantitative research, and we hope that our presentation will streamline our discussion and help students develop a stronger grasp of the most common research designs used in the quantitative tradition.

Broadly speaking, non-experimental research studies are undertaken for the following reasons: (a) to describe attributes, behaviors, or phenomena (**descriptive study**); (b) to use the relationships among attributes, behaviors, or phenomena to make predictions (**prediction study**); or (c) to test theories about how and why some attributes are related as they are, or how and why the observed differences between pre-existing groups came to be (**explanatory study**). In addition to the research objectives, how the data are collected in relation to time can be used to characterize non-experimental research. Specifically, the researcher may need to (a) collect data at one point in time (**cross-sectional study**), (b) collect data across some fixed time period (**longitudinal study**), or (c) explore whether past events are associated with observed differences among individuals (**retrospective study**).

Using these characterizations, we hope that readers will appreciate that a single study can pose questions that are descriptive, predictive, or explanatory. Likewise, all combinations of objectives and time factors are possible; for example, some research questions might require a cross-sectional explanatory study to be conducted, while other questions may require a longitudinal descriptive study. We have dedicated Chapter 7 to non-experimental research designs, and we hope that our characterization of the topic will reduce readers' confusion about the designs and the language used to describe them.

Experimental Research Designs. Compared with our introduction to non-experimental research designs, experimental research designs are a lot more clear-cut! Specifically, in the simplest two-group case, experimental research involves exposing one group of research participants to an intervention designed to influence the attributes being studied (the treatment condition) and withholding that intervention from another group (the control condition). Subsequently, the effect of the intervention is estimated by comparing the post-implementation attributes in the two groups. Under the experimental research heading, researchers can choose between implementing a **quasi-experimental research design** or a **true experimental research design**. The difference between these two specific designs rests on how the treatment and control groups are formed: In a true experimental design, the researcher creates the treatment and control groups by randomly assigning participants to one or the other group, whereas in a quasi-experimental research design, the researcher does not (or cannot) create treatment and control groups through **randomization (aka random assignment)**.

Perhaps a researcher is implementing a new instructional method in School A and comparing it with a control condition in School B. Since it is highly unlikely that the researcher was able to randomly assign students and teachers to schools, the treatment and control groups are formed non-randomly. Quasi-experimental designs are used often in school-based research and other settings where random assignment is not possible or acceptable. Overall, a true experiment is the strongest design for making claims about cause and effect.

In Chapters 7 and 8, respectively, we will revisit non-experimental and experimental research designs in more detail. We will elaborate on the essential characteristics of each design, the steps involved in conducting research with these designs, their strengths and weaknesses, and the most common threats to the conclusions that can be drawn.

Measurement and Data Collection

In Chapter 2, we described how measurement plays a pivotal role in empirical inquiry in the qualitative tradition and how trustworthy and consistent evidence is essential for making valid inferences from our data. Now, consider a research situation in which you need to weigh the individuals who are participating in your study. For example, you might be looking at the relationship between weight and self-esteem among female undergraduate athletes. In this case, it would be essential for you to use an instrument that provides you with a trustworthy and consistent measure of weight (we will come back to the self-esteem measure shortly). It would be foolhardy to draw conclusions about the relationship between weight and self-esteem if your weighing scale did not give you trustworthy measurements that would be consistent from one person to the next or from one time to the next! I am sure you would agree that the accuracy of the weighing scale would have to be evaluated before you embark on such a study.

Unfortunately, not all of the measurements we use in social science research are as straightforward as the weighing scale. In most cases, our research questions require us to measure unobservable or latent attributes; in the example above, self-esteem is a latent attribute that we can only measure indirectly through either self-report (participants indicate on a questionnaire or when interviewed) or observation of behaviors. If we had the equivalent of a weighing scale or yardstick for unobservable attributes, our lives as social science researchers would be much less difficult! Despite being unable to measure latent attributes directly, measurement is a highly sophisticated field that has continued to develop since the 19th century.

Revisiting the ideas of trustworthiness and consistency in measurement, we reintroduce the terminology most frequently used in the quantitative tradition to describe the characteristics of sound measurement: *validity* and *reliability*. A measurement instrument (think of the common weighing scales) should be measuring what it is intended to measure (valid information) and should produce consistent results from one individual to the next (reliable information). This is true for your bathroom weighing scales (i.e., it should consistently provide a credible measure of weight every time you or a family member steps on it) and also true for instruments that we use to measure latent attributes such as self-esteem, depression, mathematics achievement, or teachers' attitudes toward professional development. While these attributes are more difficult concepts to capture than weight, our goal is to use measurement instruments that are both valid and reliable.

An important point that we need to make here is that validity is not an intrinsic property of a measurement tool; rather, *validity has to do with the accuracy or credibility of the inferences made from the data provided by a measurement instrument*. So for example, while scores on a mathematics test might provide you with valid evidence about how much mathematics students know, it is unlikely to provide you with valid evidence about how much U.S. history students know! In a nutshell, the validity of a measurement instrument rests on the appropriateness of the inferences you make from the data provided by that instrument. For this reason, it is a misnomer to say that "an instrument has been validated"; rather, one should say that an instrument is valid for "these applications and under these circumstances."

Unlike validity, reliability can be considered intrinsic to the measurement instrument itself. Specifically, *reliability has to do with whether an instrument provides similar information when administered at different times to the same group*. All measurement instruments, even physical ones, have some amount of error associated with them. For example, the weighing scale in your bathroom will likely have a manufacturer-reported error indicating how much error or unreliability the user can expect from one time to the next. In the case of the weighing scale, the error might be ±0.1 pounds or some other small amount. As with the weighing scale, we need the measures that we use in the social sciences and education to provide us with reliable information about the attribute, behavior, or phenomenon we are studying.

Another important point that we wish to make is about the interconnectedness between reliability and validity. While both are essential for sound measurement, a high level of reliability on its own is insufficient for evaluating a measurement tool. That is, one can consistently measure something that does not provide valid evidence for the inferences you wish to make. For example, if you ran a thermometer along the surface of a desk, you would probably find a consistent temperature; however, if your goal were to measure its length, you would end up with invalid data because the instrument does not match to what you intended to discover. On the other hand, for the evidence from a measurement instrument to be valid, it must also be reliable. For example, if you used a ruler made from silly putty to measure the desk, you would probably get different lengths from repeated measurement; as a consequence, the data are invalid for making inferences about the length of the desk. To sum up, *reliability can be observed in the absence of validity, but reliability is a necessary condition for establishing validity*. Moreover, if one had to choose among the two, validity would be the choice, since a valid instrument is by definition a reliable instrument.

We also want to point out to our readers that establishing **instrument validity** and **instrument reliability** is an empirical endeavor that in many situations requires specialized skills in the area of measurement and psychometrics. The role of instrumentation in quantitative research is covered in more detail in Chapter 5. In the meantime, we hope that we have convinced readers of the importance of using valid and reliable measures for generating quantitative data.

Data Analysis

After a researcher has taken the steps necessary to generate valid and reliable data, appropriate methods must then be used for making sense of these data. While a complete discussion about data analysis is presented in Chapters 9 and 10, we thought it worthwhile to include a discussion here about the role of statistics and data analysis in the research process.

Without a doubt, the analysis of quantitative data presents challenges for students who are inexperienced in the quantitative tradition. To reinforce the idea first presented in Chapter 2, we remind the reader that research design and measurement are at least as important as data analysis, if not more so, since they determine the appropriate statistical tests and analysis procedures. You might recall that choosing appropriate methods for analyzing data is only 1 of the 10 quality indicators we presented in Chapter 1! Based on the order of the steps alone, we hope it is clear to the reader that the analysis procedures are predicated on the research questions, research design, and measurement components, including the types of data collected.

Statistical analyses can be broadly categorized as *descriptive* or *inferential*. That is, we use statistics to describe the attributes of a group of individuals (**descriptive analyses**), or we use statistics to make inferences from evidence we find in a sample to what we might expect to see in the larger population (**inferential analyses**). Think of a situation where you are conducting a study to look at the SAT scores for students in your local school district. Say you have access to the SAT scores for a representative sample of students in the district that completed the exam in a particular year. In this case, you could describe the typical SAT score by conducting descriptive analyses. For example, you could calculate the mean or median SAT score (the mean is the arithmetic average, and the median is the score at which 50% of the students in the sample score above and 50% below). Alternatively, you could describe the SAT scores by finding the mode among the scores (the mode is the most frequently occurring score in a group of scores). You might also be interested in exploring the distribution of SAT scores in the sample: Were most of the students bunched together with high scores (or low scores), or were the SAT scores more evenly distributed over the range of all possible scores? In this case, you can quantify the degree to which the SAT scores in the sample vary from person to person by calculating the variance or standard deviation (fear not, these terms will be described in detail in Chapter 9). Descriptive analyses play an important role in the data analysis process as they allow you to develop a more complete understanding of the patterns in your data. In fact, even when the overall purpose of the study is predictive or explanatory, and even if more advanced statistical analyses are required for addressing the research questions posed, descriptive analyses are essential for understanding data—knowing what and who you are studying is always a good starting point in quantitative research.

Now consider the situation where you wish to make inferences from the SAT data for the sample of students in the district to *all* students in the district. In this case, because you are attempting to draw conclusions that go beyond the actual data that you analyzed, you would conduct inferential analyses; you are making inferences from the data provided by the students in your data set (the sample) to all students in the district (the population). Clearly, the degree to which your sample represents the entire district will be very important to the validity of the inferences you make (Chapter 4). In Chapters 9 and 10, we provide more complete coverage of the most common types of descriptive and inferential analyses used to analyze data collected as part of the research process.

❖ STRENGTHS AND LIMITATIONS OF QUANTITATIVE RESEARCH

Quantitative research approaches have several important strengths that make them ideal for addressing the types of research questions that are posed in social science research. Specifically, quantitative methods provide us with an objective framework for testing and validating theories and hypotheses about the world around us. Predicated on having interesting and creative research questions, we can use quantitative research methodologies to objectively describe and predict behaviors and, in the case of experimental research, to look at cause and effect relationships. An important characteristic of experimental research is that of "researcher control." Recall that in an experiment, the researcher manipulates the conditions for one group while maintaining another (approximately equivalent) group as a control group. With this level of control (which is not appropriate in a qualitative study), researchers can minimize alternative or rival explanations for the results that they observe; and where appropriate, they can establish cause and effect relationships more convincingly.

More broadly, quantitative methodologies aim to allow generalizations beyond the **sample** being studied (provided that the sample is representative of the larger **population** from which it is drawn; for additional details about **sampling**, see Chapter 4). Interestingly, one of the oddities of quantitative research is that the more the researcher controls the research situation, the less generalizable its findings are likely to be! For example, in a laboratory study, the researcher controls the context of the study and so all extraneous variables are controlled (see Chapter 6 for a discussion about **internal validity** and its threats). Precisely because of this, the findings may lack generalizability beyond the laboratory (see Chapter 5 for discussion about **external validity** and its threats).

One could also assume that quantitative research studies are less time-consuming than qualitative research studies because collecting and analyzing data is faster. While this may be the case in some situations, developing theories and hypotheses that are grounded in existing literature, establishing the reliability and validity of measurement instruments, carefully selecting participants, and collecting and analyzing data in an appropriate manner, is not a quick process; rather, it requires attention to all of the 10 indicators of quality research described in Chapter 1.

If you have been an observer or a participant in the field of education since the late 1990s, you are aware that a significant change has taken place in how empirical evidence is valued. We have seen remarkable changes in federal and state education policies and in federally funded programs for educational research. Quantitative evidence and the terms associated with it are now central to the vocabularies of schools and school districts, as well as researchers in higher education. For example, terms such as accountability, data-driven decision making, annual yearly progress, and the like are ubiquitous in these arenas. It is no coincidence that this shift has occurred. While many of us may not entirely agree with this state of affairs, empirical evidence tends to be more credible for individuals in power; it can be summarized and presented for a quick snapshot of reality, and unfortunately, it can be easily misused, either unintentionally or intentionally.

Notwithstanding these strengths, research in the quantitative tradition has several weaknesses. One of the most serious weaknesses that we have to consider relates to the assumption that quantitative research is objective and value free. There is nothing intrinsic in the designs we introduced in this chapter that makes them objective; it is up to the individual researcher to aim for (but more than likely not completely achieve) objectivity and it is up to the audience to evaluate their success. The level of objectivity depends on the researcher's ability to conduct research in an impartial manner, and consumers of quantitative research findings must evaluate the actual neutrality of the research and its findings.

Quantitative research methods typically look for relationships among variables and, in some cases, aim to draw cause and effect conclusions based on the patterns observed. As such, quantitative research is limited in its ability to address some types of research questions. For example, quantitative research methods are often limited in their ability to address "how" or "why" questions, and in their ability to provide information about the context in which a study is conducted. Consider a typical situation where the researcher develops a theory and subsequent hypothesis about how two attributes are related in a population. The researcher develops valid and reliable instruments, selects a sample from the population, administers the instruments to the sample, and uses the data to test the hypothesis that the variables are related. In this situation, the researcher's ability to describe the context of the study is limited by what he measures, and his ability to generalize the findings is limited by the instruments, the representativeness of the sample, and the appropriateness of the statistical tests employed. Unfortunately, many quantitative researchers fail to acknowledge this in drawing conclusions from their research and may overstate the generalizability of their findings to their audience. Those of us who rely on research to inform our own work, whether we are conducting additional research in a specific area or are using research to guide policy and practice, are advised to remember that all research is susceptible to bias, either unintentional or intentional.

Also, following the scientific method by stating a hypothesis prior to conducting a study can limit researchers' ability to notice evidence that emerges to support competing hypotheses about how attributes or variables are associated with each other. That is, focusing on testing pre-conceived hypotheses can lead the researcher to miss important opportunities for future theory generation. Thoroughly developed hypotheses, comprehensive measures of the research context, well-defined and selected samples, careful data collection and analysis, and cautious, conditional conclusions that are based on the evidence collected can mitigate some of these weaknesses.

❖ CONNECTIONS TO QUALITATIVE RESEARCH

We identified a common purpose for both traditions in Chapter 1 by defining research as "a systematic process to make things known that are currently unknown by examining phenomena multiple times and in multiple ways" and that 10 quality indicators can be applied to both research traditions. With this as a backdrop, what follows are additional connections as discussed in this chapter.

As described in Chapter 2, terms such as *independent* and *dependent* are usually not used in the qualitative tradition. Instead, researchers are concerned with identifying linkages and patterns among the complexities that exist in their data. Quantitative researchers sometimes use "multivariate" approaches rather than univariate ones, where, instead of one independent or one dependent variable being used to try and capture reality, several variables are used simultaneously. For example, instead of trying to look at the relationship between technology and achievement, some researchers use techniques that allow them to look at the joint relationship of technology and instructional methods with both achievement and academic aspirations. In a sense, qualitative researchers are closer to this multivariate approach, since, rather than controlling or randomizing, they try to capture the complexity through identifying patterns that exist in their data rather than simplifying data in order to make sense of it. One might say that qualitative researchers tend to "complexify" rather than simplify; however, at some point, there is a need to communicate findings and insights to others, and this requires that abstruse concepts and patterns be described and explained in a way that is comprehensible. If readers can't understand what we write or our listeners can't understand what we say, then we might as well just keep our thoughts to ourselves! Perhaps, the best way to think about both quantitative and qualitative research is a dance where one step is toward complexity while the next one moves toward simplicity—a continuing movement that, in the end, results in a worthwhile performance. The traditions can be thought of as partners in this continuing dance.

Another connection relates to research hypotheses. As described above, research hypotheses can be seen as educated predictions. In quantitative research, these predictions are then tested using an appropriate statistical analysis procedure and a decision is made as to whether one accepts this hypothesis as *probably* true or rejects the hypothesis as *probably* false. While qualitative researchers do not employ this dichotomous prediction and testing procedure, they often construct "working hypotheses," where hunches and "tacit knowledge" (Polanyi, 1958) are used to construct a tentative explanatory framework for trying to understand phenomena as additional insights gradually emerge from the data. Thus, rather than state an unequivocal prediction and then steadfastly execute procedures to discover the veracity of that prediction, qualitative researchers tend to modify their "predictions" as time and understanding progress. Perhaps, we can liken the different approaches to hypothesis formulation as a snapshot versus a motion picture (or a jpeg vs. a mov file)—each provides a unique angle or perspective and both can help us further our understanding of phenomena and, thus, should be considered in relation to the problem and research questions.

Earlier in the section "Variables, Research Problems and Questions, and Research Hypotheses," we said that "researchers should have a deep understanding of the problem and how it is positioned within the field." While this goal is shared with the qualitative tradition, there is a "timing" difference regarding when this goal is achieved. This timing difference is due to the relative emphasis given to discovery and inductive learning in the qualitative tradition versus the confirmatory and deductive emphasis in the quantitative tradition. Those who use a qualitative approach tend to be predisposed to enter a research setting (whether a school or culture) with a wide lens to capture questions, complexities, and details, while those who use a quantitative approach enter the scene with a lens that is more focused to capture those aspects that are related to their hypotheses and the literature. Let us be very emphatic that we are not saying that quantitative researchers see nothing as important other than what they are looking for, while qualitative researchers see everything as equally important. Rather, the "zooming in and out" that these two traditions offer are consistent with our overall goal to unearth new understandings about phenomena—it is precisely this zooming in and out that can reveal aspects of phenomena that cannot be seen using a single approach.

Readers will also notice that quantitative research designs are often used to study the characteristics or behaviors of a large group of individuals. Quantitative research is often interested in large numbers of individuals rather than individuals per se, and therefore, one of the typical first steps, as we will see in Chapter 9 regarding descriptive data analysis, is that numerical data are first simplified or reduced by calculating some type of average with an accompanying measure of spread. Familiar measures used for indicating averages are the mean, median, and mode, while measures of spread include the range and standard deviation. While qualitative research are also concerned with groups (although a single individual can also be the sole focus), data are concerned as much with the unique characteristics of each individual member of the group as with group characteristics in aggregate. This focus on the individual in the qualitative tradition is concomitant with trying to understand phenomena from the participant's perspective; this is consistent with using a smaller number of participants, allowing researchers to devote the extensive amount of time that is often required to collect, analyze, and interpret rich oral or observational data. If we were to try and explain this in terms of the quantitative tradition, we might say that while both traditions need to "reduce" data during data analysis in order to make sense of it, data are not analyzed in the quantitative tradition until it has been collected and put into an appropriate format (e.g., Excel or SPSS). On the other hand, qualitative data are sometimes analyzed and interpreted concurrent with data collection, as additional insights and understanding emerge.

Given that "making things known that are currently unknown" is the driving force for research in both traditions, it is not surprising that this process starts with a question or questions. These research questions, the evidence we seek, together with the amount of control that we have over events and context, largely determine what research methods might be used. For example, if we want to find out which one of the two different instructional approaches (e.g., in class vs. online) work best in terms of raising student achievement as evidenced on tests and we are able to randomly assign students to receive a particular instructional approach, then an experimental research design will satisfy our goal. On the other hand, if we are interested in obtaining a deep understanding of how students perceive and experience learning under one or both conditions and we are not able to randomly assign students to conditions (nor predisposed to do so), then the methods we would use to answer our questions might best be answered by using some type of qualitative design (e.g., phenomenological) or perhaps a combination of a survey design (i.e., typically associated with the quantitative tradition) with a qualitative approach. The point here is that both traditions yield results that, when looked at together, can enable us to construct a more comprehensive framework for understanding phenomena.

Finally, while the questions asked and the control that is possible and desired lead us to appropriate quantitative and/or qualitative methods, there is an aspect of "question asking" that differs between the two traditions. Namely, the two approaches often differ with respect to *when* research questions are finalized. While both traditions seek to build on what has been learned previously, the quantitative tradition does so by posing questions and perhaps hypotheses at the outset of a study and then focuses on seeking answers to *these* questions and hypotheses that were originally posed. However, because qualitative researchers tend to analyze and interpret *during* data collection, new questions may also emerge and are often then incorporated into subsequent research efforts. This point is the essence of the philosophical difference between the inductive and deductive approaches. Some might entertain the notion that this difference is due to the fact that quantitative research tends to be more decision oriented, while qualitative research is more oriented to increasing understanding—we reserve judgment on this!

We end our "Connections" for this chapter by emphasizing that, while differences do exist in terms of processes between the two traditions, the ultimate ends are very much the same and the distinctions that exist between the two traditions should be viewed as complementary rather than antithetical.

❖ CONCLUDING REMARKS

In this chapter, we introduced research in the quantitative tradition as being characterized by objectivity, precision, empiricism, logical reasoning, generalizability, replication and verification, parsimonious explanation, and conditional conclusions in the interpretation of empirical results. As you no doubt realized while reading this chapter,

this approach requires the researcher to hold, even if it is only tempo-
rary, different philosophical assumptions about the world. We also
introduced the cornerstones of quantitative research: design, measurement, and statistics or data analysis. Each of these warrants a closer
review than was offered in this chapter, and so the remainder of this
book is dedicated to that purpose. The purpose of this chapter was to
assist the interested reader as they create an inclusive appreciation for
the complementary and supplementary nature of both research traditions. As you move through this text, we hope that you will come to
have a positive awareness about quantitative methods and the qualitative traditions.

DISCUSSION QUESTIONS

1. Which philosophical assumptions underlying the quantitative tradition do you think qualitative researchers might find most difficult to
   accept? Why?

2. If you and a team of your classmates were conducting a study to
   evaluate the effectiveness of the health care system, what variables
   would be of interest to you? Which of these variables are continuous
   and which are categorical?

3. What image comes to mind when you think of a researcher in the
   physical sciences? What about the social sciences? Are there differences in your images of researchers who engage in quantitative
   research and researchers who engage in qualitative research? What
   do you think accounts for these image differences?

KEY TERMS

Categorical variable: a variable that varies in type but not amount or
degree.

Constant: an attribute or characteristic that does not vary among individuals or groups.

Continuous variable: a variable that varies in amount or degree along
a continuum from low to high.

Cross-sectional study: a study in which data are generated at only one
point in time, thereby providing a snapshot of the attributes, behaviors,
or phenomena that the researcher is studying.

Deductive reasoning: begins with more general understanding based on theories and hypotheses and moves toward specific conclusions and examples.

Dependent variable: a variable that is hypothesized to change in response to changes in the independent variable.

Descriptive analyses: a branch of statistics in which analyses are conducted to summarize and describe data and to reveal patterns in the data that are not immediately apparent through inspecting the raw data alone.

Descriptive study: a study in which the researcher is more interested in *what* the characteristics are rather than in *why* the characteristics are as they are.

Experimental research designs: types of designs used when the goal of the research is to examine the effect of some researcher-created intervention or treatment. The researcher has at least some control over the context in which the research takes place.

Explanatory study: a study conducted to test theories about how and why some attributes, behaviors, or phenomena are related as they are, or how and why the observed differences between pre-existing groups came to be.

External validity: the extent to which the findings from a study can be generalized beyond that study to other populations (population generalizability) and contexts (ecological generalizability).

Extraneous variable: a nuisance variable that is peripheral to the research study but because it is associated with the dependent variable, can provide an alternative explanation for the results observed when uncontrolled.

Independent variable: a variable that is hypothesized to lead to changes in some other variable being studied. It may be naturally occurring (e.g., pretest scores) or may be manipulated (e.g., treatment vs. control group).

Inductive reasoning: begins with specific phenomena and moves toward a more general understanding.

Inferential analyses: a set of statistical procedures used by researchers to make inferences about the attributes or characteristics in a population using a sample from that population.

Instrument reliability: the degree to which a measurement instrument provides consistent information.

Instrument validity: the accuracy of the inferences made from the data provided by a measurement instrument.

Internal validity: the degree to which extraneous variables in a research study are controlled such that plausible, alternative explanations for the results observed are minimized.

Longitudinal study: a study in which data are generated at multiple points in time such that the researcher can describe the ways in which the attributes, behaviors, or phenomena change over time.

Non-experimental research designs: types of designs used when the goal of the research is to observe naturally occurring attributes or phenomena. The researcher does not control or manipulate the context in which the research takes place.

Operational definition: a way of defining an attribute, behavior, or phenomenon according to the actual steps taken to measure it. For example, mathematics performance as measured by Grade 8 teacher–developed end-of-year assessment.

Population: all individuals or groups that possess the characteristic that the researcher aims to investigate. The population must be defined prior to the sample being selected.

Prediction study: a study in which the researcher is interested in examining the associations among attributes or behaviors, with the ultimate aim of being able to make predictions.

Quasi-experimental research designs: a set of research designs used to examine the impact of interventions but do not use randomization to ensure group equivalence.

Randomization (aka random assignment): the process describing how individuals or clusters of individuals are assigned to treatment and control conditions, regardless of how they are sampled from the population.

Research hypothesis: a tentative statement that predicts the specific relationships, similarities or differences, or causal mechanisms that the researcher expects to observe among the attributes being investigated.

Research problem: any topic, issue, or phenomenon that the researcher is interested in studying.

Research question: distinct from, but arising from the research problem, the research question is an actual question that indicates to the audience exactly what the researcher aims to study.

Retrospective study: a study that examines the antecedents to observed differences between groups as plausible explanations for those differences.

Sample: the subset of units that is the result of the sampling process.

Sampling: the process of selecting a sample from a population that will be used in the research process.

Scientific method: an approach that involves the formulation, testing, and refinement of hypotheses; the systematic collection of empirical evidence through measurement; and in specific situations, the conduct of experiments.

True experimental research designs: a set of research designs used to examine the impact of interventions and use randomization to ensure group equivalence.

Variable: an attribute or characteristic that varies among individuals or groups.

SECTION II

The Sine Qua Non for Conducting Research in the Quantitative Tradition

The purpose of the three chapters in Section II is to identify the quantitative concepts and their counterparts in the qualitative tradition that we think should be discussed in relation to one other. One point to note here is that the order in which we present our discussion of these topics is not necessarily the order in which the research is conducted. Specifically, when conducting research, researchers follow the *design–measurement–analysis* triad. That is, after developing an understanding of the research problem and formulating research questions and hypotheses, researchers (a) select a research design that will allow the research questions to be answered (*design*); (b) collect data that will allow the research questions to be answered (*measurement*); and (c) analyze the data and make connections to the research question and research problem (*analysis*).

However, in presenting our discussion, we have re-ordered the three because we feel that our readers will be in a better position to understand and appreciate the various research designs and data analysis procedures described in subsequent chapters if they develop a solid understanding of the foundational topics covered in this section.

Specifically, in preparation for understanding the specific details of the most common quantitative research designs, the steps involved in their implementation, their strengths and weakness, as well as how to analyze the data they provide, we discuss the sine qua non for understanding conducting research in the quantitative tradition. A solid foundational understanding of these *"without which not"* concepts is essential for developing an appreciation of subsequent material covered. These topics include choosing whom to study, making generalizations, issues related to measurement and instrumentation, and minimizing alternative explanations for the results observed.

Throughout the chapters in this section, the axiom we first presented in Chapter 3 will provide a foundation for the descriptions and discussions:

> Researchers should choose research designs, procedures, data collection instruments, and data analysis methods that are appropriate for addressing the question(s) posed; allow generalizations to be made to other participants and settings beyond their study; and that minimize all feasible alternative explanations for the results observed.

In the three chapters in Section II, we discuss issues related to selecting a sample with which to conduct research and issues of generalizability (Chapter 4), ways for ensuring that the data collection instruments are appropriate and minimize bias and measurement error (Chapter 5), and describe the ways in which researchers minimize alternative explanations for the results observed (Chapter 6).

We invite readers to actively think about how concepts discussed in this chapter relate to their understanding of the qualitative tradition. While we will also try and bring some things to your attention in our "Connections to Qualitative Research" that follow each section, there is simply no substitute for recognizing and jotting down questions, insights, and observations as you read along!

4

Choosing Research Participants and Making Generalizations

Sampling and External Validity

❖ ❖ ❖

CHAPTER OUTLINE

- Sampling: Choosing Participants for Research Studies
- Probability or Random Sampling Procedures
- Non-Probability or Non-Random Sampling Procedures
- Errors Related to Sampling
- The Question of Sample Size: How Big Should a Sample Be?
- External Validity: Making Generalizations to Other Participants and Settings

R esearchers conducting studies in the quantitative tradition typically aim to *make generalizations to other participants and settings
beyond the current study.* In research parlance, the process of

selecting participants is referred to as *sampling,* and the capacity to make generalizations to other participants and settings is referred to as *external validity.* Whether a researcher is conducting an experiment to examine the effect of an intervention or is collecting survey data to simply describe some phenomenon, the philosophical assumptions of the quantitative tradition require that he or she considers whether the study's findings can be generalized beyond the individuals or groups involved in the study and beyond the context in which the research occurred (Cook & Campbell, 1976, 1979). In the case of experimental research where the researcher aims to establish a causal link between the effect of a treatment and some measured attribute, Cook and Campbell (1979) define external validity as the "approximate validity with which we can infer that the presumed causal relationship can be generalized to and across alternate measures of the cause and effect and across different types of persons, settings, and times" (p. 37). In this chapter, we describe the process of sampling and the concept of external validity.

❖ SAMPLING: CHOOSING PARTICIPANTS FOR RESEARCH STUDIES

Sampling is the process of selecting a sample from a population that will be used in the research process, and the subset of units that is the result of the sampling process is called the **sample**. Several different procedures can be used to select a sample, and sampling is the umbrella term for these procedures. In many social science research studies, the sample comprises individuals or groups of individuals. Sampling procedures are central to conducting quantitative research as they dictate the degree to which generalizations can be made beyond the current study. In fact, the use of these procedures is often what differentiates it from research in the qualitative tradition.

In the quantitative tradition, the capacity for generalization is closely related to *how* the population is defined; *who* is selected from the population to be in the study; and *how* they are selected. This is not to say that external validity is *only* a function of the sampling plan; there are several additional facets to external validity; and these will be discussed later in this chapter. However, before proceeding to discuss sampling issues, we will define some important terms.

A **population** includes all individuals or groups that possess the characteristic that the researcher aims to investigate. Beyond this broad definition of the term is a more nuanced delineation between a *target* *population* and an *accessible population*. The **target population** is the ideal population that the researcher wishes to generalize to; however, in cases where this population is not available to researchers, they must select their sample from the **accessible population**. For example, consider the situation where a researcher is interested in understanding eighth-grade public school students' mathematical ability. While researchers may wish to generalize to all eighth-grade public school students in the United States (the target population), without vast resources, it is unlikely that the entire population of eighth-grade public school students in the United States is available to them. As such, researchers might restrict the population to the eighth-grade public school students in State A to whom they have access (the accessible population). Of course, any differences between the target and accessible populations will have consequences for the generalizability of the research.

In defining the population, there are additional considerations. First, the researcher must consider the sampling element that will allow the research questions to be addressed; the **sampling element** is the unit that is selected in the population from which data will be collected and analyzed to address the research questions. In many social science studies, the sampling elements are individuals; however, at other times, the researcher will want to describe intact groups or will only have access to individuals who are clustered in groups. Regardless of whether the sampling element is an individual or clusters of individuals, the population to which the researcher wishes to generalize will need to be well-defined, thereby allowing others (e.g., other researchers attempting to conduct similar studies or individuals wishing to use the research findings to inform policy or practice) to evaluate the appropriateness of the generalizations to their own context.

In situations where all members of a population provide information, a **complete census** is conducted. However, it is usually not possible to collect data from every member of a population. This may be because the population is too large, because there is no complete list of all members of the population, or because resources (time, money, etc.) are limited. An important point that novice researchers can easily miss is that *the population must be defined prior to the sample being selected*. In this way, appropriate sampling procedures can be used to ensure that the essential characteristics of the population are represented in the sample. Without this important step, the study may lack generalizability to other participants and settings.

There are two overarching classifications of sampling procedures that a researcher can adopt: *probability sampling procedures* and *non-probability sampling procedures*. With **probability sampling procedures**, the researcher bases the selection of participants on their prevalence (with all their inherent characteristics) in the population, and every participant in the population has a *known probability* of being sampled. With careful execution, probability sampling will result in an *unbiased sample*; that is, it will result in a sample that is not systematically different from the population on the attributes that are of interest such as gender, age, years of schooling, and so on. When researchers use **non-probability sampling procedures**, the prevalence of the participants (with all their inherent characteristics) in the population is not taken into consideration and so the probability of an element being sampled from the population cannot be established. These types of sampling procedures often result in samples that are not representative and may be systematically different from the population. In comparing the two approaches, probability-based sampling procedures are more likely to result in studies that have stronger external validity; in fact, considering the importance of external validity in the quantitative tradition, probability-based procedures are considered the gold standard. Table 4.1 summarizes the most common sampling procedures available to researchers.

❖ PROBABILITY OR RANDOM SAMPLING PROCEDURES

The defining characteristic of probability sampling procedures is that every element (e.g., an individual or a cluster of individuals) has a known probability of being selected from the population. Therefore, as a first step in the probability sampling process, the researcher will need access to a complete list of every element (e.g., individuals, or groups of individuals) in the population. This is referred to as the **sampling frame**, and it is from this list that the study sample will be selected. Because every element listed in the sampling frame could potentially

Table 4.1   Summary of Sampling Procedures

Probability Sampling Procedures	Non-Probability Sampling Procedures
Simple random sampling	Convenience sampling
Stratified random sampling	Purposive sampling
Cluster random sampling	Quota sampling
Systematic sampling	Snowball sampling

be selected to be in the sample, the sampling frame should include as much information about each element as is necessary to select a sample that is representative of the population. For example, in addition to listing the contact information for each individual, the sampling frame might also include demographic information (e.g., gender, age, income level, etc.) and the geographic location (e.g., rural, urban, etc.) of every individual. That is, to minimize errors when choosing the sample, the sampling frame must be complete and have the most up-to-date information about the elements in the population; if there are gaps in the sampling frame, this might result in sampling bias (this point will be discussed in more detail shortly).

Once the sampling frame is complete, the researcher can proceed to select the sample using one of several different probability sampling procedures. Bear in mind that regardless of which probability sampling procedure is adopted, great care and attention must be paid to executing the sampling plan. For instance, the researcher should not alter the sampling plan part way through the sampling stage of the study, nor should he or she allow the implementation of the sampling plan to lapse at any point during the process. Either of these situations could result in a sample that contains known or unknown biases. There are several types of probability sampling procedures that a researcher can choose from: simple random sampling, stratified random sampling, and cluster random sampling and its extension, two-stage cluster random sampling. Systematic sampling procedures are also discussed here as a transition between probability sampling procedures and non-probability sampling procedures.

Simple Random Sampling

In a **simple random sample**, every element in the population has an equal probability of being selected to be in the sample. For example, if the population contains 1,000 elements, the probability of each element being selected is 1/1,000. While this sampling procedure will result in samples that are not systematically different from the population (i.e., it will provide the researcher with an unbiased sample), a *single* simple random sample from a population may not be completely representative of that population on all attributes or characteristics. This is because simple random sampling will result in a representative sample on average over an infinite (or very large) number of simple random samples from the population. For this reason, a single random sample, though not different in systematic ways (i.e., not biased), may not represent all the attributes of the elements in the population.

Stratified Random Sampling

In a **stratified random sample**, the population is divided into relatively homogeneous blocks or strata based on known population characteristics, and within each stratum, a sample is randomly selected. Compared with simple random sampling, stratified random sampling procedures can produce samples that are more representative of the population. This is because the distribution of attributes in the population are taken into account when choosing the sample. For example, consider the situation where the researcher wants to choose a sample in which each race category is represented in the proportion that it exists in the population of U.S. residents. If the researcher opted to use stratified random sampling procedures, he or she would use race as a **stratification variable**—a variable that is used to divide or stratify the population into multiple strata that are each racially homogeneous. Subsequent to creating the strata, the researcher would randomly sample individuals within each independent stratum in proportion to how they are represented in the entire population. Multiple stratification variables can be used simultaneously to create smaller, more homogeneous strata from which elements are then randomly selected. This process of random sampling within homogeneous strata tends to be more efficient than simple random sampling for producing a sample that is representative of the population, particularly if the sample size is moderate.

Cluster Random Sampling and Its Extensions

When we introduced the unit of analysis or sampling element earlier, we described the situation where a researcher might want to describe intact groups or only have access to individuals who are clustered within groups. Consider an example where a researcher wants to explore public school teachers' levels of satisfaction with their school leadership. In this case, the unit of analysis would be the school, and the sampling frame would list all public schools in the United States. A random sample from this sampling frame would result in a cluster random sample, and data from all teachers in each sampled school would be used to explore public school teachers' perceptions of school leadership. Technically, the term **cluster random sampling** is used to define situations where naturally occurring clusters are randomly sampled from the population and data are collected from all elements with each cluster.

Even in situations where researchers are not interested in studying groups or clusters per se, cluster random sampling may be the only option for collecting individual data. Consider again the situation where a researcher is interested in understanding eighth-grade public school students' mathematical ability. As far as we are aware, a list of all eighth-grade students in public schools in the United States does not exist. However, lists of all public schools that include eighth-grade classrooms do exist. In this case, the researcher would proceed with selecting schools as clusters and, then, could collect mathematical ability data from *all* eighth-grade students in the sampled schools. In this case, the probability of a student being selected is a function of the probability of their school being selected.

As a variant on this approach, researchers may choose to use a **two-stage cluster random sampling** procedure. In this case, the researchers randomly sample clusters at the first stage, and at the second stage, rather than collect data from every individual in the cluster, instead, sample individuals *within* the selected clusters. Consider again the previous example where the researcher samples public schools in the United States that have eighth-grade classrooms. In the previous example, the researcher collected data from all eighth-grade students in the sampled schools. It may be the case, however, that the researcher does not want to or cannot collect data from every eighth-grade student in the sampled schools; this may be due to access issues or resource (time, money, etc.) constraints. In this case, the researcher would select a sample of eighth-grade students from the sampled schools and then proceed to collect information about their mathematical ability. In cases where clusters are large and it would not be cost-effective or useful to collect data from every individual, this approach may be the most appropriate. When researchers choose to use this option, two sampling frames will need to be prepared—one that lists all clusters in the population and the other that lists all individuals within the sampled clusters.

Stratification variables can also be used with cluster random sampling and with two-stage cluster random sampling to improve the likelihood that the sample will be representative of the population. Using stratification variables that create homogeneous strata of clusters and subsequently collecting data from all elements in each cluster will result in a **stratified cluster sample**. Using stratification variables in choosing clusters *and* choosing individuals within clusters will result in a **stratified two-stage cluster sample**. Stratified cluster random and stratified two-stage cluster random sampling procedures are commonly used in large-scale studies in education. When using two-stage cluster samples, stratified or not, the probability of a student being selected is a function of the probability of their school being selected and the probability of them being selected within their school. In Chapters 9 and 10, where we describe data analysis procedures, we will briefly discuss the analysis consequences of sampling clusters from the population instead of individuals and will refer readers to more specialized texts that deal with these types of advanced data analysis methods.

Systematic Sampling

A **systematic sample** is made up of elements that are selected systematically using a fixed interval from an ordered list of elements (individuals or clusters) in the population; that is, the researcher chooses every *k*th individual from that ordered list to be in the sample. For example, say that a sampling frame contains a list of 5,000 elements from which the researcher wishes to select just 250. If from that complete list, the researcher rank orders the sample on some characteristic, then starts at a randomly chosen element, and proceeds to choose every 20th element, the result will be a systematic sample of 250 elements. This sampling procedure is presented as a transition between probability and non-probability procedures because it contains some aspects of both approaches. Specifically, while the selection process is not based on probabilities, if the list of elements is randomly ordered, the resulting sample is likely to produce an unbiased sample in the same way as would a randomly selected sample. The primary concern with systematic sampling procedures is that there may be an underlying order to the element list that is related to the attribute being studied but that the researcher has not considered or has not been made aware of. To avoid any unintended biases, researchers using systematic sampling are advised to pay close attention to how the elements are ordered (Gay & Airasian, 2003).

❖ NON-PROBABILITY OR NON-RANDOM SAMPLING PROCEDURES

Unlike the sampling procedures described in the previous section, non-probability sampling procedures do not select elements (individuals or clusters) in accordance with their incidence in the population; therefore, the probability of an element being sampled from the population cannot be established. Unlike random sampling procedures, these sampling procedures will often result in non-representative samples that may be systematically different from the population. If we were to rush to judgment about these types of sampling procedures, we could conclude that they are not very useful. However, in their defense, these sampling procedures have their place in the quantitative research tradition—as well as the qualitative tradition. Consider the situations where probability sampling might not be possible due to budget constraints, where so little might be known about the topic being investigated that only a limited study is warranted, or where the researcher might be interested in studying a low-incidence phenomenon in a population that might be geographically widespread. Although these samples tend to be less "scientific" than probability samples and generalizability of these studies is likely to be compromised, these types of situations may warrant the use of non-probability sampling procedures. In general, the conclusions drawn from studies that use non-probability sampling should be evaluated cautiously. In situations where a non-probability procedure is the only choice, researchers are advised to describe the sample in sufficient detail so that others can understand to whom, where, and when the findings are generalizable. This level of detail will be necessary as others attempt to replicate research findings. As with probability sampling procedures, there are several non-probability sampling procedures that a researcher can choose from: convenience sampling, purposive sampling, systematic sampling, quota sampling, and snowball sampling.

Convenience Sampling

A **convenience sample** is made up of elements that are conveniently available to the researcher. Consider the case where a doctoral student is conducting her doctoral thesis on how elementary students' understanding of the nature of science is associated with students' science content knowledge. The doctoral student might contact teachers she knows to request permission to conduct her research in their classrooms. The distinguishing characteristic of convenience sampling is that the individuals or clusters are not selected from the population based on some probability; rather, they are selected to be in the study because the researcher has easy access to them.

Purposive Sampling

A **purposive sample** is made up of elements that possess a particular characteristic or attribute that the researcher is interested in studying. Again, consider the case of the doctoral student who intends to examine the relationship between elementary students' understanding of the nature of science and their understanding of science content. Say that instead of contacting a group of teachers she knows, the doctoral student contacts teachers who have attended a professional development workshop aimed at helping them develop their students' understanding of the nature of science. In this way, the student purposively contacts teachers because of their specific characteristics. The distinguishing characteristic of purposive sampling is that the individuals or clusters are not systematically selected from the population; instead, they are selected to be in the study because they possess an attribute or characteristic that the researcher is interested in. Regarding the qualitative tradition, purposive sampling is essential when a researcher "purposively" selects individuals who are judged to possess or represent desired characteristics or have had experiences that the researcher wishes to investigate.

Quota Sampling

A **quota sample** is made up of elements that are selected non-randomly to represent some pre-defined population. When using a quota sampling procedure, the researcher sub-divides the population into smaller, homogeneous groups and from within those sub-sections, selects elements based on judgment or some pre-identified proportion. In this way, a sample is compiled that represents the population. This approach is similar to stratified sampling procedures with one major difference; in the case of quota sampling, the elements are not randomly selected from within the homogeneous sub-sections or strata.

Snowball Sampling

A **snowball sample** is made up of elements that are selected using a system of referrals and recommendations from one element to another. This type of sampling procedure may be useful for researchers who are studying elements (individuals or clusters) that have unique attributes that are of interest to the researcher but who cannot be recruited for a study through sites or pre-existing environments. Consider the situation where a researcher is interested in studying the effects of obsessive gaming behaviors among young adult males. In this case, the researcher may not be able to identify a large enough sample to study through traditional methods. However, with snowball sampling, the researcher could make contact with a small number of young adult males who exhibit this behavior and ask those individuals to refer him or her to additional individuals with similar characteristics. In this way, the

sample size snowballs, or increases in size, through a system of referrals to additional elements.

❖ ERRORS RELATED TO SAMPLING

To avoid samples that contain known or unknown biases, technically
known *as sampling errors*, researchers are cautioned to carefully execute
the sampling plan as it was designed. Sampling error occurs because
not all elements of the population are included in a study; **sampling
error** is the difference between the measured attributes in a sample and
the true attributes in the population. Moreover, if a large number of
samples were selected from a single population, each sample would
contain different amounts of sampling error. By definition then, all
research conducted with a sample will have sampling error. The essential question, however, is whether the error can be classified as *random
sampling error* or *systematic sampling error*.

As the name suggests, **random sampling error** is due to random or
chance differences between the sample and the intended population,
and so it is unavoidable unless the entire population is included in the
study (census). However, because it occurred by chance and is not systematic, random sampling error does not produce samples that are
systematically different from the populations from which they were
drawn. Therefore, over a large number of samples from a single population, random sampling error will average out to zero, and the effects
will be negligible.

Conversely, **systematic sampling errors** can have serious consequences for the generalizability and credibility of the findings. Systematic sampling errors can originate with the sampling frame from which
the sample is selected or with the implementation of the sampling plan.
For example, **coverage error** occurs when the population from which
the sample is drawn is not equivalent to the intended population and
will result in a sample that is systematically different from the intended
population. This may occur if the sampling frame is an incomplete list
of all the constituent elements (individuals or clusters) of the intended
population, or includes additional elements that are not part of the
intended population. Without a full list of the intended population
units and clear demarcation of who is and who is not part of the
intended population, even the best sampling plan will fail to produce
a sample that accurately represents the target population. To avoid this
error, the researcher must be conscientious about carefully defining the
members of the population, acquiring and maintaining a complete list

of the members of the intended population, developing a rigorous sampling plan that will result in a sample that represents the intended population, and ensuring that the sampling plan is implemented as designed. Although ensuring that the sampled population is equivalent to the intended population may be a painstaking task, avoiding coverage error is essential for producing sound research.

As a further point, systematic differences between the sample and the population may also occur for reasons that are unrelated to *how* the sample is selected from the population. For example, when individuals or clusters are selected to be in the sample but do not provide data (e.g., the selected individuals choose not to participate in the study or drop out of the study once it begins), the resulting sample may become systematically different from the intended population, and the consequences for the generalizability and credibility of the findings are similar to those that occur due to systematic sampling errors. Broadly, these types of errors are referred to as **non-response error**; they occur *after* the sample is selected and may have the same detrimental consequences as coverage errors. Additional details about non-sampling error are discussed in Chapter 5 related to instrumentation.

In general, researchers must be conscientious about planning for and avoiding systematic sampling errors. Without the effective controls and strategies in place to minimize these errors, the researcher is risking the credibility and generalizability of his or her findings.

❖ THE QUESTION OF SAMPLE SIZE: HOW BIG SHOULD A SAMPLE BE?

The question of sample size is often challenging for researchers who are new to research in the quantitative tradition—in fact, this is often the first question asked by students! Most research studies are conducted with limited resources, and therefore, researchers must decide on a sample size that will be feasible to select and collect data from, while also providing data that are credible and have some degree of generalizability. Therefore, researchers should be more concerned with *optimizing* the sample size, not just maximizing it. Researchers should aim for sample sizes that are large enough to allow them to "see" differences or relationships that exist and that provide generalizable findings. However, sample sizes should not be so large that they waste resources and provide results that are not practically important. This curious last point about large sample size providing results that are not practically important will be raised again Chapter 10 when we discuss inferential analyses.

Although several texts provide crude guidelines estimating the minimum sample size needed for various research designs, a precise answer to the question of sample size requires an empirical analysis. Specifically, to optimize the required sample size, the researcher must conduct a *statistical power analysis* that takes into account the following: the characteristics of the design (e.g., whether the researcher is conducting an experimental study or a non-experimental descriptive study), the degree of certainty that the researcher wants to achieve in his or her results, and an estimate of the size of effect that the researcher expects to observe. Additional information about statistical power analysis can be found in texts such as Privitera (2012), Howell (2010), Glass and Hopkins (1996), or Shavelson (1996). For the purposes of this text, we will simply describe the crude estimates of sample size that are reported for various research designs.

For descriptive studies, Fraenkel and Wallen (2011) recommend sampling a minimum of 100 individuals, while Mertler and Charles (2010) recommend sampling between 10% and 20% of the population. For correlational research designs, Fraenkel and Wallen recommend a sample size of 50 individuals, and Mertler and Charles recommend that a minimum of 30 individuals are needed. The recommended sample sizes for experimental and causal comparative research tend to be smaller, with Fraenkel and Wallen recommending 30 individuals per group, and Mertler and Charles recommending at least 15 per group. Clearly, these conflicting guidelines can leave the novice researcher more confused than ever. It is our position that the correct estimation of sample size requires empirical evidence in the form of a statistical power analysis.

❖ EXTERNAL VALIDITY: MAKING GENERALIZATIONS TO OTHER PARTICIPANTS AND SETTINGS

We began this chapter by reinforcing the clause in our axiom that stated that researchers conducting studies in the quantitative tradition typically aim to *make generalizations to other participants and settings beyond their study* and invoked Cook and Campbell's (1979) definition of **external validity** as "the approximate validity with which we can infer that the presumed causal relationship can be generalized to and across alternate measures of the cause and effect and across different types of persons, settings, and times" (p. 37). We also pointed out that while the capacity for generalization is closely related to how the population is defined, who is in the sample, and how the sample is selected, we said that there are additional aspects to ensuring the external validity of the study. This section will provide additional details on those aspects. In evaluating the external validity of a study, we must justify whether we can extrapolate the findings to other individuals or clusters and to other settings. We refer to these types of extrapolations as *population generalizability and ecological generalizability*, respectively.

Population Generalizability

As the name suggests, **population generalizability** has to do with whether the findings from a study are generalizable to other participants or clusters of participants and rests on the degree to which the sample used in the study represents the population. Recalling from the discussion about sampling designs in the previous section, the actual sample used in the study may be different from the population for several reasons, only some of which are related to the researcher's choice of sampling method. There are three primary sources of concern related to safeguarding population generalizability: (1) the difference between the target population and the accessible population, (2) the sampling method selected, and (3) the degree to which the sample remains representative throughout the duration of the study (i.e., that non-response and attrition effects are minimized).

First, consider the researcher's definition of the target population (the ideal population to which the researcher wishes to generalize) and the accessible population (the population to which the researcher has access) from which the sample will be drawn. In cases where the accessible population is systematically different from the target population or too small to be truly representative of the target population, population generalizations may not be supported. One important point to note here is that the difference between a target and an accessible population may occur for some attributes but not for others.

The researcher's choice of a sampling design will have implications for the population generalizability because sampling designs differ in their capacity to produce representative samples. For example, probability sampling procedures are more likely to produce representative samples than, say, a non-probability convenience sample. As such, the researcher's choice of a sampling design will have a direct bearing on the population generalizability. In situations where population generalizability is of concern, the researcher should choose a probability sampling procedure that results in a sample that is representative of the population.

In addition and sometimes despite a researcher's best effort to choose a sampling design that will result in a representative sample, we also described situations where sampling errors can still occur. These too, will affect the population generalizability. Specifically, sampling error can originate with the sampling frame from which the sample is selected (due to coverage error) or with the poor implementation of the intended sampling plan. A researcher can minimize or avoid these threats to population generalizability by ensuring that the sampling frame is comprehensive and complete and by safeguarding the fidelity of the sampling procedures to the intended sampling plan. Sampling errors can also arise after the sample has been selected due to non-response errors.

Overall, since research in the quantitative tradition aims to make generalizations beyond the sample involved in the study, researchers should strive to strengthen the population generalizability of their studies. The question of whether a study has population generalizability is not a yes or no decision; there are degrees of population generalizability. In an effort to strengthen population generalizability, we strongly recommend that researchers aim to know and understand the differences between their accessible population and the target population, recognize and describe the implications of these differences for their research findings, choose a probability-based sampling design and ensure that it is rigorously implemented as it was intended, and adopt procedures to minimize non-response errors. In addition, replicating the study with other samples will increase the generalizability of the findings. Achieving each of these aims will require substantial effort on the part of researchers, but the resulting research will be stronger for it.

Ecological Generalizability

The term *ecological* refers to the relationships between individuals and their environments. As such, **ecological generalizability** is concerned with whether the results observed under particular conditions or in a particular context can be generalized to other contexts. For example, it may not be appropriate to assume that an intervention shown to have positive effects on student learning in mathematics will also have the same positive effects for improving learning in English language arts. Likewise, it may not be appropriate to assume that the findings from a study conducted under "laboratory conditions" can be extrapolated to what might be observed in a "real-world" situation. This is particularly the case for studies in education where the typical classroom environment, where interruptions and complex, interconnected behaviors are routine, is likely to be very different from a controlled laboratory situation. As with population generalizability, whether a study is ecologically generalizable relates to the degree to which threats to it are minimized or eliminated completely, and in the quantitative tradition, the researcher must make every effort to anticipate and minimize common threats. These threats include (a) the degree to which the implementation of the study can be replicated in other contexts and by other researchers, (b) the extent to which the results of the study can be attributed to the factors hypothesized by the researcher, and (c) the extent to which novelty and participation effects can be minimized.

❖ CONNECTIONS TO QUALITATIVE RESEARCH

The term *subjects* is often used in quantitative studies to designate those who are selected for inclusion. On the other hand, researchers who toil in the qualitative vineyards find that because they are in more direct and prolonged contact with those that they study, a more personal relationship develops, so they typically use the term *participant, informant,* or even *co-researcher* rather than *subject*. This by no means implies that quantitative researchers are cold hearted or unfriendly, just that their tradition tries to keep "subjects" at arm's length to achieve neutrality or objectivity. Perhaps, some may find the characterization of an outside-in versus an inside-out approach a useful heuristic to differentiate between the traditions. Just keep in mind that if we believe that some approximations to reality are *more* accurate than others, this does not negate the fact that every approximation may help us get closer to that reality, and each tradition offers its own kinds of approximations.

While random sampling is the "gold standard" in the quantitative tradition, notice that both "convenience" and "purposive" sampling are recognized as sometimes appropriate if not ideal ways to select participants. Of course, for qualitative researchers, these two methods are central to their work. Because "generalizing" is accomplished via rich or thick description that may enable other researchers to match with their own work, random selection is usually not at center stage, although it certainly can be incorporated into a selection strategy using a technique referred to as *random purposive sampling*. For example, if qualitative researchers want to learn about the perspectives of employees regarding unionization by interviewing 10 individuals, they might first purposively select 25 individuals who match their selection criteria and then randomly select 10 participants from this larger group. This procedure sometimes meets with enthusiastic approval by those on dissertation committees, who were trained in the quantitative tradition!

Although this section and those that follow present terms, concepts, and underlying premises that differ from those used in the qualitative tradition, we encourage readers to make additional "connections" as we continue to describe the fundamental concerns of quantitative researchers—we are hopeful that in the end, while you may not be in agreement with everything "quantitative," you will come away with a predisposition to at least consider some of these tools for approaching your own work and for appreciating the work of your colleagues.

Since an important goal of quantitative research is to generalize findings across participants and contexts by selecting these participants via some type of random selection, the discussion that follows here aims to link the selection of subjects (participants) to the concept of "generalizability" and "external validity." For those immersed in the qualitative tradition, the intent of this term may seem somewhat confusing. As discussed in the previous "connections," qualitative researchers look to describe participants and contexts in such a rich and detailed way that readers may find themselves making linkages based on their understanding of their specific contexts and, thus, see findings as at least partially "transferable." On the other hand, quantitative researchers try to achieve their version of transferability by working to attain a context-free generalizability based on the random selection of participants. For example, medical, marketing, and government research often rely on this method to determine if a new drug is effective, whether a product is considered attractive, or whether an instructional program results in higher levels of achievement. Some would argue that because the qualitative tradition relies on rich description to ascertain transferability to other contexts while the quantitative tradition relies on random selection of participants and de-emphasizes the role of context, there exists a chasm that cannot be crossed. We believe, however, that *all* researchers would like to see their work and findings found useful by others and so they select participants based on what they are trying to discover and disseminate to a wider audience. Again, we don't see the traditions in competition; rather, they use different methods to try and discover new knowledge. The task then becomes to use this knowledge obtained by diverse methods that results in a richer symbiotic understanding.

❖ CONCLUDING REMARKS

Guided by the axiom we stated at the beginning of Section II, this chapter provided a description of the most frequently used methods for selecting study participants and introduced readers to ways for improving the generalizability of research findings to other participants and settings. The "Connections to Qualitative Research" section was written to bridge the gap between qualitative and quantitative methods and to showcase the complementary natures of the traditions.

We recognize that the material covered in this chapter was laden with technical terms and that, at times, our coverage was dense. However, conducting quality research in the quantitative tradition is predicated on having a solid understanding of the concepts and technical language introduced in this chapter. Readers trained in qualitative methods will probably agree that the concepts and technical language in that tradition can be equally arcane and may recall that it took time and practice to become au fait with them. Similar efforts are required to develop an understanding of the technicalities of quantitative research. We hope that the "Connections to Qualitative Research" sections and the list of key terms will be useful as readers work toward becoming familiar with the essential elements of research in the quantitative tradition.

DISCUSSION QUESTIONS

1. Evaluate the following statement: "The quantitative tradition seeks to generalize findings beyond samples to a larger population, whereas the qualitative tradition is indifferent to generalizing." To what extent do you think this statement is accurate? Why?

2. If you were interested in finding out how teachers felt about national testing, what are some possible methods that you might use to select participants? What are some of the strengths and weaknesses of these methods?

3. Can you think of other studies that might use a combination of probability and non-probability sampling?

4. How would you compare "ecological generalizability" as discussed in this section with qualitative researchers' concern for context?

KEY TERMS

Accessible population: the portion of the population to which the researcher has access and from which the sample is selected.

Cluster random sampling: naturally occurring clusters are randomly sampled from the population, and data are collected from all elements with each cluster.

Complete census: all members of a population provide information.

Convenience sample: a sample made up of elements (e.g., individuals, groups of individuals) that are conveniently available to the researcher.

Coverage error: coverage errors occur when the sampled population is not equivalent to the intended population and will result in a sample that is systematically different from the intended population. This may occur if the sampling frame is not a complete list of all the constituent elements (individuals or clusters) of the intended population or includes additional elements that are not part of the intended population.

Ecological generalizability: the extent to which the findings from a study can be generalized beyond that study to other contexts. Depends on the degree to which the implementation of the study can be replicated in other contexts and by other researchers, the extent to which the results of the study can be attributed to the mechanism hypothesized by the researcher, and the extent to which novelty and participation effects can be minimized.

External validity: the extent to which the findings from a study can be generalized beyond that study to other populations (population generalizability) and contexts (ecological generalizability).

Non-probability sampling procedures: the incidence of the participants (with all their inherent characteristics) in the population is not taken into consideration and so the probability of an element being sampled from the population cannot be established.

Non-response error: non-response errors occur when the elements (e.g., individuals, groups of individuals) selected to be in the sample do not provide data. For example, the selected individuals choose not to participate in the study or drop out of the study once it begins and the resulting sample may be systematically different from the intended population.

Population generalizability: the extent to which the findings from a study can be generalized beyond that study to other populations. Population generalizability. Depends on whether there are systematic differences between the target population and the accessible population, the appropriateness of the sampling design selected, and the degree to which the sample remains representative of the population throughout the study (i.e., that non-response and attrition effects are minimized).

Population: all individuals or groups that possess the characteristic that the researcher aims to investigate. The population must be defined prior to the sample being selected.

Probability sampling procedures: the selection of participants is based on their incidence (with all their inherent characteristics) in the population and every participant in the population has a known probability of being sampled.

Purposive sample: a sample made up of elements (e.g., individuals, groups of individuals) that possess a particular characteristic or attribute that the researcher is interested in studying.

Quota sample: a sample made up of elements (e.g., individuals, groups of individuals) that are selected non-randomly to represent some pre-defined population. Similar to stratified sampling procedures with one major difference; in the case of quota sampling, the elements are not randomly selected from within the homogeneous sub-sections or strata.

Random sampling errors: random sampling errors are due to chance differences between the sample and the intended population and are unavoidable since the full population is not included in the study.

Sample: a subset of units (e.g., individuals, groups of individuals) selected from the population, from whom data are collected.

Sampling element: the unit (e.g., individuals, groups of individuals) that is selected from the population from which data will be collected and analyzed to address the research questions.

Sampling error: sampling error is the difference between the measured attributes in a sample and the true attributes in the population, and it occurs because not all elements of the population are included in a study.

Sampling frame: a complete list of every element (e.g., individuals, groups of individuals) in the population.

Sampling: the process of selecting a sample from a population that will be used in the research process.

Simple random sample: a sample in which every element (e.g., individuals, groups of individuals) in the population has an equal probability of being randomly selected to be in the sample.

Snowball sample: a sample made up of elements (e.g., individuals, groups of individuals) that are selected using a system of referrals and recommendations from one element to another.

Stratification variable: a variable used to divide or stratify the population into multiple relatively homogeneous strata.

Stratified cluster sample: naturally occurring clusters are randomly sampled from the population after the population of clusters have been stratified into relatively homogeneous strata, and data are collected from all elements with each cluster.

Stratified random sample: a sample that is randomly selected from within a relatively homogeneous block or stratum of a population that has been stratified on known population characteristics.

Stratified two-stage cluster sample: naturally occurring clusters are randomly sampled from the population after the population has been stratified into relatively homogeneous strata at the fist stage, and at the second stage, individuals are sampled *within* clusters. Data are not collected from every element in the clusters.

Systematic sample: a sample made up of elements (e.g., individuals, groups of individuals) that are selected systematically using a fixed interval from an ordered list of elements (individuals or clusters) in the population.

Systematic sampling errors: systematic sampling errors are due to systematic differences between the sample and the population. These errors can originate with the sampling frame from which the sample is selected or with the implementation of the sampling plan.

Target population: the ideal population to which the researcher wishes to generalize.

Two-stage cluster random sampling: naturally occurring clusters are randomly sampled at the first stage, and at the second stage, individuals are sampled *within* clusters. Data are not collected from every element in the clusters.

REVIEW OF PUBLISHED RESEARCH ARTICLES

In this section, we describe how three published research articles describe their sampling procedures. The full articles are available online at **www.sagepub.com/odwyer.**

Article 2 (Clayton, 2011)

In this non-experimental, longitudinal trend study, the author used a purposive sample of school districts in Virginia to examine whether diversity and teacher quality predict academic performance on state-mandated tests, while controlling for school-level poverty. The districts were purposively selected to have sufficiently large minority populations to allow trends to be examined over time. From archival data provided by the Virginia Department of Education, the author compiled data for the 1997–1998, 2002–2003, and 2007–2008 school years. It is apparent from the following description that the author is interested in generalizing beyond the sample included in the study:

> To best capture the trends that existed in resegregation, it was important to examine districts that had substantial enough populations to demonstrate such shifts. Therefore, the metropolitan areas of Northern Virginia, Tidewater, and Richmond were used. Of Virginia's 132 school districts, 24 were included in the sample. On completion of the final screening, the sample included 24 districts encompassing 592 K-5 or K-6 elementary schools. Therefore, 56,046 fifth graders in the selected districts were included out of the 89,893 fifth grade students across the state representing 62% of all of Virginia's fifth graders. (p. 678)

Article 3 (Porfeli, Wang, Audette, McColl, & Algozzine, 2009)

In this non-experimental, cross-sectional study, the authors used archival data from students in 80 elementary schools from a large urban school district in the southeast region of the United States to examine the association between educational achievement and school demographics and community capital. The authors stated that 12 elementary schools in the district were excluded due to missing data but go on to say that the missing data "were not systematically associated with the principle [sic] variables employed in this study" (p. 76). In subsequent paragraphs, the authors describe how the sample is similar to the entire district and to similarly sized school districts in the United States. In saying the following, the authors are indicating their intention to generalize beyond the study sample to a larger group:

> Minority enrollments (65%) as well as socioeconomic and second language markers reflect the overall district demographics and represent

similar characteristics to those of the 100 largest public elementary school districts in the United States (cf. National Center for Education Statistics, 2003). Though we accept the limitations of conducting our study in a single school system, we believe the demographic diversity in the district was sufficient to minimize concerns that restrictions in ranges of key variables may have biased the outcomes of our analyses. (p. 76)

Article 5 (Van Voorhis, 2011)

This article described the results of a quasi-experimental longitudinal panel study conducted to examine the effect of a weekly interactive mathematics program called Teachers Involve Parents in Schoolwork (TIPS). The study was conducted over 2 consecutive school years (2004–2006) in four similar elementary schools in a southeastern urban school district. The author described the sample as follows:

> In Year 1 (the 2004–2005 school year), 135 third-grade students and their families (66 TIPS and 69 Control) participated. In Year 2, 169 fourth graders and families (80 TIPS and 89 Control) participated. In the 2005–2006 school year, students dispersed across teachers in Grade 4 so that some students used TIPS activities for 2 years, some for 1 year (in Grade 3 or Grade 4), and some not at all. For the overall sample of 153 students, 17% used TIPS for 2 years, 40% used TIPS for 1 year, and 43% were Control students who never used the TIPS intervention over the 2-year period. (pp. 319–320)

In the "Limitations and Recommendations for Future Research" section, the author acknowledged that the sample size was small by saying the following:

> Longitudinal studies of an intervention that will follow students to one or more new grade levels should start with a larger number of students. In this study, because Grade 3 students were placed in classrooms of many different teachers who were not included in this study, there were relatively few students in the TIPS 2 Year group. Future research should start with a larger number of schools, teachers, and classrooms and negotiate student placements from 1 year to the next to retain the largest possible study samples in intervention and control conditions for full longitudinal analyses of the impact of the intervention. (p. 332)

5

Measurement and Instrumentation in Quantitative Research

CHAPTER OUTLINE

- What Is Measurement?
- Measurement Scales
- Common Ways to Collect Data
- Linking Measurement Instruments to the Research Questions and Hypotheses
- Establishing the Credibility and Consistency of Measurement Instruments

W hen conducting research in the quantitative tradition, researchers *must select appropriate measurement instruments for collecting the data that will be used to address the research questions posed.* Instruments are used to measure the attributes of individuals or groups, and the scores on the instrument provide the data for answering the research questions and testing the research hypotheses. Similar to the variety of instruments we use to measure physical attributes (e.g., weighing scales for measuring weight, sphygmomanometers for measuring blood pressure, spectrometers for measuring the wavelength of light, etc.), there are a variety of instrument forms available for measuring unobservable attributes. For example, achievement tests, aptitude tests, questionnaires, and observational protocols are common instruments used to collect data. The need for appropriate data collection instruments was first introduced in Chapter 3 and was stated as part of our guiding axiom at the outset of Section II, because in the absence of appropriate measurement, even the best the research design, sampling procedures, and data analysis techniques will not produce useful results that allow generalizations to be made and that minimize all feasible alternative explanations for the results observed. The purpose of this chapter is to introduce readers to measurement and instrumentation as they are used in quantitative social science research.

❖ WHAT IS MEASUREMENT?

We are all familiar with the measurement of physical attributes in daily life. For example, in a typical day, a person might step on a bathroom scale (weight), order a beverage by referring to a particular cup size (volume), look at the outdoor thermometer before deciding what to wear (temperature), or travel a known route to work (time or distance). While most of us probably spend little time thinking about how or why we talk about pounds when referring to weight, fluid ounces when referring to volume, degrees when referring to temperature, seconds and minutes to describe time, and miles to describe distance, these ubiquitous measurement systems provide precise ways to describe the amount of an attribute that is present (e.g., the weight, volume, temperature, time, or distance). Readers are likely to have a sense of what the numbers on these measurement systems mean. For example, readers will understand that 40°F is quite a bit cooler than 70°F, and that 60 miles is a great deal shorter and would take less time to traverse than, say, 1,000 miles. In our everyday lives, experience with the numbers assigned to attributes allows us to develop a sense for the *amount* of the attribute that is being described. However, readers may be unfamiliar with other scales used to represent these same attributes. For example, the Celsius temperature scale or the metric system for distance or weight may be less familiar to some of our readers, and so the scales used to indicate the amount of the attribute may not intuitively communicate how much of that attribute is present.

Formally stated, **measurement** involves systematically assigning numbers to an attribute so as to communicate something about that attribute, and we refer to the numbers assigned as a **measurement scale**. In social science research, including educational research, measurement is not as straightforward as it is in the physical world. For example, it is not possible to use eighth-grade students' heights, weights, or blood pressure to predict how much mathematics they know or how motivated they are to learn! Instead, we must use instruments such as achievement tests, aptitude tests, questionnaires, and observational protocols to measure nonobservable attributes or constructs. In many ways, these types of instruments are more complex to develop and administer than standard physical measures, and the data produced by them can be thornier to interpret!

In our guiding axiom, we said that *researchers must select appropriate measurement instruments for collecting the data that will be used to address the research questions posed.* Based on our experiences, sound measurement can only be conducted when appropriate measurement instruments are used. Moreover, appropriate measurement instruments should (a) be relatively easy to administer, complete, and score; (b) provide objective information about the attribute being measured; (c) provide credible information about the attribute that can be used to support subsequent inferences; and (d) provide consistent information over time.

Instrument **usability** is a relatively straightforward concept: A data collection instrument should be feasible and cost-effective to administer and score, should have clear directions for the individuals providing the data, and should be appropriate for the population that is being studied. In addition to being usable, an appropriate data collection instrument must provide **objective** information that is not biased by the extraneous characteristics of the researcher, the research participants, or the context in which the measurement is conducted.

The final two characteristics are at the heart of appropriate measurement and we refer to these characteristics as *instrument validity* and *instrument reliability*, respectively. **Instrument validity** refers to the accuracy of the inferences made from the data provided by the instrument, and **instrument reliability** refers to the degree to which the instrument provides consistent information. These definitions imply that *it is possible to have reliable measures that do not support valid inferences, but in order for an instrument to support valid inferences, it must also* *be reliable.* Readers will recall that the term *validity* was used in Chapter 4 when describing the ability to make generalizations beyond a single study (external validity). However, readers are counseled not to confuse the terms *external validity* and *instrument validity*. When we discuss instrument validity, we are concerned solely with the characteristics of the data collection instruments (Table 5.1).

Readers who are new to the field of quantitative research may be unaware that there is an entire field devoted to measurement, including multiple peer-reviewed journals. The process of developing usable, objective, valid, and reliable data collection instruments is not trivial, and the psychometric details are beyond the scope of this text. For readers who are interested in learning more about instrument development, we recommend more specialized texts such as Fowler (2008), DeVellis (2011), and Netemeyer, Bearden, and Sharma (2003). In the sections that follow, we describe the most common types of measurement scales, describe a subset of commonly used data collection instruments, provide guidelines for linking the data collection instruments with the research questions and hypotheses posed, and present the concepts of instrument validity and reliability along with a description of the empirical evidence used to evaluate measurement instruments.

❖ MEASUREMENT SCALES

In Chapter 3, we described how variables may be classified as categorical or continuous, and our readers will notice that the everyday examples of measurement we referred in the previous section (e.g., the weight, volume, temperature, time, or distance) are each continuous variables. Specifically, these attributes can vary in amount, and so the numbers on the scale are designed to communicate the amount of an

Table 5.1   Characteristics of measurement instruments

Appropriate Measurement Instruments
Are relatively easy to administer, complete, and to score
Provide objective information about the attribute being measured
Provide credible information about the attribute that can be used to support subsequent inferences
Provide consistent information over time

attribute that is present. Some measurement scales, however, do not communicate anything about the amount of the attribute and, instead, communicate something about the type of attribute that is present. In Chapter 3, we used the example of eye color as a categorical variable that varied in type but not amount; the five participants were assigned numbers according to the following rule: 1 = *brown*, 2 = *blue*, and 3 = *green*. In describing this type of categorical variable, we said that the numbers assigned (i.e., the measurement scale) represented qualitative differences but not differences in the amount of the attribute.

We hope it is clear from these examples that the numbers assigned through the measurement process to represent attributes can communicate different things. In fact, beyond the binary categorical versus continuous classification of measurement scales, we can further categorize scales according to *what* they convey about the attribute. In the following discussion, we will describe Stevens's (1951, 1975) widely accepted convention for classifying measurement scales into four types: nominal, ordinal, interval, and ratio.

Nominal Measurement Scales

As the name implies, when a **nominal measurement scale** is used, the numbers assigned to represent an attribute are "in name only." This means that the values (typically numbers) assigned to the attribute indicate differences in type from one value to another but not differences in amount. This is likely to be familiar to our readers because categorical variables are measured on a nominal scale. Examples of common nominal scales include eye color (e.g., 1 = *brown*, 2 = *blue*, and 3 = *green*), sex (0 = *male* and 1 = *female*), and minority status (0 = *nonminority* and 1 = *minority*). Nominal scales are considered to be the least sophisticated type of measurement, and the values cannot be manipulated mathematically to compute sums or averages, and so on. Frequencies are primarily used to summarize the distribution of an attribute measured on a nominal scale; for example, among the sample of five individuals in Table 3.1, 60% have brown eyes and 20% each have blue and green eyes.

Ordinal Measurement Scales

Ordinal measurement scales are applied to rank ordered data and are used to convey the order in which the individuals (or groups, as the case may be) are ranked on an underlying attribute. In addition, since the attribute forms the basis for the ordinal scale, the distances between points on the scale are not necessarily equidistant from each other; we commonly say that the points on an ordinal scale are "not equal interval." Any time information is rank ordered, an ordinal measurement scale is used. As an example, consider the way in which high school students' class rank is used as part of the college admissions process; typically, a class of first-semester seniors is ranked from highest to lowest on students' grade point average (GPA) and college admissions officers may use a student's class rank to inform their decision to accept or reject that student. In this case, students' class rank (1st, 2nd, . . . 50th, etc.) is measured on an ordinal scale. However, while students' GPA forms the basis for the ranking, the ordinal scale does not represent equal intervals on this attribute. Specifically, consider the hypothetical class in which the top-ranked student has a GPA of 3.99, the second highest has a GPA of 3.92, and the student ranked third has a GPA of 3.91. On the ordinal scale, the interval between Rank 1 and Rank 2 is the same as the interval between Rank 2 and Rank 3; however, these intervals are not equal on the underlying GPA attribute; the distance between 3.99 and 3.92 is not equivalent to the distance between 3.92 and 3.91. To sum up, an ordinal scale is used when data are rank ordered, but the scale is not equal interval in that it does not convey how much of the underlying attribute exists at each rank position.

Interval Measurement Scales

An **interval measurement scale** is similar to an ordinal measurement scale in that it conveys an order on some attribute, but since the interval scale is also equal interval, it conveys information about how *much* of the attribute exists at each point on the scale. Moreover, a value of zero on an interval scale does not mean the absence of the attribute. The classic examples of this are the most common scales used to represent temperature, the Fahrenheit and Celsius scales. On these scales, temperature can be ranked from hottest to coldest *and* the distance between points on the scale is equal interval all along the scale. For example, say that the temperatures on three consecutive days were 55 degrees, 65 degrees, and 50 degrees. Like the ordinal scale, the numbers assigned to the attributes on the interval scale convey that there is more of the attribute (temperature) on the second day than in the other days. However, since the scale is equal interval, the difference between 55 degrees and 60 degrees is the same as the difference between 60 degrees and 65 degrees. Anyone who has been outside on a day when the temperature is zero degrees (on either the Fahrenheit or Celsius scales) will also notice that zero on these scales does not mean the absence of the attribute; instead, it is quite cold, particularly if it is zero degrees on the Fahrenheit scale! As this example illustrates, zero on an interval scale is simply another point that conveys how much of an attribute exists and does not mean the absence of the attribute.

Many of the instruments used to measure educational outcomes (e.g., achievement tests, aptitude test, attitude scales, etc.) are assumed to provide data on an interval scale. For example, SAT scores have the following characteristics: They convey information about how much ability students possess in the domain being assessed (i.e., mathematics, critical reading, or writing), the distance between pairs of adjacent SAT scores on different parts of the SAT scale will be equivalent, and zero does not mean the absence of ability. We use the word *assume* at the start of this paragraph because the creation of an interval level scale for educational or behavioral attributes is a complex task that requires specialized expertise and resources, typically only available among professional instrument developers (e.g., The College Board, ETS, etc.). The specifics around developing interval-level scales are beyond the scope of this book, and readers interested in this topic are referred to van der Linden and Hambleton (1997), DeMars (2010), or Hambleton and Swaminathan (2010) for additional information.

The most useful characteristic of data provided by an interval scale is that it can be manipulated mathematically. However, in the absence of zero, it is not possible to interpret the data using ratios; for example, it is not possible to conclude that a high school student with an SAT mathematics score of 600 has twice as much of the attribute (i.e., knowledge in the domain) as a student with a SAT score of 300. In sum, numbers on an interval scale convey an order on some attribute, and since the scale is equal interval, it also conveys information about how much of the attribute exists at each point on the scale.

Ratio Measurement Scales

Ratio measurement scales possess all the qualities of ordinal and interval scales, and in addition, zero on the scale represents the absence of the attribute. Specifically, on a ratio scale, the score provides rank order information on an attribute; conveys the amount of an attribute that is present; conveys that the distance between pairs of adjacent scores on different parts of the scale will be equivalent; and because zero means the absence of the attribute, conclusions involving ratios can be made. This final point means that, for example, one could conclude that an individual with a score of 10 on a ratio scale possesses twice as much of the attribute as an individual with a score of 5 on that scale. Many attributes in the physical world are measured on ratio scales. For example, weight, volume, distance, and height are all represented on ratio scales. In sum, ratio scales are equal interval, and zero means the absence of the attribute.

Unfortunately, true ratio-level measurement is rare in social science and education. Although it does not seem possible according to the four-level classification system we just outlined, the measurement scales we use in several fields, such as education, typically provide us with data that lie somewhere between ordinal and interval. That is, instruments that provide interval-level information are not always used to collect data, and yet the data collected are analyzed as though they are interval data! For example, researchers often collect data using ordinal Likert scales that range from *Strongly disagree* to *Strongly agree*. Once the data are collected, the researcher assigns numbers to the response options (e.g., 1 = *Strongly disagree* to 5 = *Strongly agree*) and proceeds to calculate sums and averages and to formulate prediction models with the data. In this way, the researcher is treating the ordinal data provided by the Likert scale as though it is interval data. While this is common practice, we urge our readers to be cautious when analyzing ordinal data and to understand its inherent limitations.

❖ COMMON WAYS TO COLLECT DATA

There are a variety of instrument forms available for measuring the types of unobservable attributes we encounter in social science research. In this section, we will discuss a subset of the most commonly used data collection instruments—achievement and aptitude tests, questionnaires, and observation protocols. It is important to note that most research studies use multiple types of instruments to collect data. For example, in a school setting a test and a questionnaire might be administered to students and an observational protocol used to observe classroom activities.

Achievement and Aptitude Tests

It is unlikely that any of our readers reached college or graduate school without having completed dozens of tests; readers have probably completed standardized and unstandardized achievement tests and aptitude tests, and some of our musically inclined readers have probably also completed performance tests. Even from this short list of examples, it is evident that there are many different types of tests, often requiring different types of information from the test-taker and often serving different purposes for the test administrator. Technically speaking, the term **test** is an umbrella term for a set of instruments used to measure a specific domain. Tests present test-takers with a sample of questions or performances from a particular domain, and the test-taker is required to respond to the prompts on the test or to perform some action. Tests can be classified as *achievement or aptitude tests, standardized or unstandardized tests,* and *norm-referenced or criterion-referenced tests,* and more often than not, more than one classification will apply to a single test.

The primary difference between an achievement test and an aptitude test is their purpose. While **achievement tests** measure whether test-takers have mastered material taught in a particular domain, **aptitude tests** measure knowledge acquired through formal and informal process with the goal of predicting some future performance or behavior. For example, teacher-made classroom assessments are archetypal achievement tests because their purpose is to provide the teacher with a measure of how much of the taught content has been learned. The College Board's SAT and ETS's Graduate Record Examination (GRE) are examples of aptitude tests because their purpose is to provide a measure of knowledge that can be used to predict future performance. The data provided by these measures allow undergraduate and graduate college admissions committees, respectively, to predict how well students will perform in undergraduate and graduate programs.

You will also notice that the examples we provided for achievement and aptitude tests are very different from each other, and the differences go beyond just their purpose. For example, teacher-made classroom assessments are *unstandardized,* while tests like the SAT and GRE are *standardized.* Standardized and unstandardized tests differ from each other in their psychometric rigor and in how they are administered; a **standardized test** is usually developed by professional test developers and administered under standardized conditions, whereas **unstandardized tests** tend to be developed and administered by non-testing professionals. Pearson Assessments' Stanford Achievement Test (Stanford 9) and CBT McGraw-Hill's Terra Nova are examples of standardized achievement tests, and The College Board's SAT and ETS's GRE are examples of standardized aptitude tests. Teacher-developed tests such as those administered at the end of the semester are examples of unstandardized achievement tests; unstandardized aptitude tests tend to be rare.

It is also possible to classify tests as either norm referenced or criterion referenced. In a **norm-referenced test**, a test-taker's score is assigned based on a comparison with the scores of a norm group, a representative sample from the population of likely test-takers. Therefore, scores are assigned to test-takers in comparison to the performance in the norm group, and in addition to a numerical score on the measurement, scores are often reported as percentile ranks. Tests such as the Stanford 9 and Terra Nova are norm-referenced, standardized achievement tests, and the SAT and GRE are norm-referenced, standardized aptitude tests.

In comparison, **criterion-referenced tests** are tests in which scores are assigned to test-takers in comparison to some criterion (e.g., mastery of particular criterion concepts or a pre-established minimum score on the test). In K-12 education, many of the state tests that have been developed over the past decade to meet federal reporting mandates under the No Child Left Behind Act (NCLB) are criterion-referenced, standardized, achievement tests because they aim to measure whether students have mastered the content taught under state curriculum frameworks. For example, state tests such as the Massachusetts Comprehensive Assessment System (MCAS) or the New England Common Assessment Program (NECAP) are standardized criterion-referenced achievement tests; these are psychometrically rigorous tests administered under standardized conditions, and mastery of the material taught is evaluated against a particular criterion. Classroom teachers and college professors administering end-of-semester tests are likely to use criterion-referenced, unstandardized, achievement tests; first, these professionals are unlikely to have norm groups against which scores can be compared, and second, their intention is to evaluate whether the test-takers have mastered the material taught. To sum up, norm-referenced and criterion-referenced achievement tests differ in how mastery of the domain is established; norm-referenced achievement tests evaluate mastery compared with a norm group, whereas criterion-referenced achievement tests evaluate mastery relative to some criterion score.

Since improving students' performance and ability are the core goals of education, and students' test scores remain the currency for evaluating learning and innovations in education, achievement and aptitude tests, standardized and unstandardized tests, and norm-referenced and criterion-referenced tests are staples in educational research conducted in the quantitative tradition.

Questionnaires

A **questionnaire** is a measurement instrument on which research participants self-report about particular attributes. Questionnaires are frequently referred to as surveys; however, in an effort to avoid any confusion between survey research design and surveys used to generate or collect data, throughout this section and in subsequent discussions, we will use the term *questionnaire* in place of the term *survey*. Moreover, questionnaires can be administered as part of any type of research design and are not exclusively used when conducting survey research. It is probably safe to assume that all of our readers have completed a questionnaire at some point and so are familiar with the format of these instruments: Study participants provide responses to questions or items (e.g., answer questions, endorse statements, report on behaviors, etc.), and their responses become the data used to address the research questions. Typically, questionnaires also include questions about demographic characteristics (e.g., gender, race/ethnicity, income, etc.). Questionnaires are extremely versatile in terms of the amount and type of information that can be collected, and this makes them a very popular form of data collection instrument in social science research.

The self-reported nature of the questionnaire, combined with the fact that study participants are often physically and geographically removed from the researcher often result in *non-response errors*. As a reminder, we first introduced this term in Chapter 4 when we described possible threats to external validity. The challenge of non-response is particularly salient when questionnaires are used as part of a survey research design where the purpose is to describe some attribute in the population by administering a questionnaire remotely (e.g., via regular mail or electronically) to a sample from the population. **Non-response error** occurs when two conditions are met: (1) when significant numbers of individuals (or if a cluster random sampling design is used, clusters of individuals) in the sample fail to provide responses to the questionnaire and (2) those units are systematically different from those that did provide responses. As a consequence, the selected sample may no longer represent the population in systematic ways. In Chapter 4, we likened non-response errors to coverage errors; while coverage errors occur during the formulation of the sampling frame and in the implementation of the sampling plan, non-response errors occur *during* the study. Despite this central difference, both types of error can affect the external validity of research studies.

Non-response errors can take two forms: (1) *total non-response* and (2) *item non-response*. **Total non-response error** occurs when individuals or clusters do not respond to a questionnaire at all, while **item non-response error** occurs when there are uncompleted questions or items on a questionnaire. Both types of non-response can have a detrimental effect on the validity of the research findings; each may result in a sample that is no longer representative of the population and may reduce the size of the sample. Unfortunately, in situations where the researcher is not physically present for the completion of the questions, non-response errors can be an intractable issue. In any kind of research, we can expect that some individuals will fail to complete the measurement instruments or will only partially complete them. As such, researchers should plan to minimize non-response during the entire research process—during the planning phase, the data collection phase, and the data analysis phase by adhering to the guidelines that follow.

During the planning phase, the researcher should plan to devote resources (i.e., expertise, time, funding, etc.) in order to ensure that non-response is minimized. For example, sending an introduction letter or e-mail or placing a telephone call prior to sending the questionnaire can increase the response rate. Likewise, providing an incentive such as a nominal monetary sum or the chance to win a prize may also increase the response rate. These additional steps may require the allocation of additional resources and should be projected at the planning phase. During the data collection phase, the researcher should keep a detailed account of the questionnaire return rate and should send follow-up letters or e-mails or make a telephone call to the respondents who have not returned their completed questionnaire in an effort to increase the response rate.

During the data analysis phase, researchers should evaluate the effects of total non-response by comparing what is known about the individuals (or clusters) who responded to the questionnaire to those who did not. For example, if the researcher has demographic information for all individuals in the sample, he or she can compare the demographics of the two groups. In this case, systematic differences between the demographic characteristics may indicate that total non-response errors have resulted in the sample that is systematically different from the population.

For item non-response, the researcher should compare the characteristics of the individuals who answered a question or item with those who did not, and this should be repeated for every occasion on which responses are missing. In fact, statistical software packages such as SPSS and STATA have very useful algorithms that allow the researcher to identify patterns in missing responses to items. Depending on whether the item responses appear to be missing-at-random or systematically missing, the researcher may choose to remove respondents from the sample (this option should be used judiciously) or choose to replace the missing values. The process of replacing missing item responses in a data set is referred to as **data imputation**. A complete discussion of this process and its consequences is beyond the scope of this text, and the reader is referred to Allison (2001), Howell (2007), van Buuren (2012), Enders (2010), or Heeringa, West, and Berglund (2010) for further information. Suffice it to say that there are several effective strategies available for ameliorating the effects of item non-response.

There are many different ways to administer questionnaires, and typically, budget and time constraints need to be considered when deciding how to administer a questionnaire. In the past, questionnaires were typically administered via mail; however, in the past decade, Internet or web-based surveys have become more popular. In general, mail, phone, and web-based questionnaires tend to be most popular modes of administration, and each has its own strengths and weaknesses. Survey administration techniques are described in depth in texts such as Dillman, Smyth, and Christian (2008), Rea and Parker (2005), Fowler (2008), Groves, Fowler, Couper, and Lepkowski (2009), Fink (2012), and Wright and Marsden (2010).

Observation Protocols

Observation protocols are data collection instruments used to record information when observing the behaviors or attributes of individuals or groups in a specific situation. Unlike the previously discussed data collection methods, the researcher plays a central role when using an observation protocol. Instead of developing a test or questionnaire and subsequently administering it, the observation protocol requires the researcher to be an unobtrusive observer of the behaviors and attributes being studied. The observation protocol is a natural complement to the questionnaire—since self-reported data sources are vulnerable to bias (due perhaps to social desirability or attitude threats), the data collected via an observational protocol provides opportunities to triangulate the findings.

Adhering to the guidelines we laid out for appropriate measurement, observational protocols must be usable, must provide objective information about the attributes and behaviors being observed, and must provide valid and reliable information that supports subsequent inferences. For these reasons, standardized procedures should be in place when observational protocols are used for research in the quantitative tradition. For instance, the observation protocol, often a checklist or rating scale–type instrument, should provide the observer with very specific prompts about what data will be recorded, and when. In addition, prior to using the observational protocol in the research setting, observers should be trained in how to behave in an unobtrusive manner and how to use the protocol and should be provided with multiple opportunities to familiarize themselves with the protocol's use.

A common way to use observational protocols in the quantitative tradition is to sample the attributes and behaviors being studied at particular time intervals. For example, an observer might record precisely what is taking place in an elementary school classroom in 2-minutes intervals every 10 minutes throughout a 2-hour observation period. Depending on the purpose of the protocol, he or she might record the positions of the students and teacher, the number and type of student-to-student interactions and student-to-teacher interactions, and what material is being covered. Observational protocols typically provide data in the form of behavior or attribute counts, frequencies, or percentages when used as part of a quantitative research design.

❖ LINKING MEASUREMENT INSTRUMENTS TO THE RESEARCH QUESTIONS AND HYPOTHESES

The essential first step in selecting appropriate data collection instruments is for the researcher to consider the following question: *What attributes and characteristics do I need to measure in the sample in order to address the research questions and to test the research hypotheses?* This question is essential because the attributes and characteristics measured in the sample become the evidence used to answer the research questions and support or refute the research hypotheses. Without a clear understanding of how the data will address the research questions and hypotheses, and shed light on the research problem, the researcher may fail to collect data that is necessary for addressing the research problem and questions. A comprehensive understanding of the research problem and how the research questions are positioned within the extant body of literature on the topic is a prerequisite for researchers' being able to select the most appropriate instruments. This is because prior research on the topic will be crucial to defining the attributes or characteristics that need to be measured, and can alert the researcher to important additional phenomena that should be measured or to nuisance phenomena that need to be controlled for during the data analysis phase. While this may seem like an obvious point, it occasionally happens that the researcher has only a limited understanding of the research problem and so inadvertently fails to collect the essential data.

Consider the example where a researcher is conducting a study to compare the mathematics ability of a group of eighth-grade students who have been exposed to a new teaching method with a comparison group who used the old method. In this case, the researcher will need an appropriate measure of eighth-grade mathematics ability, and there may be several different options available. For example, he could use scores on a teacher-made test that is used to assign end-of-course grades, scores on a state test that is aligned with state standards, or perhaps even scores on an aptitude test that measures mathematical abilities typically not taught as part of the school curriculum. Ultimately, the inferences that can be made about students' mathematics ability as a result of the new teaching method will depend on which instrument the researcher chooses. In the case of the teacher-made test, the researcher would be able to make inferences about what students have mastered from the content presented during the course of the semester. Using the state test, the researcher would be able to make inferences about whether the students have mastered the content defined in the state standards. From a standardized mathematics aptitude test, researchers may be able to make inferences about how students compare with a norm group and may be able to predict their potential to do well on mathematics assessments in the future. These inferences are not necessarily equivalent, and depending on the purpose of the research, using one in place of the other may result in a misalignment of the research purpose and the measurement instruments. If the research purpose was to examine whether the new teaching methods improved students' scores on the state test (i.e., used as part of the state's federal reporting mandates), scores on the teacher-made test or the aptitude test would not be appropriate for addressing the overall purpose of the research. Likewise, if the purpose of the research was to examine whether the group that received the new method had better mastery of the content they were exposed to during the semester, the teacher-made test would be more appropriate than either the state test or the aptitude test; in this case, both the state and aptitude tests may not be measuring the content domain with a sufficient level of precision to be able to draw conclusions about the effectiveness of the new intervention. As this example shows, the selection of measurement instruments should be carefully aligned with the goals of the research and the research questions.

❖ ESTABLISHING THE CREDIBILITY AND CONSISTENCY OF MEASUREMENT INSTRUMENTS

In the section "What Is Measurement?" we defined instrument validity as the accuracy of the inferences made from the data provided by the instrument, and instrument reliability as the degree to which the instrument provides consistent information. We also said that it is possible to have reliable measures that do not support valid inferences, but that the opposite is not possible; for an instrument to support valid inferences, it must also be reliable. Establishing that an instrument is providing valid and reliable information is a central concern when conducting research in the quantitative tradition, and the evidence used to establish instrument validity and reliability should be reported as a part of every research study. However, the complexity involved in presenting this evidence will vary from study to study. This is because the level and type of evidence required will depend on whether the researcher is developing new data collection instruments or whether pre-existing instruments whose measurement properties have been extensively examined and reported are being used. We wish to point out that adopting an instrument whose measurement properties have *not* been examined is not a choice we recommend; instruments whose measurement properties have not been studied should never be used in a research study without first conducting an empirical study of their properties.

The process of developing new data collection instruments and establishing their measurement properties, or even establishing the measurement properties of a pre-existing instrument, is not trivial and requires specialized knowledge about item development and psychometrics. For those readers who are interested in instrument development, we recommend spending additional time reviewing more specialized texts such as DeVellis (2011) or Netemeyer et al. (2003) to develop a deeper understanding of the instrument development process. Here, we will focus on defining instrument validity and reliability and will discuss the types of evidence that researchers use to establish both. We hope that our discussion in the subsections that follow will corroborate the fact that establishing instrument validity and reliability is an empirical endeavor that is central to the research process.

Instrument Validity

Instrument validity relates to the appropriateness of the inferences made from the data provided by the instruments, and as such, it is not an intrinsic characteristic of the instrument itself. Rather, instrument validity has to do with *how* the instrument is used. Consider for example, a mathematics test that the researcher carefully developed to provide truthful (i.e., valid) information to support inferences about how much students have learned during the academic year. In this case, the researcher could infer that low-scoring students had mastered less of the content than high-scoring students. Therefore, the inferences made from students' test scores about their mathematics ability are likely to be valid. However, if the scores on that mathematics test were instead used to make inferences about students' mastery of U.S. history, the inferences would not be valid. As this example shows, instrument validity is not a characteristic of the instrument itself but instead relates to whether the inferences made from the instrument are appropriate. We caution our readers to avoid concluding that an "instrument is valid," or worse, that an "instrument has been proven to be valid" because both conclusions are incompatible with the precise definition of instrument validity. According to Messick's seminal work (1989, 1996a, 1996b), instrument validity is a "unitary concept" but evidence is gathered from multiple sources. Specifically, *content, criterion,* and *construct validity evidence* are used to establish instrument validity.

Content validity is concerned with whether the sample of items (e.g., survey questions or test questions) on an instrument represents the universe of behaviors that define the attribute. Examining this aspect of instrument validity is typically one of the first steps researchers take in establishing overall instrument validity. Developing a sample of items that represents the universe of behaviors that define the attribute requires the researcher to have a deep understanding of the attribute being measured and a clear definition of the behaviors that constitute the attribute (points that have been emphasized throughout this chapter). In the absence of this knowledge, the researcher may fail to include items on the instrument that are essential for capturing the attribute (**construct under-representation**) or may include items that are irrelevant for representing the attribute (**construct irrelevance**), thereby lengthening the instrument and increasing the burden on the research participants.

Content validity is typically established by having experts, who are knowledgeable about the attribute being measured and the population being studied, participate in a systematic review of the items on the instrument. In this way, content validity rests on the judgment of experts. The questions at this stage of the validation process might include the following types of questions:

- Does the sample of items adequately represent the universe of behaviors or characteristics that define the attribute?

- Is each item essential for representing the attribute?

- Are any items irrelevant to measuring the attribute?

- Does the content appear biased against any group (e.g., females, minorities, or low income individuals)?

- Are the directions for completing the instrument clear and unambiguous?

- Is the format of the instrument (e.g., the layout and the response options) and the vocabulary and sentence structure appropriate for the intended research participants?

Content validity alone is insufficient for establishing instrument validity. Rather, the evidence provided through the expert review process must be used in conjunction with empirical evidence about how the instrument functions.

Criterion validity is concerned with whether the information provided by the instrument is systematically related to information provided by another, criterion instrument. More specifically, scores on an instrument should be related to scores on other instruments measuring the same attribute (*convergent validity*) and should not be related to scores on instruments that are measuring theoretically unrelated attributes (*divergent validity*). Researchers are typically concerned with two types of criterion validity evidence: (1) *concurrent validity evidence* and (2) *predictive validity evidence*. As the name suggests, **concurrent validity evidence** is garnered from the relationship between scores provided by the instrument and scores on some other criterion instrument administered at the same point in time. On the other hand, **predictive validity evidence** is concerned with whether the information provided by the instrument is related to performance on some criterion measure administered at some point in the future.

Overall, evidence of criterion validity is provided by the empirical relationships between scores on the instrument used in the research and scores on criterion instruments that measure the same and different attributes. In technical terms, evidence of criterion validity is provided by the size and direction of the *correlation coefficient* (*r*) that represents the relationship between the scores provided by the instrument under study and the scores on other instruments. In Chapter 9, we will describe it in more detail, but for now the following description of the correlation coefficient will suffice: *A* **correlation coefficient** *indicates the* *strength and direction of the relationship between two measures taken on the same individual, and its value ranges from –1 to +1.* A positive correlation coefficient indicates that higher scores on one measure are associated with higher scores on the other measure, negative correlations indicate that as scores on one measure increase scores on the other measure tend to decrease, and values close to zero indicate that there is no relationship between the scores on the two measures. Furthermore, correlation does not imply that one attribute causes the other. Based on this description, there should be a relationship between the scores on two instruments measuring the same attribute (**convergent validity evidence**) and a correlation close to zero between the scores on two instruments measuring theoretically unrelated attributes (**divergent validity evidence**).

From our description, it is probably evident to the reader that gathering evidence of criterion validity is not always straightforward. For example, a valid and reliable criterion measure may not be available or even exist for some attributes, and it may not be feasible or cost-effective to administer two instruments as part of a research study.

Construct validity is concerned with whether an instrument is providing the researcher with meaningful information about the attribute being studied. Since construct validity has to do with whether an instrument is measuring what it is supposed to be measuring, establishing construct validity is at the core of establishing overall instrument validity. In fact, construct validity is predicated on the instrument demonstrating both content and criterion validity. Moreover, beyond these two forms of validity evidence, construct validity is established (a) by linking the information provided by the instrument to the theory underlying its purpose and (b) by ruling out alternative explanations for the scores observed.

Consider for example, the situation where a researcher develops a test to measure students' mastery of the mathematics content covered in eighth grade. First, the researcher must establish the content validity of the test. Specifically, she must define the content domain by describing the mathematical concepts that were covered and the skills that students were required to master. For example, she may find that the eighth-grade curriculum covers mathematical processes, numbers and operations, algebra, geometry and measurement, and data analysis, statistics, and probability. As a first step, representative items must be carefully developed to sample the content knowledge and skills within each sub-domain. After developing these test items, an expert review is required to judge the content validity of the test.

Second, the researcher must gather criterion validity evidence by examining the correlation between scores on the test and external criterion measures. For example, the researcher might examine the correlation between scores on the test and the teacher-assigned course grades, the criterion measure. In this case, the researcher would expect to find that scores on the test are positively related to course grades; convergent validity is being established because students who had high scores on the researcher-developed test would be expected to have high course grades.

Going beyond the evidence necessary for establishing content and criterion validity, construct validity is concerned with whether the variability among students' scores on the test is due to variability in their mathematics content knowledge or whether there is some alternative source of variation. For example, lengthy word problems may in fact be measuring reading skills (vocabulary and comprehension) instead of mathematics skills. Likewise, problems that use cultural references familiar only to the nonminority students may inadvertently place minority students at a disadvantage for demonstrating their mathematical skills, the rightful attribute the test was designed to measure. As such, the researcher must gather evidence to establish that the instrument is truly measuring what it was designed to measure and to rule out alternative explanations for the variability among students' scores.

Since participants' responses to the items on an instrument are manifestations of the attribute being measured (e.g., mathematics ability in the previous example), the inter-relatedness of the responses to the items on an instrument are used to support the theory, or theories, on which the instrument was predicated. For example, if the researcher's theory is that students' eighth-grade mathematics content knowledge is a function of their knowledge of multiple sub-domains, that is, mathematical processes, numbers and operations, algebra, geometry and measurement, and data analysis, statistics, and probability, she would examine whether the responses to the items cluster together according to this theory. If the theory holds, responses to items within each sub-domain will be more highly correlated with other items measuring the same sub-domain than they are to the responses to the items tapping other sub-domains. Stated more broadly, the relationships among the items on an instrument are used to establish whether the instrument is measuring the attribute it was designed to measure. Additional details about analysis procedures used to explore the inter-relatedness of the items on an instrument can be found in more specialized texts such as Thompson (2004), Walkey and Welch (2010), Mulaik

(2009), or Fabrigar and Wegener (2011) that are devoted to factor analytic techniques (e.g., common factor analysis, principal components analysis, etc.).

Additional evidence supporting construct validity may be gathered from sources external to the instrument being studied, either external measures of the same and different constructs or from individuals who are not part of the research study. Using external measures of the same and different constructs, the **multitrait multimethod approach** first proposed by Campbell (1957) provides a framework for evaluating the convergent and divergent validity of an instrument. Under this framework, researchers examine the correlations among measures of multiple attributes using multiple measurement methods, expecting to see a particular pattern among three relationships. *First, there should be a positive relationship between two measures of the same attribute, measured in the same way.* Using the previous example, there should be a positive correlation between scores on the researcher-made paper-and-pencil mathematics test and scores on a teacher-made paper-and-pencil mathematics test. *Second, there should be a positive correlation between two measures of the same attribute, measured in different ways.* For example, there should be a positive correlation between scores on the researcher-made paper-and-pencil mathematics test and students' performance on an oral test of mathematics skills. *Third, there should be no correlation between measures of theoretically unrelated attributes, measured in the same way* and *no correlation between measures of theoretically unrelated attributes, measured in different ways.* For example, if mathematics and reading skills are theoretically unrelated, there should be no correlation between scores on the researcher-made paper-and-pencil mathematics test and students' performance on a paper-and-pencil reading test. Likewise, there should be no correlation between scores on the researcher-made paper-and-pencil mathematics test and students' performance on an oral test of reading skills.

Individuals who are not part of the research study may also be used to provide evidence supporting construct validity. Specifically, the **known-group method** can be used to examine whether an instrument can discriminate between individuals who are either known to possess or have high levels of the attribute being measured and individuals who either do not possess or have low levels of that attribute. Again using the mathematics example, the test should be able to discriminate between a group of 12th-grade students who have mastered and surpassed the content covered in 8th grade and a group of 8th-grade students who have recently learned the content.

Instrument Reliability

In the section "What Is Measurement?" we said that appropriate measurement should not only provide data that can be used to support truthful inferences but that it should also provide consistent information. We introduced this as *instrument reliability*, and as with instrument validity, the reliability of the information provided by an instrument must be established empirically and should be reported as part of any research summary. Instrument reliability is related to the concept of measurement error. Technically, **measurement error** is the difference between the "true amount" of an attribute and the value that is obtained through the measurement process. This type of error is made up of two pieces: (1) *random error* and (2) *systematic error*. **Random measurement error** occurs due to random fluctuations in the "amount" of an attribute when measures are taken at multiple points in time. Overall, random errors average out to be zero and have negligible effects. Conversely, **systematic measurement error** is the result of faulty measurement and over multiple time points—this type of error does not average out to be zero.

To explain this further, consider the common bathroom scale. If you measure your weight three times in quick succession, there is a chance that you will get slightly different results each time. Each measure is likely to be within the random error range reported by the manufacturer of the scale (depending on the scale, it may be as small as ±0.01 pounds or as large as ±0.10 pounds), and over an infinite number of weigh-ins, this error will average to zero. Now consider the situation where the scale consistently reported that your weight was 10 pounds heavier than you know yourself to be; that is, the scale indicates that you are 10 pounds over your "true amount of weight." In this situation, there is systematic error in the measurement instrument (the weighing scale) that is biasing the observed results. To avoid systematic measurement errors, the conscientious researcher must devote resources (time, money, psychometric expertise, etc.) to the development of a reliable instrument. Furthermore, as we stated in our introduction to the section "Establishing the Credibility and Consistency of Measurement Instruments," in cases where previously developed instruments are being used, prior accounts of instrument reliability should be reported alongside estimates of reliability calculated using the data collected as part of the study.

Conceptually, an instrument is reliable if it provides similar information when administered at different times to the same group. In technical terms, there should be a strong, positive correlation between the data provided by an instrument at two different points in time.

Moreover, just as we expect our bathroom weighing scale to provide us with similar estimates of our weight on two consecutive days, we also expect that the instruments we choose to use when measuring unobservable attributes will provide similarly consistent estimates. For example, an achievement test administered on two separate occasions to the same individuals should provide us with approximately equivalent estimates of students' ability. As before, we would expect to see small, random variations in the estimates. We should not, however, expect to see large systematic differences between the estimates.

As you probably noticed in this example, administering the same instrument on different occasions can lead to other challenges. For example, students may remember the questions on the test from one time to the next, particularly if the time between administrations is short. Moreover, having been alerted to the questions on the test, students could study those topics between administrations. These are generally referred to as *practice effects*. Finally, it may not be feasible to administer the same instrument more than once because of time, cost, or access restrictions. These challenges point to the reasons why there are two distinct approaches to estimating instrument reliability; ones that require multiple administrations of an instrument (*test–retest and equivalent forms methods*) and others that rely on a single administration of an instrument (*internal consistency methods, including split-halves and Cronbach's alpha methods*). Subsequent to discussing these methods, we also describe inter-rater reliability as a means for establishing the degree of reliability among scores assigned by multiple raters.

The **test–retest method** for estimating reliability requires at least two administrations of an instrument to the same group. For example, a researcher interested in establishing the reliability of a test of mathematics content knowledge could administer the test on two different occasions to the same group of students. The researcher would evaluate the reliability of the instrument by examining the correlation coefficient that indicates the relationship between students' scores on the test at Time 1 and the scores at Time 2 and would expect to see a strong, positive correlation between the two sets of scores. In fact, the magnitude of this correlation, referred to as the *reliability coefficient*, is used to estimate instrument reliability. A test–retest reliability coefficient of +1 for an instrument indicates that the data provided by the two administrations are perfectly, positively correlated, and so the instrument would be deemed perfectly reliable. Conversely, a correlation of zero indicates that the instrument is perfectly unreliable. In general, researchers aim to have reliability coefficients as close to +1 as possible. As an aside, a negative reliability coefficient should prompt the researcher to carefully review the instrument and the data file for the data entry mistakes. As we pointed out in our earlier discussion, administering the same instrument on more than one occasion can be problematic due to practice effects and so on.

The **equivalent forms method** is similar to the test–retest method in that it requires two administrations of an instrument and uses a correlation coefficient as the reliability estimate. However, the equivalent forms method aims to avoid practice effects by administering two psychometrically equivalent forms (sometimes referred to as *parallel forms*) of the same instrument and, subsequently, calculating the reliability coefficient as the correlation between individuals' scores on each form. The term *psychometrically equivalent* means that both forms of the instrument measure the same attribute, include items that are similarly difficult for the population being measured, include an equal number of items, and are scored and interpreted in precisely the same way. As with most things we have discussed in this chapter, psychometric equivalence is established empirically. While one would not expect a classroom teacher to have the resources to be able to create psychometrically equivalent forms of his or her classroom assessments, commercial test and instrument publishers frequently develop multiple equivalent forms of the same instrument, conduct studies to establish instrument equivalence, and report equivalent forms reliability evidence. For example, the Test of Written Language (TOWL), developed and commercially distributed by Multi-Health Systems (MHS), is available in Form A and Form B (www.mhs.com). Likewise, Pearson Assessments produces two equivalent forms of the Peabody Picture Vocabulary Test (PPVT; www.pearsonassessments.com). While using equivalent forms of the same instrument minimizes or eliminates practice effects, additional resources have to be applied for a second administration of the instrument, and continued access to the individuals or groups being studied is required. As with the test–retest method, a correlation coefficient close to +1 indicates that the data provided by the two administrations are strongly positively correlated and so the instrument would be deemed reliable, a correlation close to zero indicates unreliability in the instrument, and therefore, researchers aim to have reliability coefficients as close to +1 as possible.

Internal consistency methods for estimating reliability are unlike the previous methods in that they require only one administration of an instrument. As such, these methods prevent practice effects, eliminate the costs associated with re-administering the instrument, and avoid the need for additional access to the individuals or groups beings studied. For these reasons, internal consistency methods such as the split-halves approach and the Cronbach's alpha approach are more appealing.

Split-halves method is a form of internal consistency that uses the correlation between the scores on each half of an instrument as an estimate of the reliability of the instrument as a whole. According to this method, individuals are administered one instrument, and responses to the items on one half of the instrument are used to calculate the first semitotal score for each individual, while the responses to the remaining half are used to calculate a second semitotal score for individuals. Subsequently, the correlation coefficient representing the relationship between the two semitotal scores is the reliability coefficient. As before, reliability coefficient values close to +1 are optimal.

The fact that only half the items are used to calculate the semitotal scores on which the reliability coefficient is calculated is a weakness of this approach. As you recall from our discussion about instrument validity earlier in this section, the items on an instrument should be a representative sample of the population of items that could be used to measure a particular domain. It makes sense then that using many items to measure a domain will likely provide a better (i.e., more valid) measure of the attribute, but it also makes sense that providing individuals with multiple opportunities to be measured via the items on the instrument will lead to a more consistent (i.e., more reliable) estimate of the attribute. Stated more directly, the more items on an instrument used to measure an attribute, the more reliable the instrument will tend to be. It follows then that calculating semitotal scores using half the items for each and subsequently calculating the correlation between them could result in an underestimation of the reliability of the instrument as a whole. Of course, the longer the instrument, the less likely this is to be a problem (and vice versa). Due to this issue, it is recommended that the Spearman–Brown adjustment is applied; this adjustment estimates the instrument reliability if psychometrically equivalent items were added to increase the length of the halves to the full-length instrument.

Another significant challenge associated with using this approach lies with selecting the most appropriate way to split the instrument. For example, one could split the instrument in the middle, split by even and odd question numbers, split the instrument into halves that are balanced in terms of content and difficulty, or one could randomly assign items to each half. Depending on the attribute being measured, one or more of these methods may not produce satisfactory results, and in fact, different splitting decisions could produce dissimilar reliability coefficients. Consider, for example, a 50-item test that is designed to measure students' mathematics knowledge. Splitting the test in the middle may produce unsatisfactory results because students' performance on the second half of the test could be affected by fatigue or item positioning that results in different difficulty levels (e.g., easier items may have been placed at the start of the test, whereas more difficult items may have been placed toward the end) and because the two halves may not be matched in terms of the content they measure (e.g., algebra and geometry may be measured by the items at the start of the test, whereas statistics and probability may be measured by the items toward the end of the test). Splitting by odd- and even-numbered questions would avoid the effects of fatigue, but the possibility of the two halves being unmatched in terms of content or difficulty remains. The most appropriate approach may be to use a combination of the two final splitting options: This would involve dividing the instrument into its content sub-domains, matching pairs of items within each sub-domain on content and difficulty, and then randomly assigning items from each pair to each half. Because this final approach produces halves that are approximately psychometrically equivalent, it is likely to produce the most credible estimate of reliability.

Instead of an achievement test, now consider the splitting decisions that could be made if the instrument was a 20-item scale designed to measure students' test anxiety. Referring again to our discussion on instrument validity earlier in this section, the items chosen to measure test anxiety should be a representative sample of the population of items that could measure test anxiety behaviors. In this case, it may not be possible to even approximate equivalent halves due to the fact that each item contributes to the measurement of the entire domain; as such, splitting the instrument in two may result in measures that are not equivalent in terms of the domain being measured. Overall, the split-halves method for estimating reliability provides some advantages over the test–retest method and equivalent forms methods because only one administration is required. However, underestimating the reliability of the entire instrument and selecting the most appropriate way to split the instrument can be intractable issues.

Cronbach's alpha (α) is similar to the split-halves approach in its advantage over the test–retest and equivalent forms approaches; namely, that the instrument need only be administered one time. However, Cronbach's α offers significant advantages over the split-halves internal consistency approach: First, the semitotal scores are not used to estimate the reliability of the complete instrument, and, second, no decisions need to be made regarding appropriate ways to split the instrument. Unlike the previous methods, Cronbach's α is not a straightforward correlation between two sets of scores for the same individuals. However, it is measured on the same scale, with zero indicating unreliability and values close to 1 indicating higher reliability. Values of Cronbach's α equal to, or greater than 0.70 are deemed optimal as they indicate that *at least* 70% of the observed person-to-person differences in the responses to the items on the instrument is due to person-to-person differences in the "true amount" of the attribute being measured. Stated differently, 30% or less of the observed person-to-person differences in the responses to the items on the instrument is due to random error. The phrase *at least* is used when interpreting Cronbach's α because it is considered to be a lower bound estimate of reliability.

Conceptually, the observed value of Cronbach's α is a function of the average differences among the responses to each item (i.e., the variability among the responses to each item), the average differences among the responses to the instrument as a whole (i.e., the variability among the total scores on the instrument), and the number of items on the instrument. Fortunately, the most common statistical software packages (e.g., SPSS, Stata, SAS) can be easily used to calculate Cronbach's α.

Note that Cronbach's α is a more general form of previously developed methods called the Kuder–Richardson (KR) approaches; the two KR approaches (KR-20 and KR-21) were first published in 1937, whereas Cronbach's α was not developed until the early 1950s (Kerlinger, 1973). The primary difference between Cronbach's α and the earlier KR approaches lies with the types of data that can be used. Whereas Cronbach's α can be used to calculate the reliability of an instrument that produces dichotomous scores (e.g., scores on a multiple choice item; 1 = *correct* and 0 = *incorrect*) or polytomous scores (e.g., scores on an essay item or Likert-type scale; 0, 1, 2, 3, etc.), the KR approaches are more limited. Specifically, the KR-20 and KR-21 approaches can only be used to estimate the reliability of instruments that produce dichotomous scores, and in fact, the KR-21 assumes that each item is equally difficult. Overall, Cronbach's α provides more flexibility in the types of data that can be used.

Inter-rater reliability is an estimate of the degree of reliability in scores assigned by multiple raters. To ensure maximum objectivity, inter-rater reliability is calculated when data are collected using instruments that may be deemed subjective or when researchers assign scores on an instrument that could be considered subjective (e.g., observation protocols or open-ended short answer or essay questions). One of the ways that this is accomplished is to use multiple "raters" (observers, scorers, judges, etc.) and to establish the amount of agreement among raters. Technically, **inter-rater reliability** is a measure of the amount of agreement in the scores assigned by multiple raters. Agreement levels greater than 80% are deemed optimal.

As we described in the earlier sections, it is necessary to provide raters with adequate training and opportunities to practice using subjective instruments. As such, we recommend training and practice for the raters prior to considering inter-rater reliability. Once raters have been trained and have practiced, the most straightforward way to calculate inter-rater reliability is to have at least two raters independently assign scores to a sample of behaviors, and subsequently, the correlation between the assigned scores is calculated. If the correlation between the ratings is lower than optimal, additional training or practice is warranted. These steps should be repeated until the degree of agreement is 80% or higher.

❖ CONNECTIONS TO QUALITATIVE RESEARCH

Measurement and the instruments that are used to generate data are central elements in the quantitative tradition because any conclusions that are drawn from a study depend squarely on the quality of the evidence that is collected. Perhaps the most compelling sentence that could be used to argue that the chasm is wide between the traditions is the oft-stated phrase in the qualitative tradition that "the researcher is the primary instrument." As described in this section, measurement in the quantitative tradition has received a great deal of attention in relation to the types of variables under study, the kind of instruments used to collect data about these variables, and the reliability and validity of these data generated by these instruments. The discussion about "measurement" in the qualitative tradition is at once both simpler and more complex. Even though things like semistructured interviews and observation protocols are used to guide data collection efforts, the fact that qualitative researchers recognize that they are the primary instrument simplifies the range of options. On the other hand, assuming the mantle of "primary instrument" places an added burden on qualitative researchers because rather than being able to point to established validity and reliability coefficients of a test or questionnaire, they must be able to convince readers that they have exercised due diligence in achieving the analogues for validity and reliability (see Quality Question 6 in Chapter 1). These analogues include techniques specific to the qualitative tradition such as triangulation and audit trails (Guba, 1981; Yin, 2012).

It should also be noted that not all instruments used in the quantitative tradition are of the "off the shelf" variety with acceptable psychometric properties. Rather, there are a great number of instruments used in research projects and dissertations that are researcher or teacher developed (e.g., questionnaires used in survey designs) because there are no existing instruments that can address the specific research questions being asked. In these cases, researchers must develop their instruments with care and rigor—much like qualitative researchers' need to exercise similar care when developing interview and observation protocols.

Notwithstanding the need to construct researcher-made instruments due to a lack of appropriate existing instruments, research in both the traditions could benefit by at least posing similar or related questions that have been asked in related studies. The collection of related data across studies versus a myriad "stand-alone" studies could increase our understanding about phenomena (see Moss et al., 2009). In concert with conducting a *relevant* literature review, using similar instruments and questions across studies could go a long way toward creating a cumulative knowledge base in the social sciences comprising quantitative and qualitative findings that could help practitioners in fields such as education to transform empirical findings into actual practice—an ever-elusive goal!

❖ CONCLUDING REMARKS

We hope that our coverage of measurement and instrumentation has convinced our readers of the importance of appropriate measurement and instrumentation and the need to present empirical evidence of appropriateness when describing the instruments used. As a final note, we want to provide our readers with some guidelines for summarizing the characteristics of the instruments as part of a research report (e.g., a master's or doctoral dissertation, a journal article, or report for funding agencies). Typically, research reports such as these have a section dedicated to describing the instruments used, and depending on whether the researcher developed a new instrument or used a pre-established one, the level and type of information required can vary significantly. At a minimum, the instrumentation section of a research report should (a) provide a detailed description of the attribute being measured by the instrument; (b) indicate the source of the instrument (researcher-developed or pre-established); (c) describe how the instrument was administered (online, paper-and-pencil, etc.);

(d) indicate the number of items on the instrument and what types of data the items provided (e.g., open-ended responses, Likert scale responses, etc.); (e) provide evidence of instrument reliability; and (f) provide evidence of instrument validity.

DISCUSSION QUESTIONS

1. If you decided to investigate a problem in your field using both quantitative and qualitative approaches, how might you equate the notion of "instrument validity" in the quantitative tradition to "trustworthiness" in the qualitative tradition?

2. How might you contrast the concept of "instrument reliability" in the quantitative and qualitative traditions?

3. If quantitative researchers want to use some "open-ended" questions as part of a questionnaire composed primarily of Likert scale items, what advice might you give them to allow participants to reveal "richer" information?

4. How would you respond to the assertion that instrument development is more "technical" in the quantitative tradition than in the qualitative tradition?

KEY TERMS

Achievement test: a test that measures whether test-takers have mastered the material taught in a particular domain.

Aptitude test: a test that measures knowledge acquired through formal and informal process with the goal of predicting some future performance or behavior.

Concurrent validity evidence: criterion validity evidence garnered from the relationship between scores on a measurement instrument and scores on a criterion instrument administered at the same point in time.

Construct irrelevance: when a measurement instrument includes items that are irrelevant for measuring a particular attribute.

Construct under-representation: when a measurement instrument does not include all questions or items necessary for measuring a particular attribute.

Construct validity: relates to whether an instrument is providing the researcher with meaningful information about the attribute being studied. It is predicated on the instrument demonstrating both content and criterion validity and is established by linking the information provided by the instrument to the theory underlying its purpose and by ruling out alternative explanations for the scores observed.

Content validity: relates to whether the sample of items (e.g., survey questions or test questions) on a measurement instrument represents the universe of behaviors that define the attribute.

Convergent validity evidence: when scores on an instrument are related to scores on other measurement instruments measuring the same attribute.

Correlation coefficient: a number ranging from −1 to +1 that indicates the strength and direction of the relationship between two measures taken on the same individual. A positive correlation coefficient indicates that higher scores on one measure are associated with higher scores on the other measure, while negative correlations indicate that as scores on one measure increase scores on the other measure tend to decrease. Values close to zero indicate that there is no relationship between the scores on the two measures.

Criterion validity: relates to whether the information provided by a measurement instrument is systematically related to information provided by another, criterion instrument. Criterion validity evidence may be concurrent or predictive.

Criterion-referenced test: a test in which scores are assigned to test-takers in comparison to some criterion (e.g., mastery of particular criterion concepts or a pre-established minimum score).

Cronbach's alpha (α): an internal consistency approach that provides a reliability estimate that is a function of the variability among the responses to each item on an instrument, the variability among the total scores on an instrument, and the total number of items on an instrument.

Data imputation: the process of replacing missing item responses in a data set.

Divergent validity evidence: when scores on an instrument are not related to scores on other measurement instruments that are measuring theoretically unrelated attributes.

Equivalent forms method: a method for estimating instrument reliability that requires the administration of psychometrically equivalent forms of the same instrument.

Instrument reliability: the degree to which a measurement instrument provides consistent information.

Instrument validity: the accuracy of the inferences made from the data provided by a measurement instrument.

Internal consistency methods: approaches for estimating instrument reliability that do not require multiple administrations of the instrument. Internal consistency methods include the split-halves and Cronbach's alpha methods.

Inter-rater reliability: an estimate of the amount of agreement in the scores assigned by multiple raters. Agreement levels greater than 80% are deemed optimal.

Interval measurement scale: the numbers on an interval scale convey information about how much of the attribute exists at each point on the scale and are equal interval, and a value of zero does not mean the absence of the attribute.

Item non-response errors: errors that occur when elements selected to be in the sample do not complete all questions or items on the measurement instruments.

Known-group method: a method for examining whether an instrument can discriminate between individuals who are either known to possess or have high levels of an attribute being measured and individuals who either do not possess or have low levels of that attribute.

Measurement error: related to instrument reliability, measurement error is the difference between the "true amount" of an attribute and the value that is obtained through the measurement process. Measurement errors may be random or systematic.

Measurement scales: the numbers assigned to an attribute that communicate something about that attribute.

Measurement: the systematic assignment of numbers to an attribute so as to communicate something about that attribute.

Multitrait multimethod approach: a framework first proposed by Campbell (1957) for evaluating the convergent and divergent validity of an instrument.

Nominal measurement scale: the numbers on a nominal scale are "in name only" and indicate differences in type from one value to another but not differences in amount.

Non-response error: errors that occur when significant numbers of elements in a sample fail to provide responses to a measurement instrument, and these elements are systematically different from those that did provide responses.

Norm-referenced test: a test in which the test-takers' scores are assigned based on a comparison with the scores of a norm group, a representative sample from the population of likely test-takers.

Objective: the concept that a data collection instrument must provide information that is not biased by the extraneous characteristics of the researcher, the research participants, or the context in which the measurement is conducted.

Observation protocol: a data collection instrument used to record information when observing the behaviors or attributes of individuals or groups in a specific situation.

Ordinal measurement scale: the numbers on an ordinal scale convey the rank order on an underlying attribute. The distances between points on an ordinal scale are not necessarily equal interval.

Predictive validity evidence: criterion validity evidence garnered from the relationship between scores on a measurement instrument and performance on some criterion measure collected at some point in the future.

Questionnaire: a measurement instrument on which research participants self-report about particular attributes.

Random measurement error: measurement errors due to random fluctuations in the "amount" of an attribute when measures are taken at multiple points in time. Over multiple time points, random errors average out to be zero and have negligible effects.

Ratio measurement scale: the numbers on a ratio scale convey information about how much of the attribute exists at each point on the scale and are equal interval, and a value of zero means the absence of the attribute.

Split-halves method: an internal consistency approach that uses the correlation between the scores on each half of an instrument as an estimate of the reliability of the instrument as a whole.

Standardized test: a test that is administered under standardized conditions.

Systematic measurement error: measurement errors due to faulty measurement. Over multiple time points, this type of error does not average out to be zero.

Test: a term used to describe a type of measurement instrument used to collect data in a specific domain.

Test–retest method: a method for estimating instrument reliability that requires the administration of a single instrument to the same group at least twice.

Total non-response errors: errors that occur when elements selected to be in the sample do not provide any data (i.e., fail to respond to measurement instruments completely).

Unstandardized test: a test that is not administered under standardized conditions.

Usability: the concept that a data collection instrument should be feasible and cost-effective to administer and score, should have clear directions for the individuals providing the data, and should be appropriate for the population being studied.

REVIEW OF PUBLISHED RESEARCH ARTICLES

In this section, we describe how three published research articles describe the measurement and instrumentation components of their studies. The full articles are available online at **www.sagepub.com/odwyer**.

Article 1 (Yang, Cho, Mathew, & Worth, 2011)

The authors administered online and paper-based questionnaires to students, and the self-report data were used to address the research questions. Specifically, the questionnaires generated data about students' "team learning orientation" and "sense of classroom community (SOCC)" and the "effort they expended" in class. The authors did not develop any new instruments as part of this study. Instead, they adapted a pre-existing measure of team orientation and used pre-existing measures of SOCC and effort. With respect to the team orientation measure, they said the following:

> We measured students' team learning versus individual learning orientations using the 15 items adopted from the individual/collectivism scale (Wagner, 1995; for example, "I prefer to work with others than work alone" and "People in a group should be willing to make sacrifices for the group's well being"). (p. 625)

In describing the team learning measure, the authors reported previous studies that not only examined the psychometric properties of the measure (p. 625) but also described how they conducted their own psychometric analyses. Using data they collected as part of the current study, they empirically established that the team learning measure comprises four sub-domains (they referred to these as "factors"). For each sub-domain and for the team learning scale as a whole, they reported reliability information in the form of Cronbach's alpha (an internal consistency measure). They stated the following:

> Factor 1 was labeled as "supremacy of team goals" (STG), Factor 2 as "team work" (TW), Factor 3 as "team reliance" (TR), and Factor 4 as "supremacy of team interests" (STI). Internal consistency coefficients for the four factors were 0.82 (STG), 0.85 (TW), 0.67 (TR), and 0.71 (STI). This revised scale produced an overall reliability coefficient of 0.69, which is minimally acceptable because reliability is considered satisfactory when coefficients of reliability are around or above 0.70 (Cohen, 1977; Nunnally, 1978). (p. 625)

To measure students' SOCC, they used a scale that one author (Cho) had developed previously. They provided information about the five sub-domains that were measured by the scale and went on to state the number of items used on each sub-domain measure:

> We measured students' SOCC using the Integrative Sense of Community Scale (Cho et al., 2010) that has five components: shared goals and responsibility, student–instructor interaction, value and interest, peer respect, and emotional connection. (pp. 625–626)

Subsequently, the authors reported the reliabilities of the sub-domain scales and the SOCC as a whole.

> The internal consistency coefficients of the subscales for the overall sample were 0.93, 0.94, 0.91, 0.88, and 0.66, respectively. A composite score for each subscale was created by averaging the item scores and was used in subsequent analyses. The overall Cronbach's α for the scale was .96. (p. 626)

Article 3 (Porfeli, Wang, Audette, McColl, & Algozzine, 2009)

The authors used archival data from an end-of-grade reading and mathematics achievement tests to examine the association between educational achievement and school demographics and community capital. The authors justify their use of this particular test of achievement as follows:

> Since data from the end-of-year statewide testing program contribute to district comparison reports and filing requirements under *No Child Left Behind* and other federal, state, and local accountability rules and guidelines, we reasoned that they represented the best markers for school achievement in our study. (p. 78)

The authors went on to describe how long the tests took to complete (approximately three and one-half hours over multiple days, p. 79), the format of the tests (multiple choice, p. 79), and when the tests were administered (during the final 3 weeks of school, p. 79). Although the authors do not provide any evidence of the validity or reliability of the achievement tests, they provide a detailed description of the domains measured on each test (also on p. 79).

Article 6 (Booksh, Pella, Singh, & Gouvier, 2010)

The authors of this study conducted a true experimental cross-sectional study to examine college students' ability to simulate attention-deficit hyperactivity disorder (ADHD) symptoms on neuropsychological and self-report measures. To generate the data used to test the research hypotheses (p. 328), the authors used multiple types of instruments. Specifically, they used structured interviews, questionnaires, diagnostic interviews, computer-based measures, paper-and-pencil tests, tests of intelligence, self-report symptom scales, and memorization tests. The battery of instruments included measures developed for the purposes of this study (e.g., the structured clinical interview, p. 328), measures adapted from pre-existing ones (e.g., the ADHD Knowledge and Opinions Survey—Revised), and pre-existing measures without adaptations (e.g., four subtests from the Wechsler Adult Intelligence Scale—III or WAIS-III).

The authors did not report the results of any psychometric analysis of the measures they used in this study; however, they pointed the reader to the original sources for each instrument. For example, when they described WAIS-III, a highly regarded and widely used test designed to measure intelligence in adults and older adolescents, the authors wrote the following:

> The ADHD sample in the normative studies for the WAIS-III (Wechsler, 1997) performed more poorly on the digit symbol coding (DSC), digit span (DS), symbol search (SS), and letter–number sequencing (LNS) subtests, hence these four subtests were employed in the present study. (p. 329)

Likewise, when they described the Attention Deficit Scales for Adults (ADSA), they said the following:

> The ADSA (Triolo & Murphy, 1996) is a 54-item self-report of adult ADHD symptoms. Along with nine clinical scales, it also has an internal consistency measure and a total score. The clinical scales include the following: attention–focus–concentration, interpersonal, behavior-disorganized activity, coordination, academic theme, emotive, consistency-long term, childhood, and negative-social. The total score has been found to reliably discriminate ADHD adults from controls with a cutoff of 45 points. (p. 329)

6

Minimizing Alternative Explanations for Research Findings

Internal Validity

CHAPTER OUTLINE

- Defining Internal Validity
- Common Threats to Internal Validity
- The Relationship Between External Validity and Internal Validity

R eferring back to the axiom we stated in our Overview to Section II, when conducting research in the quantitative tradition, researchers aim to *minimize probable alternative explanations for the results observed*. In research parlance, minimizing alternative explanations by controlling nuisance variables that may be associated with the attributes or characteristics being studied is referred to as *minimizing threats to the internal validity of a study*. The concept of "internal validity" is somewhat parallel to the term *credibility* under the qualitative tradition, a connection we make in the section "Connections to Qualitative Research." Campbell and Stanley (1963) were the first to delineate the various types of extraneous variables that can plague the most common research designs. Over the years, Cook, Campbell, and their colleagues (Cook & Campbell, 1979; Cook & Shadish, 1994; Shadish, Cook, & Campbell, 2002) continued to contribute to our understanding of the threats posed by extraneous variables. Given the importance of minimizing alternative explanations for the results observed in a research study, this chapter is devoted to defining internal validity and discussing the most common threats in quantitative studies.

❖ DEFINING INTERNAL VALIDITY

In the case of experimental research designs where the researcher creates a treatment group and a control group with the aim of establishing a causal link between the treatment effect and the dependent variable, Cook and Campbell (1979) wrote that internal validity "refers to the approximate validity with which we infer that a relationship between two variables is causal or that the absence of a relationship implies the absence of cause" (p. 37). In this case, membership in the treatment or control group (manipulated independent variable) is hypothesized to lead to changes in the measured attribute (the dependent variable), and no other plausible explanations exist for the results observed.

However, issues of internal validity are also highly relevant in non-experimental research designs, and researchers must ensure that the results observed in non-experimental research studies are free from the effects of extraneous variables that may confound the interpretation of the results. Generalizing beyond the definition of internal validity for experimental research designs, we say that the **internal validity** of a study is a function of the degree to which **extraneous variables** are controlled and possible alternative explanations for the results observed are minimized. As is implied by this definition, we generally cannot conclude, for example, that Study A has internal validity or that Study B does not have internal validity. Instead, we evaluate the degree to which common threats to internal validity are controlled for or minimized in a study and the degree to which any threats that might exist could have plausibly produced the results observed. In this sense, internal validity is not an either/or condition, and moreover, the onus is on the researcher to choose an appropriate design, implementation procedures, data collection instruments, and analysis methods so that all threats to internal validity are controlled for or minimized.

When we describe these common threats in the sections that follow, readers are advised to notice that threats do not always act in isolation; threats to internal validity can occur simultaneously in the same direction and result in inflated study findings or work simultaneously in opposition to result in the negation of research findings (Shadish et al., 2002). As we hope will become apparent in the discussion that follows, the source of threats to internal validity are many and varied, and so researchers need to be conscientious about monitoring and minimizing threats from multiple sources. Where possible, researchers should also provide evidence that any threats that might exist are not likely to be *plausible* alternative explanations for the results observed.

We also want to avoid any confusion on the part of the reader by pointing out that internal validity differs from the concept of external validity that we introduced in Chapter 4 as well as instrument validity that we introduced in Chapter 5. While internal validity has to do with controlling for, or minimizing the effects of extraneous variables, external validity is concerned with the generalizability of the research findings, and instrument validity is concerned with the trustworthiness or credibility of the inferences you make from the evidence provided by a measurement or data collection instrument. However, the fact that these are different concepts does not mean that they are unrelated! In fact, inappropriate or poor measurement and instrumentation may threaten the internal validity of a study, and without a high degree of internal validity, the external validity of a study may be compromised. We hope that these points will become clear as readers progress through the sections that follow.

❖ COMMON THREATS TO INTERNAL VALIDITY

In our descriptions of the most common threats to internal validity, we will focus on the two most straightforward research designs for elucidating these threats—quasi- and true experimental designs. When using these designs, the researcher creates conditions (two, in the simplest case) by placing participants into different conditions and, subsequently, applies an intervention to one group (treatment group) and not the other (control group). The primary difference between these two designs rests with how the researcher places participants in the groups. In a true experiment, the researcher randomly assigns individuals to treatment and control conditions, but in the quasi-experiment, participants are not randomly assigned to conditions. In the case of both quasi- and true experiments, the researcher manipulates an independent variable and measures how the dependent variable changes as a result of the intervention. In Chapters 7 and 8 respectively, we provide additional information about the particular internal threats common to non-experimental and experimental research. While these threats are described here as discrete challenges, they can occur together and result in additive threats.

Subject Characteristics Threat

A **subject characteristics threat** occurs when individuals in the groups being compared are not equivalent to each other prior to the application of the intervention. In this case, equivalence implies that on average, the two groups are approximately the same on all measured *and* unmeasured attributes or characteristics prior to the intervention. Without group equivalence, the researcher cannot be confident that any observed post-intervention differences between the groups were in fact caused by the intervention; rather, prior differences between the groups would have to be considered a plausible alternative explanation for post-intervention effects. In fact, in many instances, the researcher cannot be sure whether selection bias has inflated or negated the true intervention effects. This threat is prevalent in quasi-experimental research designs in which groups are not created through a random assignment process; in most situations, randomly assigning individuals to treatment and control conditions, as is the case with true experimental research designs, will help mitigate this threat. Additional information about the process of random assignment, the theory of randomization, and how it minimizes subject characteristics threats is presented in Chapter 8.

History Threat

A **history threat** to internal validity refers to situations in which unplanned or unforeseen events occur during the study that affect the implementation of the treatment and, subsequently, the attributes or characteristics being studied. Moreover, researchers must be concerned about whether this threat occurred for both the treatment and control conditions, or whether it occurred for just one of the groups. Either way, the consequence of this threat is to weaken the researcher's confidence in any post-intervention differences observed. By definition, these unplanned or unforeseen events are hard to avoid, particularly, when conducting research in real-world situations, such as in schools. However, the researcher is advised to be familiar with the research setting and to collect as much supplementary information as possible about the conditions under which the study was conducted. For instance, it is more egregious to have no knowledge of a history threat and to interpret the results as though an event had not occurred than to acknowledge the threat and to interpret the results in light of that threat.

Location Threat

A **location threat** occurs when the physical environment in which a study is conducted or in which data are collected affects the attributes or characteristics being studied. Consider the situation where a researcher compares student learning in two classrooms or training rooms, one in which a new teaching method is used and the other in which the traditional approach is used. A location threat would be unlikely if both classrooms provide approximately equivalent learning experiences. However, in the extreme situation where one classroom or training room is relegated to a poorly lit and noisy classroom, the location in which the instruction takes place may influence student learning. That is, the location becomes a nuisance variable that may be an alternative explanation for the results observed. To avoid this threat, researchers are advised to keep the location constant, or at a minimum, to ensure that the locations are approximately equivalent. In the absence of control over the physical location, the researcher should keep a record of any unusual or possibly disruptive issues related to the physical environment in which the study is conducted.

Maturation Threat

A **maturation threat** occurs when participants in the study "mature" during the course of the study, thereby affecting the attributes or characteristics being studied. For example, a researcher conducting a study with fifth graders between September and June would be more likely to encounter a maturation threat than say, a researcher who is conducting a study with *Fortune* 500 CEOs during the same period. A maturation threat is only likely to be a plausible explanation of any post-intervention differences observed if there was evidence that one group matured at a faster rate than the other group. This might occur if the groups were not formed through a random assignment process and so were not equivalent prior to the application of the treatment; in this case, a subject characteristics threat is interacting with a maturation threat. However, with random assignment to treatment and control conditions, the researcher can be more confident that even if maturation were to occur, it would occur at the same rate in both groups.

Instrumentation Threat

Instrumentation threats occur when the ways in which the measurement instruments are administered or scored provide an alternative explanation for the results observed. With respect to how the instruments are administered, who collects the data, and where the data are collected can affect the data itself. For example, the characteristics of the individual collecting the data (e.g., gender, race, education level, occupation, etc.) may produce responses from the participants that do not reflect the true attributes being studied. Likewise, where the data are collected can produce uncharacteristic responses. As an extreme example, consider the situation in which the researcher administers a questionnaire to adolescents to measure their attitude toward law enforcement personnel. If the researcher hires uniformed police officers to distribute and collect the questionnaire or administers the questionnaire at the local police station, it is likely that the data will not reflect the adolescents' true attitude. To avoid this type of threat, researchers should aim to minimize any data collector characteristics that could affect the data collected and aim to standardize the characteristics of the locations where the data are collected.

An instrumentation threat can also occur if the scores assigned to the attributes change during the duration of the study. This threat is more likely to occur when collecting observational data or when scoring open-ended responses that may be scored somewhat subjectively. This happens because observers and scorers typically become more familiar with the attributes being recorded or evaluated as time passes, and this may lead to discrepancies between the measures at different time points. To avoid this, training and opportunities to become familiar with the attributes being studied should be part of the research effort. Using multiple individuals to observe or score instruments and monitoring the degree of overlap among the scores generated (interrater reliability) will also help minimize this threat to internal validity.

Attrition Threat

An **attrition threat** (also referred to as a mortality threat) occurs when individuals drop out or leave a study, thereby affecting the equivalence of the groups being compared or the representativeness of the sample. This can be especially problematic in studies that are conducted over extended periods of time. In addition, differential attrition from the treatment and control groups and/or situations where the individuals who drop out are somehow different from the individuals who remain in the study can greatly weaken the internal validity of a study. Both of these scenarios can result in treatment and control groups that are no longer equivalent (i.e., a subject characteristics threat), even in cases where random assignment was used, and can lead to samples that are so diminished in size that subsequent analyses may be compromised. This threat has consequences similar to those that result from sampling errors (see the discussion on sampling in Chapter 4) and non-response errors (see the discussion on measurement and instrument in Chapter 5). In fact, the effects of each error can be equated, except that attrition threats and non-response errors occur during the course of the research, after the sample is selected (Shadish et al., 2002). To avoid or at least minimize this threat, researchers should aim to encourage the continued participation of all individuals in the study. At a minimum, researchers should collect as much information as possible about the individuals who drop out of the study, thereby allowing comparisons with those who remain. Small or no differences between the groups on these measured characteristics may allow the researcher to contend that attrition was not a plausible explanation for any post-intervention differences observed. Of course, unmeasured variables may still be a concern in this situation.

Testing Threat

A **testing threat** may occur in research designs that use the same tests to collect pre-intervention and post-intervention data. In this case, there is a practice effect for the individuals in the study, and this practice effect may be a plausible alternative explanation for any post-intervention differences. Eliminating the pre-intervention measure would resolve this issue; however, this is unadvisable, as it would preclude the researcher from empirically comparing the groups prior to the intervention. As an alternative, and if resources and time allow it, the researcher could create equivalent pre- and post-intervention measures (Chapter 5) and/or increase the time between the testing periods. In fact, a researcher might well argue that since a testing threat is likely to be occurring in both groups, its effect on the post-intervention comparisons can be ignored.

Regression to the Mean Threat

Regression to the mean threat is a statistical phenomenon whereby, on average, extreme scores at the low or high end will tend to be less extreme on subsequent measures. As a consequence, the researcher might see pre- to post-intervention changes that are simply artifacts of one extreme random event being followed, on average, by a less extreme event. This type of threat is particularly troublesome for researchers conducting studies with extreme groups, such as students in academically gifted classrooms or students receiving remedial instruction. If however, the treatment and control conditions both comprise extreme participants, the researcher might contend that since regression to the mean is likely to be occurring in both groups, any effect from it can be ignored. Of course, this argument would hold only if the treatment and control groups were created through a random assignment process; if not, then a subject characteristics threat could be confounded with a regression to the mean threat (Shadish et al., 2002).

❖ THE RELATIONSHIP BETWEEN EXTERNAL VALIDITY AND INTERNAL VALIDITY

Now that we have discussed both external validity (Chapter 4) and internal validity, the next obvious question relates to how they are related to each other. Recall that the seminal definitions set forth by Cook and Campbell (1979) for experimental research designs state that external validity "refers to the approximate validity with which we can infer that the presumed causal relationship can be generalized to and across alternate measures of the cause and effect and across different types of persons, settings, and times" and that internal validity refers to "approximate validity with which we infer that a relationship between two variables is causal or that the absence of a relationship implies the absence of cause" (p. 37).

Given the ways that we outlined for increasing external validity and internal validity, it would appear that there is a tension between the two. On the one hand, one could expect that the steps taken to increase the internal validity of a study might in fact, reduce the external validity of that study. For example, one could argue that the results from a study in which all possible extraneous variables are controlled through design and/or implementation procedures (e.g., perhaps conducted under laboratory-like conditions) would not be generalizable to real-world situations. On the other hand, one could argue that a study cannot have external validity in the absence of strong internal validity; controlling for or minimizing threats to internal validity is a necessary condition for external validity. For example, the results from a study fraught with threats to internal validity would likely be so compromised in terms of their overall credibility as to preclude valid generalizations.

In fact, both positions related to the connection between internal and external validity may be appropriate, and each has been raised in seminal texts on the topic. For example, with regard to the first position, Campbell and Stanley (1963) wrote that "both types of criteria are obviously important, even though they are frequently at odds in that features increasing one may jeopardize the other" (p. 5). Related to the second position, Hogarth (2005) wrote that "internal validity is a necessary but not sufficient condition for external validity" (p. 262).

It is our position that the researcher must take a balanced approach to maximizing *both* the internal validity and the external validity of their study by selecting the most appropriate *research designs, procedures, data collection instruments, and data analysis methods* available for addressing the research questions posed. We take this approach because we recognize that a single study cannot tell us everything we want or need to know about a phenomenon, or how phenomena relate to each other. Instead multiple studies, each building on previous research contribute to the body of knowledge about a particular phenomenon and in most cases, research conducted in one context and with one sample will point to the need for the research to be *replicated* in other contexts and with other samples. It is because, as we first pointed out in Chapter 3, *replication* is so central to research in the quantitative tradition that we do not favor either position above the other.

❖ CONNECTIONS TO QUALITATIVE RESEARCH

As described in the section "Defining Internal Validity", "*the internal validity of a study is a function of the degree to which extraneous variables are controlled and possible alternative explanations for the results observed are minimized.*" The term *credibility* under the qualitative tradition also connotes a desire to produce findings that can be understood and defended as reasonable. However, while the quantitative paradigm seeks to focus on a discrete set of independent and quasi-independent variables by relying on control and random assignment, the qualitative tradition feels more comfortable hanging on to complexity and then using techniques such as extended engagement, triangulation, and member checking to discern patterns in the data. Do these two paradigms differ "axiomatically?" Certainly, they do. However, in combination, they can reveal a great deal more about phenomena because at various points along the quantitative–qualitative continuum, there is both overlap and complementary evidence. We also think that there are points where evidence diverges, and rather than being viewed as ammunition to be used by one tradition against the other, we think it offers an opportunity for synthesis and new perspectives that transcend what has been discovered thus far within each solitary tradition.

Because qualitative research is conducted in naturalistic settings and is therefore relatively free from reactive experimental effects, the competing demands and tensions between the demands of internal validity and external validity that is sometimes played out in the quantitative tradition is lessened. This is why replication is so important in quantitative studies. While people jest about the fact that today drug "X" is found effective and tomorrow it is found ineffective or even dangerous, it simply underscores the fact that the quantitative tradition does not claim to be infallible. Rather, it recognizes that because of a focus on a limited number of cases using a particular type and quantity of independent variable (e.g., 10 mg of a drug), that results are looked on as tentative even if threats to both internal validity and external validity have been dealt with in a rigorous manner. Consequently, replication with perhaps somewhat different amounts, participants, and contexts is often necessary to have a greater sense of confidence about results. So too in qualitative research do we profit by conducting related research in somewhat different settings and thereby extend our knowledge and understanding of phenomena. In fact, "prolonged engagement" might be thought of as a kind of replication where individuals and settings are examined in different ways and at different times so as to obtain more confidence in discerning what we see and hear. By having evidence that is considered "valid" or "credible," we have a much firmer basis on which to interpret our findings.

❖ CONCLUDING REMARKS

As is evident by our description of internal validity and its most common threats, researchers must pay close attention to all possible threats to the internal validity of their study. Where possible, the researcher should aim to avoid or control for the threat, and in situations where this cannot be accomplished, the researcher should aim to minimize the threats and also interpret the results cautiously and in light of any threats that have occurred. In general, addressing threats to internal validity during the planning or implementation phase is the preferred method for ameliorating any negative consequences.

DISCUSSION QUESTIONS

1. What might be some examples where a quantitative study has a large degree of internal validity but only limited external validity?

2. What might be some examples where a qualitative study has a large degree of credibility but little transferability?

3. To what extent can any of the eight "threats" to internal validity be related to studies in the qualitative tradition?

4. If you were asked to support the position that threats to internal validity under the quantitative tradition are more formidable than threats to credibility under the qualitative tradition, what arguments might you make? If you were asked to take the opposite position, how might you respond?

KEY TERMS

Attrition threat: occurs when individuals drop out or leave a study, thereby affecting the equivalence of the groups being compared or the representativeness of the sample. It is also referred to as a mortality threat.

Extraneous variable: nuisance variable that is peripheral to the research study but because it is associated with the dependent variable, can provide an alternative explanation for the results observed when uncontrolled.

History threat: occurs in situations where unforeseen events occur during the study that affect the results observed.

Instrumentation threat: occurs when the ways in which the measurement instruments are administered or scored provide an alternative explanation for the results observed.

Internal validity: the degree to which extraneous variables in a research study are controlled such that plausible, alternative explanations for the results observed are minimized.

Location threat: occurs when the physical environment in which a study is conducted or in which data are collected affects the attributes or characteristics being studied.

Maturation threat: occurs when participants in the study mature during the course of the study, thereby affecting the attributes or characteristics being studied.

Regression to the mean threat: a statistical phenomenon whereby, on average, extreme scores at the low or high end will tend to be less extreme on subsequent measures.

Subject characteristics threat: occurs when individuals in the groups being compared are not equivalent to each other prior, thereby providing a plausible alternative explanation for the results observed.

Testing threat: occurs when researchers use the same instruments to collect data from participants on more than one occasion.

REVIEW OF PUBLISHED RESEARCH ARTICLES

In this section, we describe how three published research articles address the most common threats to internal validity. The full articles are available online at **www.sagepub.com/odwyer**.

Article 1 (Yang, Cho, Mathew, & Worth, 2011)

In this non-experimental study, the authors examined three primary research questions. First, they examined whether there were gender differences in students' effort in online versus face-to-face courses. Second, whether after controlling for gender, team learning orientation predicted student effort in online versus face-to-face courses. Finally, controlling for the potential effects of gender and team learning orientation, they examined whether students' sense of classroom community predicted their effort in an online versus face-to-face class.

In an effort to minimize the internal validity threats to this non-experimental study, the authors made decisions about the data collection process and also used statistical controls. While these efforts aim to minimize other plausible explanations for the results, they do not allow strong cause-and-effect conclusions to be drawn.

With respect to the data collection process, the authors aimed to minimize the possibility of an instrumentation threat (i.e., the presence of the course instructor). They said the following:

> Participants were instructed to select either an online or face-to-face course and keep that course in mind while completing a survey about their SOCC, team learning orientation, and the amount of effort they put into that class. They also provided general demographic information. Students were not required to report the course that the researchers visited nor the course they selected to reflect on for the study. This alleviated the potential pressure caused by

instructor presence and encouraged more candid responses. Therefore, the students completed the survey based on different courses of their choice (either online or face-to-face). (p. 624)

Subsequent to conducting descriptive analyses, the authors used hierarchical regression analyses that included statistical controls, often referred to as covariates. For example, they statistically controlled for gender when they examined whether team learning orientation predicted students' effort in online versus face-to-face courses. Likewise, they statistically controlled for gender and team learning orientation when they examined whether students' sense of classroom community predicted their effort in an online versus face-to-face class.

Article 5 (Van Voorhis, 2011)

The quasi-experimental longitudinal panel study described by the authors was conducted to examine the effect of the TIPS (Teachers Involve Parents in Schoolwork) program on family involvement, emotions and attitudes, and student achievement in four elementary schools. The study is characterized as a quasi-experimental design because the author was unable to randomly assign students to classrooms. In an effort to ameliorate the effects of a subject characteristics threats to the internal validity of the study, the author too attempted to minimize the differences between the treatment and control conditions. First, the author stated that "this intervention study took place over 2 consecutive school years (2004–2006) in four *similar* [italics added] elementary schools in a southeastern urban school district" (p. 319).

However, the author does not provide additional information about the characteristics on which the schools are similar. The author goes on to say,

> At each school, one teacher was randomly assigned to implement the Teachers Involve Parents in Schoolwork (TIPS) interactive math homework assignments weekly along with other homework, and the other teacher used "regular" math homework assignments in a matched Control classroom. Thus, teachers were randomly assigned to the intervention and Control conditions. (p. 319)

The researcher strengthened the quasi-experimental design by assigning teachers to conditions within schools—this decision had the effect of minimizing any systematic school-to-school differences as plausible explanations for the results observed. The author provides somewhat weak information about how the students were matched or how likely there were to be differences among the classrooms: "Although students were not randomly assigned to classrooms, every effort was made to select similar, 'average' classrooms of students in Grade 3" (p. 319).

Article 6 (Booksh, Pella, Singh, & Gouvier, 2010)

The authors of this true experimental cross-sectional study aimed to maximize the internal validity of their study using design elements. Most important, the 110 participants "were randomly assigned to the control or simulated malingering conditions" (p. 329). This ensured that the groups were probabilistically equivalent on all measured and unmeasured variables. In addition, the authors limited their sample according to the following description:

> Because it is assumed that a number of those malingering during an ADHD [attention-deficit/hyperactive disorder] evaluation do not actually meet criteria for ADHD, the researchers thought it was necessary to use participants from a normative sample to obtain a more generalizable sample. So too, we elected to screen out other conditions that may otherwise account for participants' performance on the cognitive measures. Therefore, exclusion criteria were as follows: age less than 18 years, history of LD [learning disability], and diagnosis of ADHD or current complaints of significant problems with ADHD-related symptoms or neurological problems. (p. 328)

In addition, the authors developed and administered a structured clinical interview that was used to "obtain the demographic information (i.e., gender, race, age, etc.), ADHD knowledge, and to screen for exclusion criteria" (p. 328). This additional check minimized the plausibility of this particular subject characteristics threat.

SECTION III

Research Design and Data Analysis in the Quantitative Tradition

I n this section, we describe the most common research designs and data analysis procedures used in the quantitative tradition. These designs and data analysis procedures are tried-and-tested approaches for answering the types of research questions that are best addressed by quantitative research. Notice that our language here is very deliberate—we did not say that these were the types of designs used by quantitative researchers. Instead, we wish to emphasize that the research designs and data analysis procedures we discuss have been established as viable methods for generating and analyzing information to address important issues in the social sciences. In other words, these designs should be placed right alongside those discussed in Chapter 2 as viable approaches for discovering new knowledge.

Our guiding axiom will continue to serve as the foundation for our descriptions and discussion in this section:

> Researchers should choose research designs, procedures, data collection instruments, and data analysis methods that: are appropriate for addressing the question(s) posed; allow generalizations to be made to other participants and settings beyond their study; and that minimize all feasible alternative explanations for the results observed.

There are two overarching research approaches possible in the quantitative tradition—non-experimental research and experimental research. The choice between these two approaches will depend on the purpose of the research and the research questions that are posed. The essential question is whether the purpose of the study is to describe, predict, or explain naturally occurring attributes, behaviors, or phenomena or whether the goal is to examine the effect of an intervention or treatment. This decision will dictate whether the research is non-experimental or experimental.

Choosing Between Non-Experimental and Experimental Research

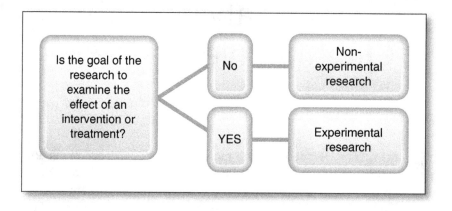

In Chapters 7 and 8, we describe non-experimental and experimental research designs, respectively. In each case, we describe the essential characteristics of the design, the steps undertaken during implementation, the strengths and limitations of the design, as well as common threats to external and internal validity. In addition, we will point readers to the pertinent sections of Chapter 9 that describe associated data analysis procedures and will continue to include our "Connections to Qualitative Research" sections.

In Chapters 9 and 10, we introduce descriptive and inferential analyses, respectively, as the basic data analysis procedures used to analyze the data generated by quantitative research designs.

The methods used to analyze qualitative and quantitative data are quite different; given the types of data that are collected in each tradition, this is not surprising. However, despite the differences, analyses in both traditions seek to make sense of the collected data using tried-and-tested analysis approaches.

Two Branches of Statistical Analysis

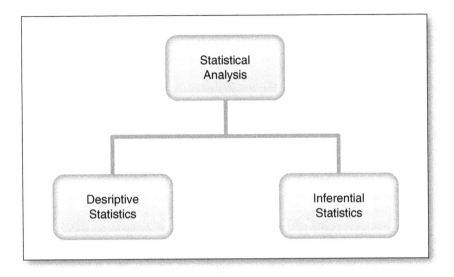

Research design and analysis are intimately connected under both the quantitative and qualitative traditions. For example, if we decide to examine the shared experiences of graduate students in relation to online education, we might decide to use a phenomenological design where data would be analyzed in a way that would help illuminate the essence of these shared experiences. Similarly, under the quantitative tradition, this same kind of symbiotic relationship holds between design and methods of analysis. For example, if we want to determine if online education is as effective as traditional education for promoting the academic achievement of graduate students, we might decide to use an experimental design where data would be analyzed using the appropriate type of statistical analysis. We hope that in reading this section, readers will continue to develop an appreciation for the fact that the unifying goal of qualitative and quantitative research is to discover new knowledge that can help describe, explain, and predict the world around us. Although designs and analyses may differ, both traditions require that we use both creativity and a disciplined approach to achieve this aim.

7

Non-Experimental
Research Designs

CHAPTER OUTLINE

- Essential Characteristics of Non-Experimental Research Designs

- Steps in Conducting Non-Experimental Research

- Strengths and Limitations of Non-Experimental Research

- Threats to External and Internal Validity in Non-Experimental Research

- Strengthening the Inferences From Non-Experimental Research Designs

The purpose of this chapter is to introduce readers to quantitative, non-experimental research designs as a way for generating data to address important research questions. In describing these designs, we refrain from categorizing them as discrete entities and instead present descriptions to how the designs are used and how the data are generated.

❖ ESSENTIAL CHARACTERISTICS OF NON-EXPERIMENTAL RESEARCH DESIGNS

Non-experimental research designs are appropriate when the goal is to examine naturally occurring attributes, behaviors, or phenomena that cannot be experimentally manipulated by the researcher. This may be because it is impossible or unethical to manipulate these characteristics, or because the events occurred sometime in the past. For example, consider the situation in which a researcher wishes to examine whether preschool attendance is associated with higher academic outcomes among middle school students. It would likely be impossible and even unethical for the researcher to assign students to a control condition in which preschool education was withheld. Similarly, if the researcher is studying students who are currently in middle school, the researcher would not be able to manipulate their preschool attendance as it occurred several years in the past. In technical terms, the researcher cannot create a *manipulated independent variable* (Chapter 3) in non-experimental research.

Since non-experimental designs are used to study naturally occurring attributes or phenomena, they generally preclude strong cause-and-effect conclusions and are instead limited to more descriptive and correlational conclusions. Generally, non-experimental research studies are conducted with the following objectives: (a) to describe attributes, behaviors, or phenomena (*descriptive study*); (b) to use the relationships among attributes, behaviors, or phenomena to make predictions (*prediction study*); or (c) to test theories about how and why some attributes are related as they are, or how and why the observed differences between pre-existing groups came to be (*explanatory study*). Time also plays a role in how we characterize non-experimental research because the researcher may need to collect data at one point in time (*cross-sectional study*), across some fixed time period (*longitudinal study*), or the researcher may need to explore whether past events are associated with observed differences in individuals (*retrospective study*).

Before we discuss these broad objectives and how we characterize data collection, we want to remind readers that the questions posed by the researcher at the outset of a non-experimental study will dictate whether the objective of the study is descriptive, predictive, or explanatory and whether cross-sectional, longitudinal, or retrospective data are most appropriate. This point reaffirms what we have said several times so far in this text and is implicit in our guiding axiom; namely, that researchers must have a solid and deep understanding of the body of research on the topic they are researching. This will ensure that they are primed to select the most appropriate research design and data generation procedures that will minimize plausible alternative explanations for the results observed, a particular challenge when conducting non-experimental research.

Research Objectives: Descriptive, Prediction, and Explanatory Studies

In describing the difference between the objectives of descriptive, prediction, and explanatory research, we will use a hypothetical example in which a researcher aims to examine whether teachers' use of technology is associated with the number of years they have been teaching. The researcher administers a questionnaire that asks teachers to indicate how often they used technology for various purposes while teaching during the previous month. Based on teachers' responses to multiple items on the questionnaire, the researcher creates a continuous variable ranging from 0 to 10 to represent teachers' technology use, with 0 = *no use* and 10 = *habitual use*. The researcher also asks teachers to indicate the number of years they had been teaching and represents this information in two ways: first, as a continuous variable that takes on values ranging from, say, 1 to 35 years, and second, as a dichotomous variable where 0 indicates having taught for 15 years or fewer, and 1 indicates having taught for 16 years or more. Note that a *dichotomous variable* is a categorical variable with just two categories.

Descriptive Studies

When conducting a **descriptive** non-experimental study, the researcher is more interested in *what* the characteristics are rather than in *why* the characteristics are as they are. Depending on the research question, descriptive research may be conducted to characterize attributes, behaviors, or phenomena in isolation or may be conducted to summarize how attributes, behaviors, or phenomena are related to each other. Most research studies have a descriptive component, even if the eventual goal of the research is predictive or explanatory. This is because prior to the researcher examining how one attribute or behavior predicts another, or how past events are associated with current observed differences, the researcher will want to describe the characteristics of participants in the study.

Survey research is the quintessential descriptive research design because it is used when the purpose of the research is to describe the characteristics of a population by making inferences from a sample drawn from that population. Most of us are familiar with survey research; we have received a questionnaire in the mail, or have received a phone call or email asking for 5 to 10 minutes for our time to answer some questions. The questionnaire is the primary measurement tool used in survey research; it is a self-report instrument where the study participants respond to items (e.g., answer questions, endorse statements, report on behaviors, etc.), and their responses become the data that the researcher will analyze. However, any kind of data collection instrument can be used to generate data for a descriptive study, including academic or cognitive performance measures (achievement or aptitude tests), observation protocols, or interviews.

Using the hypothetical research situation, the researcher could describe technology use and years teaching in isolation in accordance with the following research questions: "How frequently do teachers in the sample use technology in the classroom?" or "What is the average length of time that teachers in the sample have been teaching?" To answer these questions, the researcher would use descriptive analysis procedures such as frequency distributions or averages to summarize the patterns in the data (Chapter 9).

Similarly, the research would also be characterized as descriptive if the research question was "What is the relationship between teachers' use of technology and number of years teaching?" To answer this question, the researcher would calculate the strength and direction of the correlation coefficient to describe the association between teachers' use of technology and number of years teaching; a correlation coefficient indicates how much and in what direction the two attributes vary together (Chapter 9). The researcher could also pose a *descriptive* question using the dichotomous version of the years teaching variable: "Is use of technology different for teachers who have been teaching for 15 years or fewer and teachers who have been teaching for 16 years or more?" In this case, the researcher would describe and compare the average amount of technology use for the two groups of teachers. Subsequently, a test of the difference between average technology use across the two groups could be conducted, allowing the researcher to estimate whether the difference in technology use between the two groups of teachers was sufficiently large to warrant the conclusion that it was unlikely to have occurred by chance. This type of statistical test, the *t*-test, will be discussed further in Chapter 10.

Prediction Studies

Researchers are often interested in examining the associations among attributes or behaviors when conducting non-experimental research, with the ultimate aim of being able to make predictions. Recall that even in the absence of being able to manipulate the independent variable in non-experimental designs, these types of studies can be useful for identifying attributes, behaviors, or phenomena that could be manipulated experimentally in subsequent research. In a **prediction study**, statistical models are formulated to predict one attribute or behavior (the dependent variable) from another (the independent variable). This prediction model is subsequently applied to another group for whom only the independent variable is known to predict their potential value on the dependent variable. Prediction models are applied in many real-world situations, not only when conducting research in the quantitative tradition. For example, college admissions officers formulate prediction models using information about students accepted in prior years and use those models to predict which new applicants are likely to be successful at their university. Likewise, loan underwriters use prediction models based on past loan recipients to predict the likelihood that new loan applicants will repay their loan in full and on time.

Returning to the hypothetical research example, the purpose of the study would be predictive if the research question was "Does number of years teaching predict how teachers use technology?" Using information provided by the correlation between the two measures, a statistical model would be formulated to predict teachers' technology use from the number of years they have been teaching, and this prediction model would subsequently be used to predict technology use for teachers for whom only the number of years teaching is known. In this case, either the continuous or categorical version of the years teaching variable could be used. Prediction models also (known as *regression models*) can easily be used with continuous or categorical predictor variables.

Explanatory Studies

Explanatory studies are conducted to test theories about how and why some attributes, behaviors, or phenomena are related as they are, or how and why the observed differences between pre-existing groups came to be. The procedures and analyses conducted for an explanatory study are identical to those used in descriptive or prediction studies; the only difference being that in an explanatory study, the researcher is testing a specific theory about the observed relationship or difference between pre-existing groups.

Again returning to the hypothetical example, the purpose would be explanatory if the research aimed to test the theory that "teachers who have been teaching for 15 years or fewer are more likely to use technology than teachers who have been teaching for more than 15 years." In this case, the observed data can be compared with a theoretical model for how the attributes are related to each other, and the fit of the data to the model could be evaluated empirically. Often, the purpose of this type of analysis is to investigate possible causal relationships using non-experimental data. We refer readers back to our introduction in Chapter 3 to support our decision to refrain from using the term *causal comparative* or *ex post facto* to describe this design. Like any form of non-experimental research, explanatory studies generally cannot support strong causal inferences but, with additional controls for extraneous variables, may be able to suggest some causal linkages.

Figure 7.1   Schematic for selecting a research design

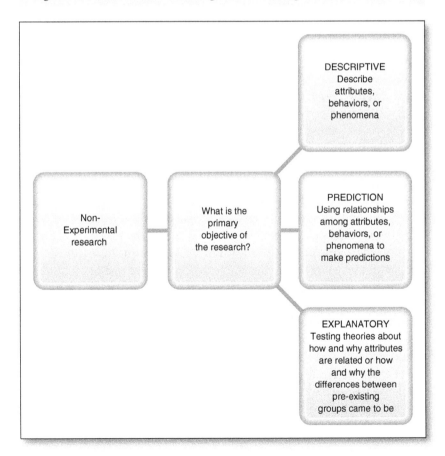

Cross-Sectional, Longitudinal, and Retrospective Studies

Regardless of whether a non-experimental study is descriptive, predictive, or explanatory, the next essential question is whether the research questions *require information about the attributes, behaviors, or phenomena at a single point in time*, whether the research questions *require information about the ways in which the attributes, behaviors, or phenomena change over time*, or whether the research questions *require data to be examined retrospectively*. Again, the researchers' response to this question should dictate which approach is most appropriate.

In a **cross-sectional research design**, data are generated at only one point in time, thus providing a snapshot of the attributes, behaviors, or phenomena that the researcher is studying. Conversely, longitudinal non-experimental research is conducted over a period of time, such that the researcher can describe the ways in which the attributes, behaviors, or phenomena change over time. In the longitudinal case, the researcher can either use the same sample of individuals over time (*a panel study*) or use a different sample of individuals from the same population over time (*a trend study*).

Again, taking the example in which the researcher is interested in examining teachers' use of technology. A cross-sectional research design would be most appropriate if the researcher's question was "How did teachers use technology during the current academic year?" A sample of teachers would be selected, they would be asked how they currently use technology in school, and the data would provide the researcher with a cross-sectional snapshot during that academic year.

Say instead that the researcher asks "Has teachers' use of technology changed over a 10-year period?" In this case, the researcher would need to use a **longitudinal design** in which data are generated at multiple points in time and has some additional decisions to make. Specifically, the researcher will need to decide whether the research question warrants collecting data from the same teachers at multiple time points (e.g., once per year) over a decade to see how their use of technology changes (a type of longitudinal design called **a panel study**), or whether it is more appropriate to collect data from a different group of teachers selected from the same population of teachers once per year (a type of longitudinal design called **trend study**). In both cases, the data would provide the researcher with information about how teachers' use of technology changed over a 10-year period.

Some non-experimental research studies are considered **retrospective** because they examine the antecedents to observed differences between groups as plausible explanations for those differences. In

Chapter 3, we described these studies as ex post facto studies because, "after the fact," the researcher aims to explore whether past attributes, behaviors, or phenomena may be explanations for observed differences among groups. For example, a researcher might be interested in whether children who attended preschool had better academic outcomes in middle school compared with children who did not attend preschool. In this case, the researcher cannot manipulate the antecedent (preschool attendance) to the outcomes being studied (academic performance) and yet aims to establish whether it is possible that past behaviors are associated with current outcomes. While this design may provide correlational information about how past attributes, behaviors, or phenomena are associated with current outcomes, it generally cannot support strong causal inferences. For example, a child's attendance at preschool may also be correlated with parental education, resources in the home, parental aspirations around education, and possibly a host of other family and community characteristics. As such, subject characteristics threats (Chapter 6) abound with these types of studies.

❖ STEPS IN CONDUCTING NON-EXPERIMENTAL RESEARCH

When conducting non-experimental research, the researcher first defines the research problem, develops clear research questions that are grounded in the literature, and, that if answered, will elucidate the research problem. In cases where the purpose of the research is purely descriptive, formal research hypotheses may not be stated. Once the research questions have been finalized, the researcher defines the target and accessible populations and chooses the most appropriate sampling procedures to select a sample from the population (Chapter 4). Readers are reminded that the population should be defined before the sample is selected.

Next, the researcher must choose an instrument for measuring the attributes being studied and decide on the most appropriate method for administering that instrument. For example, the researcher may choose to administer an achievement or aptitude test, a questionnaire via snail mail, electronically, by phone, or face-to-face or use an observational protocol. These types of instruments are used to operationalize the attributes, behaviors, or phenomena that are being researched, and the data generated by these instruments are used to address the research questions (Chapter 5). The number of data collection points will depend on whether the study is cross-sectional or longitudinal. Once the data have been generated from the sample, paying close attention to the research problem and research questions that were stated at the outset of the study, the researcher analyzes and interprets participants' responses. Regardless of whether the purpose of the study is descriptive, predictive, or explanatory, the steps are as follows:

1. Define the research problem and state the research questions.

2. Define the target and accessible populations and use appropriate methods to select a sample from the population.

3. Develop or select appropriate instruments that will operationalize the attributes, behaviors, or phenomena being studied and that will generate valid and reliable data for addressing research questions.

4. Decide whether data will be collected using a cross-sectional design or a longitudinal design, or whether a retrospective study will be conducted.

5. Use the most appropriate method for administering the instruments to the participants so that valid and reliable data are generated in a cost-effective and timely manner.

6. Analyze participants' responses to the instruments using descriptive and/or inferential data analysis procedures.

7. Summarize and interpret the findings by making connections to the research problem and research question.

Throughout the study, researchers must be aware of, and aim to minimize, the most common types of errors that can occur. These can occur during the phase when the target and accessible populations are defined, during the sampling phase, during the instrument design or selection phase, or during the data collection phase. *Coverage error* and *sampling error* (Chapter 4) occur during the phases when the target and accessible populations are defined and during the sampling phase; *measurement error* can be attributed to the instrument design or selection decisions; and *non-response error* can arise during the data collection phase (Chapter 5). The possibility of these errors occurring should be given careful attention by the researcher; in fact, a scrupulous researcher can almost completely eliminate coverage error, sampling error, and measurement error, and can greatly reduce non-response error. Without the effective controls and strategies in place to minimize these errors, the researcher may seriously degrade the internal and external validity of the research.

❖ STRENGTHS AND LIMITATIONS OF NON-EXPERIMENTAL RESEARCH

Non-experimental research designs are popular in social science research for several reasons. First, these designs can be implemented to study several attributes at the same time and can be used to study attributes that cannot be easily investigated with an experimental design, considered the gold standard for isolating cause-and-effect mechanisms. Using the example of studying the relationship between teachers' technology and number of years teaching, it would not be possible to create an intervention to examine whether teachers who had been teaching for more years were less or more likely to use technology. Specifically, it would not be possible to assign individuals to become teachers and to remain in the classroom for a set number of years. The opposite is also true: It would not be possible to assign teachers to use technology in the classroom, then study how long they remained in the classroom, and attribute attrition from the classroom to having been assigned to use technology. Due to logistical or ethical constraints, many of the attributes that are interesting to social science researchers are not manipulable, and so non-experimental research designs are a mainstay in our field. Having said this, the findings from non-experimental studies can often identify attributes, characteristics, or phenomena that may be experimentally manipulated in subsequent research efforts.

Second, compared with more costly and time-consuming experimental designs, non-experimental research designs are relatively easy and cost-effective to conduct. Finally, the analyses conducted as part of these designs are straightforward to conduct and typically do not need specialized skills or software. For example, Microsoft Excel, a standard application on most computers, can be used to calculate descriptive statistics and correlation coefficients, to formulate prediction models, and to test the difference between means.

As an aside, not all research questions and data structures lend themselves to these simple analyses, and in these cases, specialized software and/or skills may be needed. For example, in Chapter 4, we discussed two-stage random sampling procedures whereby clusters are sampled from the population at the first stage, and individuals within those clusters are sampled at the second stage. In discussing this sampling approach, we noted that the analyses conducted with such samples were generally more complex than those required in situations where a simple random sample of individuals was selected from the population. This is because from a statistical perspective, individuals nested in clusters (e.g., teachers in schools, students in classrooms, etc.)

tend to provide fewer pieces of unique information than a simple random sample of individuals from a population; in plain terms, individuals who share a context tend to be more like each other than they are like individuals in other contexts. In fact, statistical inferences made from correlation coefficients or prediction models that are formulated with nested data may produce misleading results. As such, specialized skills and/or software may be required. Likewise, causal modeling conducted as part of an explanatory study may require specialized training and software. In Chapter 9, we will provide some additional details about these analysis procedures and, where appropriate, will refer the reader to more specialized texts on these topics.

The most significant weakness of non-experimental designs is the lack of control over threats to internal validity that limits researchers' capacity to make causal inferences from non-experimental data. For example, consider a study in which only the dependent variable A and the independent variable B are measured, and they are found to be correlated at $r = .90$. This strong positive correlation means that knowing an individual's score on the independent variable B allows us to predict their score on the dependent variable B with a high degree of precision. However, based on the correlation alone, it is not possible to judge whether changes in A are leading to changes in B, whether changes in B are leading to changes in A, or whether an unmeasured variable C is leading to the changes observed in both A and B. In this case, attribute C is an extraneous variable that may not be controlled for or even measured, and so despite the magnitude of the correlation coefficient, it is only possible to say that the relationship between A and B is strong and positive.

❖ THREATS TO EXTERNAL AND INTERNAL VALIDITY IN NON-EXPERIMENTAL RESEARCH

Non-experimental research designs are susceptible to external and internal validity threats, some of which are common to any type of research conducted with a sample from a population, and researchers must minimize the effects of these threats. The most common threats to the internal validity of non-experimental designs are subject characteristics threats, location threats, instrumentation threats, as well as testing and attrition threats. Moreover, these threats may operate simultaneously in the same or opposite directions, making it difficult for the researcher to estimate the true relationships or differences between groups. Again, consider the example in which the researcher is studying technology use and number of years teaching. If, for example, the less experienced teachers (≤15 years teaching) dropped out of the study at higher rates than the more experienced teachers (>16 years teaching), a subject characteristics threat would be confounded with an attrition threat. Likewise, if the less experienced group completed the research instruments in a location that affected their responses but this did not occur for the more experienced teachers, a subject characteristics threat would be confounded with a location threat. In general, when implementing non-experimental designs, researchers are advised to pay close attention to the possibility that extraneous variables are affecting the results observed and to take all steps possible to minimize these effects. Some possibilities for strengthening the internal validity of non-experimental research are discussed in the next section.

❖ STRENGTHENING THE INFERENCES FROM NON-EXPERIMENTAL RESEARCH DESIGNS

In many situations, non-experimental research does not support causal conclusions. As a general rule, conclusions about attribute A *causing* attribute B, would only be possible if three conditions are met: (1) A must occur before B, (2) changes in A must be associated with changes in B, and (3) all other possible explanations for the observed association between A and B are controlled. Since non-experimental designs are concerned only with naturally occurring attributes, behaviors, or phenomena, the third condition cannot be easily met. As such, in the absence of controls, the possibility of explanations for the results cannot be ruled out.

Despite this general guideline, it is possible to make tentative or conditional causal inferences using non-experimental research when some conditions are met. Specifically, causal inferences may be possible when (a) extraneous variables are held constant or controlled during a study, (b) extraneous variables are built into the design and subsequently used as statistical controls during the data analysis phase, or (c) matching is used in the comparison of pre-existing groups.

As the term suggests, *holding extraneous variables constant* requires that the researcher controls variables that are not central to the research, yet if left uncontrolled could plausibly explain the results observed. Again, we will use the example of research conducted to examine the relationship between teachers' use of technology in the classroom and number of years teaching. Now, let us assume that the researcher suspects that teachers' attitude toward technology use in general might be an extraneous variable. To control for this variable, the researcher might choose to only analyze data from teachers who had positive attitudes toward technology in general; this controls the extraneous variable by making it constant for every teacher in the study. However, controlling for extraneous variables can affect the generalizability of the results; in this case, for the example, the findings from the study could only be generalized to teachers with positive attitudes toward technology.

To avoid limiting the generalizability of the results, extraneous variables could be measured as part of the design and subsequently used as statistical controls during the data analysis phase. For example, instead of analyzing only data from teachers with positive attitudes toward technology, the researcher could use data from all teachers and include a measure of teachers' attitude toward technology as an additional independent variable in the analysis. In interpreting the findings, the researcher makes conclusions about the relationship between teachers' use of technology in the classroom and the number of years teaching, after controlling for teachers' attitude toward technology. While this may sound like an appealing approach, we caution our readers that causal inferences based on designs where statistical controls are used are generally weaker than the inferences possible when design elements are used to control for extraneous variables.

When comparing pre-existing groups, the researcher could also use *matching* in an effort to minimize the subject characteristics differences between those groups. Specifically, the researcher manually matches individuals in the groups on some attribute, or attributes, and when analyzing the data, only includes the pairs of matched individuals in the analyses. Using multiple attributes to match individuals will serve to improve the chances that the pre-existing groups comprising the pairs of individuals are approximately equivalent, thereby minimizing a subject characteristics threat. However, it can be difficult to find appropriate matches on more than a small number of attributes. While matching does not eliminate all possible sources of subject characteristics threats between the groups and may lead to a drop in the size of the groups because unmatched individuals are excluded from the analyses, it may mitigate some of the pre-existing differences between non-randomly formed groups.

In sum, researchers conducting non-experimental research are advised to identify all possible extraneous variables at the planning phase; where possible, add design controls to hold the extraneous variables constant (e.g., limiting the study to a single location or subgroup); and if not possible to hold constant, include measures of the extraneous variables and statistically control for them in the subsequent analyses. Our readers are advised that these steps are only possible when the researcher has a deep understanding of the literature and the research problem, when reliable and valid measures of the extraneous variables are available, and when the researcher is trained to conduct analyses that incorporate statistical controls.

❖ CONNECTIONS TO QUALITATIVE RESEARCH

While we contend that the research questions should determine what type of research design to use, it is not always quite that simple. As noted previously, sometimes researchers have multiple objectives when conducting a single study, such as being interested in descriptive findings *and* explanatory findings. For example, if you want to learn about senior citizens' use of technology, a questionnaire might ask them to answer not only questions about this issue but also some "demographic" questions such degree of education, income range, number of children, and so on. Based on data generated, it might then be determined not only how seniors use technology but also whether there are discernible associations (correlations) between any of these demographic variables and their responses about technology use.

In a related fashion, we sometimes use multiple designs and approaches in qualitative research as we define our purpose for doing a study. For example, while conducting an ethnographic study in a veteran's hospital, a researcher might simultaneously analyze emerging data from a phenomenological approach or begin to explore a grounded theory approach. Creswell (2007) in his last chapter uses the phrase "turning the story" and demonstrates how a substantive study can be approached using different designs. While he advocates competency in the different designs and their associated procedures, he shows that the same researcher (or multiple researchers), by approaching a study from a different perspective and using a different design or combination of designs, can garner unique but complementary knowledge and insights about phenomena. We likewise encourage readers to learn about the various quantitative designs but also keep in mind that the purpose of these research designs is to help us understand a reality that is often complex, and therefore purity of design, while perhaps aesthetically pleasing, is not always compatible with this reality.

The mainstay of data collection for qualitative researchers is extended observation, in-depth interviews, and important artifacts. Questionnaires can also be used to generate qualitative data that can be used to supplement the quantitative data that are typically collected from questionnaires used in a survey design. We think if approached with care, this can result in useful insights that may not be obtained from using only closed-ended items. However, while we hope that it is clear that we view both traditions as equally valid ways to discover new knowledge, we do not endorse approaches that water down the value of either or both traditions. In the case of non-experimental research that uses a questionnaire to collect data, some researchers may think that by including a few open-ended questions, they have produced a quality mixed methods study. While we know of no yardstick to determine at what point a study can legitimately be called mixed methods, we do know that reflection, critical thought, and an appreciation of participant perspectives are hallmarks of the qualitative tradition. To the extent that non-experimental designs incorporate these characteristics, they come closer to being able to claim that they approach a mixed methods study.

As can be discerned from the above discussion, a lot of thought and care needs to be exercised in order to produce quality research using quantitative non-experimental research designs. While it might seem overwhelming at times, our advice is to begin with the *purpose* for conducting your study—what do you want to find out? After you wrestle with and finally define that most important question, we suggest that you look to identify which designs and methods housed in your qualitative and quantitative repertoires either alone or in combination can best satisfy this purpose and answer your research questions. By becoming familiar with the most important components of the designs already discussed and those that follow, you will have within your reach ideas for asking questions that you may not have considered previously. You might also engage in methods either alone or with the help of others that were formerly quite foreign to you—quite an accomplishment!

❖ CONCLUDING REMARKS

In this chapter, we described the essential characteristics of non-experimental research conducted in the quantitative tradition. Rather than focus on the discrete classifications that are often used in other quantitative research methods textbooks to describe non-experimental research, we described the procedures for conducting the research according to its objectives (descriptive, prediction, or explanatory) and how data are generated (cross-sectionally, longitudinally, or whether retrospective data are used). Readers should be assured that the way that we have presented the information is not at odds with other textbooks. In fact, all the characteristics of the classic types of research approaches (e.g., survey research, ex post facto research, or causal comparative) are encompassed by our descriptions. We hope that the way in which we presented the descriptions avoids giving our readers the impression that there is a set of non-overlapping, non-experimental research designs and that a researcher's design can only fall under one heading. In fact, researchers conducting quantitative research will draw on many different procedures, each complementing the others, and each contributing to a better understanding of the world around us.

DISCUSSION QUESTIONS

1. What are some similarities that you see between qualitative research designs and non-experimental quantitative research designs? What about differences?

2. What concepts and procedures used for cross-sectional, longitudinal, and retrospective studies might help inform how you conduct qualitative studies?

3. Choose a research problem of interest. For example, if you are interested in technology, perhaps a problem to investigate is "the effects of technology on academic achievement." How might you investigate this problem using a cross-sectional design? If you decide to "turn the story," how might you investigate the same problem using a longitudinal design? How about a retrospective approach?

4. The section "Strengthening the Inferences From Non-Experimental Research Designs" discusses how to strengthen the inferences that can be made from non-experimental designs. Can you identify any related ways where inferences can be supported under the qualitative tradition?

KEY TERMS

Cross-sectional research design: a study in which data are generated at only one point in time, thereby providing a snapshot of the attributes, behaviors, or phenomena that the researcher is studying.

Descriptive study: a study in which the researcher is more interested in *what* the characteristics are rather than in *why* the characteristics are as they are.

Explanatory study: a study conducted to test theories about how and why some attributes, behaviors, or phenomena are related as they are, or how and why the observed differences between pre-existing groups came to be.

Longitudinal research design: a study in which data are generated at multiple points in time such that the researcher can describe the ways in which the attributes, behaviors, or phenomena change over time.

Panel study: a longitudinal study in which the researcher collects data from the same sample of individuals over time.

Prediction study: a study in which the researcher is interested in examining the associations among attributes or behaviors, with the ultimate aim of being able to make predictions.

Retrospective study: a study that examines the antecedents to observed differences between groups as plausible explanations for those differences.

Trend study: a longitudinal study in which the researcher collects data from a different sample of individuals drawn from the same population over time.

REVIEW OF PUBLISHED RESEARCH ARTICLES

In this section, we describe three published research articles that use non-experimental research designs. The full articles are available online at **www.sagepub.com/odwyer.**

Article 2 (Clayton, 2011)

This non-experimental, longitudinal trend study used retrospective data. The author stated that the purpose of the study was to "determine the relationships and predictability of poverty, teacher quality, and diversity of schools on Grade 5 reading and mathematics Virginia Standards of Learning (SOL) examinations for student subgroups in selected districts" (p. 677).

This study typifies the situation in which a researcher must use a non-experimental research design. In this case, the researcher cannot create a manipulated independent variable and cannot use random assignment to create probabilistically equivalent groups. For example, it would not be possible to randomly assign students to live in poverty or to attend a high-poverty school.

This type of study is also common because its goals were both descriptive and predictive; readers will notice that descriptive and prediction studies often go hand-in-hand. The author described the design of the study as follows: "To address these questions, the design of this study included a combination of causal comparative, correlational, and descriptive research methods" (p. 677).

The author's characterization of the design aligns with the nomenclature we used in Chapter 7 to describe non-experimental research designs; however, it could be misleading because it implies that multiple, discrete designs were used (causal comparative study, correlational study, or descriptive study). According to the ways in which we described the non-experimental designs, the author could have described the study as a "longitudinal study that used retrospective data to describe and predict behaviors." Our description avoids the confusion associated with the term *causal-comparative*; namely, that it implies that causal conclusions are warranted.

When conducting the predictive analyses using multiple regression, the author used statistical controls in an effort to improve the strength of the inferences possible from the results. Specifically, in the multiple regression model formulated to explore whether teacher quality and ethnic diversity (the independent variables) predicted academic performance, she included an indicator of poverty. She said the following:

> The process was used to evaluate whether school diversity levels and teacher quality were able to predict pass and advanced pass rates on the SOL test for math and English reading pertaining to Grade 5 Black, Hispanic, and White students over and above the expected predictor of poverty. (p. 683)

While these types of statistical controls can improve the estimates of the regression effects, they are not as effective as design controls.

Article 3 (Porfeli, Wang, Audette, McColl, & Algozzine, 2009)

In this non-experimental study, the authors compiled archival data for students in 80 elementary schools from a large urban school district in the southeast region of the United States. Their goal was to examine the association between educational achievement and school demographics and community capital. As in Article 2, this type of question could not be addressed using an experimental research design as it would not be feasible to assign students to schools with varying levels of community capital. The authors described the study as follows: "The nature of this causal-comparative (*ex post facto*) archival research allows us to document existing differences among the participating schools and to explore the cause, or reason, for them" (p. 79).

Based on this statement, it appears that the authors are using the terms *causal comparative* and *ex post facto* interchangeably. As we first said in Chapter 3, this is a point of confusion among those who are new to the quantitative tradition. While both these designs are non-experimental in nature, there are differences between them. As we understand it, the term *ex post facto designs* refer to studies in which data are gathered retrospectively, and the term *causal comparative* is used to describe studies in which data are gathered from pre-formed groups and the independent variable is not manipulated as in an experiment. According to this distinction, the authors' study may best be characterized as an ex post facto design.

Article 4 (Núñez, Sparks, & Hernández, 2011)

The authors of this study used a non-experimental, cross-sectional study to examine the factors that are related to Latino students' enrollment in 2-year Hispanic-serving institutions (HSIs). As with the two previous articles, it would not be possible for the researchers to randomly assign students to attend HSIs. The authors used archival data from the Beginning Postsecondary Students Longitudinal Study 2004. Since the authors used data only from 2004, the study was cross-sectional. The authors did not provide an explicit description or name for their research design. However, according to our nomenclature, this non-experimental study could be characterized as a "cross-sectional study that used retrospective data to describe and predict behaviors."

8

Experimental Research Designs

The purpose of this chapter is to introduce readers to experimental research designs as a way for generating data to address important research questions. We begin by reinforcing for our readers the difference between quasi-experiments and true experiments and proceed to describe some of the most common experimental research designs used in social science research studies.

❖ ESSENTIAL CHARACTERISTICS OF EXPERIMENTAL RESEARCH

If the researcher's aim is to examine the effect of a treatment or intervention on some attribute or outcome (e.g., whether a new teaching or therapeutic method can lead to better outcomes compared with a traditional method), *experimental research* may be the most appropriate. In the simplest case, experimental research requires the implementation of a treatment with one group (the treatment group) and not with another (the control group). In this way, the independent variable is manipulated by the researcher. Subsequent to applying the intervention to the treatment group, the researcher compares the two groups on the attribute or outcome hypothesized to respond to the treatment. The primary purpose of experimental research is to be able to establish "cause and effect" or, more technically, to make causal inferences. That is, the researcher aims to conclude that the treatment *caused* the difference that was observed between the groups on the attribute that is being studied. Recall that it is only possible to conclude that attribute *A* causes attribute *B* when (a) *A* occurs before *B*, (b) changes in *A* are associated with changes in *B*, and (c) all other possible explanations for the observed association between *A* and *B* are controlled. The final condition, that all other possible explanations are controlled, differentiates experimental research from non-experimental research.

In cases where the researcher only wishes to describe an attribute, to quantify the relationship between attributes, or to examine the differences between pre-existing groups on some antecedent attribute, experimental research is not appropriate. While we are certainly in favor of conducting rigorous research that supports causal inference, we are of the opinion that experimental research is not always appropriate. For example, when the extant body of knowledge relating to a research problem is not yet fully developed, it may be unwise to expend resources developing an intervention. In this situation, non-experimental research may be more appropriate as it may contribute to a deeper understanding of the problem and suggest future directions for the development of interventions that can subsequently be evaluated using an experimental research design. In fact, the results of a qualitative inquiry can lead to ideas for designing an experimental study if the researcher is inclined to do so.

As we have mentioned previously (Chapter 3 and in the Overview to Section III), under the experimental research heading, there is a distinction between **quasi-experimental research designs** and **true experimental research designs**. While both designs are used to examine the impact of interventions and both require the researcher to

create treatment and control conditions (the manipulated independent variable), they differ in one very important characteristic;
namely, the way in which the researcher creates the treatment and
control groups. In a true experiment, the researcher creates the treatment and control groups by randomly assigning individuals or clusters of individuals to the treatment and control condition prior to the
implementation of any intervention. The presumed effect of the randomization process is to make the groups probabilistically equivalent
prior to the implementation of the intervention so that any differences on outcomes can be attributed to the intervention.

On the other hand, in a quasi-experiment, the researcher creates
the treatment and control conditions through a non-random process.
As such, the intervention is implemented with treatment and control
groups that may or may not be equivalent. The absence of randomization means that the groups are not probabilistically equivalent, and this
can significantly weaken the causal conclusions that are supported.
Other than the process by which individuals are assigned to the treatment and control conditions and its consequences for making causal
inferences, quasi-experiments and true experiments are similar in
terms of their purpose and design characteristics, as well as their limitations and weaknesses. Where possible, we recommend that researchers
use a true experimental design to evaluate the impact of a treatment.
However, since it is often not possible to randomly assign individuals
to groups (especially in schools), quasi-experimental research remains
prevalent in social science research.

We must make two important points here. First, some readers may
confuse a quasi-experiment with the type of design in which the
researcher compares pre-existing groups (we referred to this as a causal
comparative in Chapter 3). Readers are cautioned to notice that in a
quasi-experiment, the researcher does, in fact, create a manipulated
independent variable by forming groups, but he or she does not use a
random assignment process. In the type of design referred to as causal
comparative, the data are gathered from pre-formed groups and the
independent variable is not manipulated by the researcher. As a consequence of this difference, quasi-experimental designs are classified as
experimental designs and causal comparative designs are classified as
non-experimental designs.

Second, **randomization (aka random assignment)** to treatment
and control conditions is different from the random selection procedures we described in Chapter 4. Random selection procedures are
used to "select" a representative sample of individuals or clusters
from the population. Conversely, random assignment, relates to how

individuals in a study are "assigned" to treatment and control conditions, regardless of how they are sampled from the population. The process of random assignment is used to ensure the equivalence of the groups prior to the implementation of the intervention, and if after the intervention the groups differ on the attribute, it allows the differences to be ascribed to the intervention.

One other point to note is that random assignment does not necessarily result in groups that are exactly the same on all characteristics. Rather, according to the theory of randomization, the groups are only **probabilistically equivalent**. This means that on average, across an infinite number of repeated random assignments to the treatment and control conditions, the groups are equivalent on all measured and unmeasured attributes. This also implies that the observed treatment effect (i.e., the difference between the treatment and control conditions after the intervention) will only differ from the "true" treatment effect in the population by chance (Shadish et al., 2002; Shavelson & Towne, 2002). Randomization and the quantitative procedures that depend on this process are not infallible; rather, they provide assurance in a probabilistic (vs. a definitive) manner.

When conducting experimental research, the researcher must pay attention to the **unit of assignment** when deciding whether individuals or clusters of individuals (e.g., classrooms, schools, etc.) will be assigned to conditions. In many cases of experimental research, individuals are assigned, randomly or otherwise, to the treatment and control conditions, and so the unit of assignment is the individual. However, in some research situations, clusters of individuals (e.g., intact classrooms) are assigned, and so the unit of assignment is the cluster. In situations where every individual within a cluster is randomly assigned to the same condition, this design configuration is referred to as a **cluster randomized trial**, and the treatment effect is calculated between the clusters in the control group and the clusters in the treatment group. This type of design is commonly used in large-scale studies conducted to examine the effectiveness of educational interventions. Using clusters as the unit of assignment and analysis has consequences of the types of analyses that can be conducted, and these will be further described in Chapter 9.

Finally, there are a set of designs that share some characteristics with quasi-experimental and true experimental research, yet are significantly weaker in terms of their internal validity and, consequently, in their ability to support causal conclusions. These designs, referred to as **pre-experimental research designs** by some authors (e.g., Fraenkel & Wallen, 2011), are similar to quasi-experimental and true experimental research designs in that the researcher implements an intervention and aims to examine the impact of that intervention on some attribute. However, these designs lack a control group, and so no counterfactual evidence is available for comparison with the observations in the treatment group. For example, a *pretest–posttest no control group design* does not permit the researcher to ascertain whether the results observed on the post-implementation measure are attributable to the treatment; any observed post-intervention differences may have resulted from other causes. These types of designs are not on par with quasi-experimental designs or true experimental research designs for making causal inferences and so should be avoided by the conscientious researcher.

We recognize that our coverage of experimental research (quasi- and true experimental) is limited. For example, we only discuss **between-subjects designs** in which participants can be in a treatment or control group, but not in both. Although we do not describe them in the sections that follow, **within-subjects designs** are also popular in social science research. In a within-subjects design, every participant is exposed to the treatment and individuals act as their own controls. For more detailed information on these and other quasi- and true experimental research designs, we refer the reader to more specialized texts such as Shadish et al., (2002), Kirk (2012), or Keppel and Wickens (2004) for more detailed coverage.

❖ QUASI-EXPERIMENTAL BETWEEN-SUBJECTS RESEARCH DESIGNS

Quasi-experiments are conducted when researchers wish to examine the impact of an intervention but cannot use randomization to ensure that the group receiving the intervention and the group that does not are probabilistically equivalent on all measured and unmeasured attributes. The absence of randomization in quasi-experimental designs means that pre-existing differences between the treatment and control conditions may pose a subject characteristics threat to the internal validity of the study, thereby weakening the causal inferences. For reasons of logistics, resources, or ethics, quasi-experimental research designs may be the only option available to researchers wishing to examine the effect of an intervention.

Despite the lack of randomization in quasi-experimental designs, conditional causal inferences may still be possible if steps are taken to control the *plausible* threats to the internal validity of the study that are identified. Similar to the points we made in our discussion on approaches for improving non-experimental research designs (Chapter 7), the inferences from quasi-experimental research can be strengthened by holding extraneous variables constant, by building extraneous variables into the design and subsequently using them as statistical controls during the data analysis phase, or through the use of matching. Again, we remind our readers that causal inferences based on designs where statistical controls are used tend to be weaker than the inferences possible when design elements such as randomization are used to control for extraneous variables.

Steps in Conducting Quasi-Experimental Between-Subjects Research

As a first step in conducting a quasi-experiment, the researcher must first design or have access to an intervention that is hypothesized to affect the attribute or behavior (outcome or dependent variable) that is of interest to the researcher. Second, in the simplest case, the researcher creates treatment and control conditions without random assignment. Recall that quasi-experimental designs also do not specify that groups are randomly selected to be representative of the population; while it may increase the generalizability of the results, random selection of the sample is not a condition for implementing the design. Third, the researcher collects pre-implementation data from the two groups so as to empirically examine the equivalence of the treatment and control groups on all measured attributes. While this does not ensure that the groups are truly equivalent (e.g., they may differ on unmeasured attributes), this step provides weak evidence about the groups prior to the intervention. Fourth, the researcher implements the intervention with one group and not with the other group while maintaining maximum control over all possible threats to internal validity. Fifth, at the end of the intervention phase, the researcher collects post-implementation data from the two groups and analyzes the data to compute the treatment effect (i.e., the difference between the two groups on the post-implementation measure). Finally, the researcher must summarize and interpret the findings by making connections to the research problem, research questions, and research hypotheses. During this final phase, the researcher must consider the extent to which threats to the internal validity of the study were controlled. Specifically, the steps are as follows:

1. Design or gain access to an intervention that is hypothesized to affect the attribute or behavior (outcome or dependent variable) that is of interest to the researcher.

2. Identify at least two non-randomly formed groups with which the study will be conducted.

3. Collect pre-implementation data from the groups and empirically examine their equivalence on all measured attributes.

4. Implement the intervention with one group and not with the other group while maintaining maximum control over all possible threats to internal validity.

5. Collect post-implementation data from the groups and analyze the data to compute the treatment effect.

6. Acknowledge the extent to which threats to the internal validity of the study were controlled, and summarize and interpret the findings by making connections to the research problem, research questions, and research hypotheses.

When conducting quasi-experimental research, there are several tried-and-tested configurations to choose from, not all of which include each of the six steps we outlined. Here, we will discuss three of the most common quasi-experimental configurations. In the following design schematics, "NR" indicates non-random assignment to treatment and control conditions, "O" indicates a time point at which data are observed or collected, and "X" indicates the implementation of the intervention.

The Posttest-Only Quasi-Experimental Between-Subjects Design

When implementing this design, the researcher collects only post-implementation data from the treatment and control groups.

Treatment Group	NR	X	O
Control Group	NR		O

In the absence of pre-implementation measures, it is not possible to evaluate the equivalence of the groups prior to the implementation of the intervention or to use pre-implementation information as a statistical control. As such, under this design, pre-existing differences between the groups may be the basis for any differences observed on the post-implementation measure; that is, a subject characteristics threat cannot be ruled out. In addition, without pre-implementation information, it is not possible to know whether individuals withdrew from the study, and if so, how those individuals may have differed from the individuals who remained, or whether the rates of attrition from the study was different in the treatment and control conditions. Therefore, the researcher cannot critically evaluate the impact of attrition on the findings from the study. Perhaps the only redeeming characteristic of this design is that the testing threat has been eliminated, and even this does not outweigh the weaknesses of this configuration.

The Pretest–Posttest Quasi-Experimental Between-Subjects Design

This design adds a data collection point prior to the implementation of the intervention and so is stronger than the posttest-only design.

Treatment Group	NR O X O
Control Group	NR O O

With the addition of the pre-implementation measure, the researcher can empirically compare the groups on the attribute that the treatment is designed to affect prior to implementation, can include the implementation data as a statistical control during the analysis phase, and can monitor attrition from the study. However, the researcher can only evaluate the equivalence of the groups on the attributes and characteristics that are measured; unmeasured attributes could be related to how the intervention affects the treatment group. As such, a subject characteristics threat may still be a concern here. Matching, holding extraneous variables constant, or building extraneous variables into the design and subsequently using them as statistical controls can all be used to improve this design.

The inclusion of the pre-implementation measure introduces the possibility of a testing threat, whereby the individuals in the study have been exposed to the measurement instrument, and this may alert them to the behavior that the intervention is designed to alter and/or could provide them with practice on the measure (in the case of an achievement or performance measure). Administering different, but psychometrically equivalent, pre- and post-implementation measures and/or maximizing the time between data collection points may reduce these effects. Overall, researchers who implement this design are advised to collect extensive pre-implementation information and to interpret the findings in a prudent manner, discussing the plausibility of alternative explanations for the results observed.

The Pretest–Posttest Quasi-Experimental Between-Subjects Design With Multiple Pretests

In this design, an additional wave of pretest data are collected from the two groups.

Treatment Group $\quad \overline{N_R \quad O_1 \quad O_2 \quad X \quad O_3}$

Control Group $\quad \overline{N_R \quad O_1 \quad O_2 \quad \quad O_3}$

The addition of the second pretest allows the researcher to examine whether maturation or regression to the mean is occurring and, if so, whether it is confounded with subject characteristics threats. For example, if no changes are observed for either group between measurement points O_1 and O_2, the researcher can tentatively conclude that maturation and regression to the mean threats have been minimized. Similarly, any observed differences between the groups between points O_1 and O_2 would allow the researcher to evaluate whether maturation or regression to mean was occurring to a similar degree in the non-randomly assigned groups. In addition to increasing the length and cost of the study, this configuration is vulnerable to testing threats. As before, administering psychometrically equivalent pre- and post-implementation measures and/or maximizing the time between measures may reduce these effects. Also as before, researchers can use matching, can hold extraneous variables constant, or can build extraneous variables into the design to bolster the validity of the causal inferences.

In summary, the results from all quasi-experimental research designs must be interpreted cautiously. The absence of randomly formed treatment and control groups, the essential characteristic that differentiates these designs from the true experiment, may lead to the conflation of subject characteristics with the treatment effects, may necessitate the use of additional safeguards during implementation, and may only support weak causal conclusions.

❖ TRUE EXPERIMENTAL BETWEEN-SUBJECTS RESEARCH DESIGNS

True experimental research studies are conducted when the researcher wishes to examine the impact of an intervention *and* can randomly assign individuals or clusters to the treatment and control conditions.

Randomization ensures that the treatment and control conditions are probabilistically equivalent on all measured and unmeasured variables, and the observed treatment effect (i.e., the difference observed between the treatment and control group on the post-implementation measure) will only differ from the population treatment effect by chance and not in any systematic way.

Steps in Conducting True Experimental Between-Subjects Research

In a true experimental design, individuals or clusters of individuals are randomly assigned to the treatment or control condition, pre-implementation data are collected, the intervention is implemented with one group and not with the other, and at the end of the intervention phase, post-implementation data are collected. As an alternative to the order of these steps, the researcher could randomly assign to treatment and control conditions *after* the pre-implementation data are collected. In this case, the researcher uses the data gathered from the individuals at the pre-implementation stage (e.g., race, gender, socioeconomic status, etc.) to create homogeneous strata, and from within these strata, the researcher randomly assigns individuals to either the treatment or control condition. Compared with the simple random assignment process that relies just on chance to make the groups equivalent, the latter procedure will likely result in treatment and control groups that are more similar to each other on the measured attributes, particularly if the sample size is small. As an aside, this process is analogous to using stratification variables when choosing a random sample from the population (Chapter 4). Regardless of which randomization process is used, the researcher must adhere strictly to the randomization plan that is established ahead of time; this will avoid what Shadish et al. (2002) refer to as "haphazard random assignment." Apart from how the treatment and control conditions are formed, the steps for conducting a true experiment are similar to those outlined for quasi-experimental designs:

1. Design or gain access to an intervention that is hypothesized to affect the attribute or behavior (outcome or dependent variable) that is of interest to the researcher.

2. Create at least two groups using a random assignment process with which the study will be conducted.

3. Collect pre-implementation data from the groups and empirically examine their equivalence on all measured attributes.

4. Implement the intervention with one group and not with the other group while maintaining maximum control over all possible threats to internal validity.

5. Collect post-implementation data from the groups and analyze the data to compute the treatment effect.

6. Acknowledge the extent to which threats to the internal validity of the study were controlled and summarize and interpret the findings by making connections to the research problem, research questions, and research hypotheses.

Again, researchers have several tried-and-tested true experimental research design configurations to choose from when conducting their study. Here again, we will discuss some of the most common true experimental configurations. In the following design schematics, "R" indicates random assignment to treatment and control conditions, and as in the previous section, "O" indicates a time point at which data are observed or collected, and "X" indicates the implementation of the intervention.

The Basic True Experimental Between-Subjects Design

Under this configuration, the researcher randomly assigns individuals or clusters to treatment and control conditions and collects only post-implementation data from the treatment and control groups.

Treatment Group	R	X	O
Control Group	R		O

Despite using random assignment and a control condition, the absence of pre-implementation measures weakens the strength of this design. Specifically, the researcher has no way to evaluate the equivalence of the treatment and control conditions prior to the intervention and so must entrust the equivalence of the groups to the randomization process. In addition, no pre-implementation data are available to include as statistical controls during the analysis phase. With small sample sizes, this type of design could result in groups that are quite different on measured and unmeasured variables. In addition, without a pre-implementation measure, the researcher cannot monitor or evaluate the impact of differential attrition rates from the treatment and control groups. The only real strength of this design lies with the fact that the researcher can avoid any testing threats to internal validity.

The Pretest–Posttest True Experimental Between-Subjects Design

Using randomization, pre- and post-implementation measures, and a control group, this configuration is one of the most commonly used true experimental research designs.

Treatment Group	R	O	X	O
Control Group	R	O		O

Alternatively,

Treatment Group	O	R	X	O
Control Group	O	R		O

The addition of the pre-implementation measures results in a stronger design than the basic true experimental design because it allows the researcher to empirically examine the equivalence of the treatment and control groups on the measured variables and statistically control for pre-existing differences on the pre-implementation measure and allows the researcher to monitor attrition rates in the treatment and control groups. Again, there is the possibility of a testing threat to the internal validity of the study, but this can be mitigated by using psychometrically equivalent pre- and post-implementation measures and/or maximizing the time between data collection points.

Alternatives to the Pretest–Posttest True Experimental Between-Subjects Design

It is common for researchers to want to compare more than one treatment and control conditions. For example, when examining the efficacy of an intervention, a researcher might want to know exactly *which* components of the intervention produce the best outcomes. Consider the example of the researcher who wishes to examine the efficacy of the technology-based intervention on student learning in science. He or she may want to know whether hands-on activities, in addition to the technology intervention, are necessary in order to produce positive gains in student learning compared with the control condition. In this case, the researcher may randomly create three groups: (1) a group of students that receives the technology intervention and the hands-on activities, (2) a group that receives the technology intervention but no hands-on activities, and (3) a control group that receives instruction in science using "business-as-usual" classroom conditions. Using randomization to avoid subject characteristics threat, the researcher can implement the following three-group configuration:

Treatment Group A	O R XA O
Treatment Group B	O R XB O
Control Group	O R O

With this design, the researcher can minimize subject characteristics threats with randomization, evaluate the equivalence of the groups on the pre-implementation measures, determine whether there is differential attrition across groups, and compare the outcomes across the three conditions to determine which treatment, or amount of treatment, produces the greatest effect. Another variation on this design would be to eliminate the pre-implementation measures; this may ameliorate the effects of a testing threat but would also preclude evaluating the equivalence of the groups and the attrition rates. Yet another variation would be to eliminate the no-treatment control group for the configuration; in cases where the effectiveness of intervention compared with a no-treatment control group has already been established in previous studies, this variation may be appropriate. Likewise, if access to participants or resources is a concern, the researcher may have no option other than to eliminate the control condition. In general, it is advisable to include a control group for comparison, as this gives the researcher the greatest opportunity to evaluate the effect of the intervention.

Longitudinal True Experimental Between-Subjects Designs

The final true experimental design configuration we will describe is the longitudinal experimental design. Under this design, the researcher randomly assigns individuals or clusters of individuals to treatment and control conditions, collects data from both groups over some period of time prior to the implementation of the intervention, implements the intervention in the treatment group, and subsequently collects data from both groups at multiple points after the intervention has been implemented. The following configuration shows measures at four time points, pre- and post-implementation, but the researcher can include as many as are feasible:

Treatment Group	R	O	O	O	O	X	O	O	O	O
Control Group	R	O	O	O	O		O	O	O	O

Because multiple measures of an attribute provide a more stable and consistent (i.e., reliable) estimate compared with a single measure, the researcher can have greater confidence in his or her measurement of the attribute in the groups. In addition, this type of configuration allows the researcher to formulate statistical models of change over time as a consequence of the intervention. This approach would be particularly useful if say, maturation was expected to be a concern. In this case, the researcher could build a measure of maturation into the design and, during the data analysis phase, could explicitly model maturation while also examining the effect of the intervention. Finally, the multiple post-implementation measures allow the researcher to examine the immediacy of the treatment effect and whether the effect endured over time. This virtue makes longitudinal designs ideal for examining interventions that aim to create sustainable change in attributes or behaviors.

Despite these strengths, however, this configuration has several weaknesses, some of which may preclude its implementation and others that can weaken the validity of any causal claims. Specifically, longitudinal designs are vulnerable to testing threats, particularly if the same measurement instruments are used at each time point. Overall, longitudinal designs are costly and time-intensive to implement, and depending on the research area, it can be difficult to recruit participants to studies that are conducted over long periods of time. Related to this is the fact that longitudinal studies are particularly weak with regard to attrition. Depending on the duration of the study and the extent of the commitment required on the part of the participants, it can be difficult and costly to maintain (through regular contact, follow-up calls, etc.) a sufficiently large sample that also remains representative of the population.

❖ STRENGTHS AND LIMITATIONS OF QUASI- AND TRUE EXPERIMENTAL BETWEEN-SUBJECTS RESEARCH DESIGNS

The clear advantage of experimental research designs rests on their capacity for supporting causal inferences. With the combined virtues of random assignment and counterfactual evidence provided by a control group, true experimental research designs are the gold standard for isolating cause-and-effect mechanisms and provide stronger evidence than quasi-experimental designs.

The corollary of this virtue is that experimental designs are only useful in situations where the researcher has an intervention he or she wishes to study and evaluate; as such, they are not always appropriate for addressing researchers' questions. For example, social science researchers are often interested in attributes such as socioeconomic status or parental involvement, which cannot be manipulated experimentally. In situations where this is the case, non-experimental research designs are more appropriate. Second, experimental designs are generally difficult to implement in real-world environments such as classrooms and schools. For example, it is usually difficult to assign (randomly, or otherwise) teachers within schools to different conditions, to assign students to classrooms, and to assign students to different conditions within classrooms. In addition, it can be difficult to maintain the fidelity of the treatment implementation across teachers and schools. Third, experimental designs are considerably more expensive to conduct than non-experimental designs. This is because interventions are usually costly to develop and require substantial resources (e.g., researchers' time, etc.) to implement. In addition, and as a consequence of the difficulty in assigning teachers and students within schools, experimental designs in education often use schools (i.e., clusters) as the assignment unit; schools, along with every teacher and student in that school, are assigned to either the treatment or control condition. This approach requires many schools, and as such, the cost of these types of studies may be very high.

To summarize, experimental research designs provide the strongest evidence for cause-and-effect relationships, and true experimental research is stronger in this regard than quasi-experimental research. However, since the research design should always be linked to the purpose of the research, these types of designs are not always appropriate for meeting researchers' needs. On balance, readers are encouraged to select research designs that allow the research questions to be answered and the research hypotheses to be tested, even if those designs are non-experimental.

❖ COMMON THREATS TO EXTERNAL AND INTERNAL VALIDITY FOR QUASI- AND TRUE EXPERIMENTAL BETWEEN-SUBJECTS RESEARCH DESIGNS

Despite being the strongest designs for examining cause-and-effect relationships, quasi-experimental and true experimental research designs remain susceptible to external and internal validity threats. For example, experimental research designs are often limited in their generalizability. As we first pointed out in Chapter 3, the more the researcher controls the research environment, the less generalizable the findings from the study are likely to be. Consider the extreme situation where a researcher is studying the impact of a new method of instruction and conducts an experiment under laboratory conditions at his or her university. In the laboratory, the researcher randomly assigns the students to receive either the new method of instruction or the traditional method. In implementing the design, the researcher not only controls subject characteristics threats through random assignment but also maintains tight controls over how the new method of instruction is implemented by the teachers and controls the classroom environment by eliminating the types of interruptions and distractions that can occur in a typical classroom. If students receiving the new method of instruction were found to outperform the control group, the researcher may not be able to assume that the same results would be observed in a typical classroom setting. That is, the findings may only hold under idealized conditions and may have limited ecological generalizability. This example reaffirms the point that we made in previous chapters about the need for conducting replication studies.

As with any other type of research, even with non-experimental designs, population generalizability depends on the representativeness of the sample and whether systematic sampling errors and non-response errors are minimized. Moreover, it is certainly possible to implement an experimental design with a representative sample from a population. Likewise, systematic measurement error can threaten the generalizability of the findings from experimental research.

As is evident from the various experimental designs we presented in the previous section, individual designs vary in their capacity to minimize threats to internal validity. As a reminder, randomization does not eliminate all possible threats to the internal validity of a study; rather, it minimizes the likelihood that differences in subject characteristics across groups (subject characteristics threats) are conflated with the effect of the intervention. Subject characteristics threats are particularly problematic in quasi-experimental designs, and additional steps are recommended (e.g., matching, statistical controls, etc.) for minimizing this threat.

Furthermore, while other possible threats to internal validity (e.g., history, implementation, instrumentation, etc.) can remain, randomization reduces the possibility that these threats will have differential impacts across the treatment and control conditions. For example, when subject characteristics threats are minimized through random assignment, internal validity threats such as testing, maturation, attrition, and regression to the mean are expected to be equivalent in both groups and so would not be expected to bias the treatment effect. To minimize threats to the internal validity of experimental designs, readers are advised to use randomization when possible, maintain control over all extraneous variables, build extraneous variables into the design and use them as statistical controls during data analyses, and/or use matching.

❖ CONNECTIONS TO QUALITATIVE RESEARCH

If you are a researcher trained in the qualitative tradition, the X and O discussion may leave you wondering how this way of portraying a research strategy can possibly connect with the way you go about thinking, reflecting, and discovering! This is certainly understandable since the authors are quite sensitive to these kinds of differences between the two paradigms. We are also convinced, however, that at their core, these paradigms with their associated designs offer ways of learning about phenomena that neither approach can accomplish alone. Even though ethnographic and phenomenological research differ dramatically from quantitative designs in how the study is framed, what constitutes data, and how participants are enlisted, they are connected via their essential purpose. As described in Chapter 1, "Research is a systematic process to make things known that are currently unknown by examining phenomena multiple times and in multiple ways." When you think about "multiple ways," we hope that you now see quantitative designs and their associated methods of data collection and analysis (discussed in Chapter 9) as good candidates for "making things known that are currently unknown." Multiple designs and methods that focus on what you would like to discover, whether these studies are conducted by the individual researcher or have been conducted by others, can yield a richer perspective of phenomena.

❖ CONCLUDING REMARKS

This chapter was designed to provide readers with an overview of the experimental research designs that are most frequently used for addressing questions in education and other social and behavioral sciences. Similar to our remarks and recommendations at the end of Chapter 7, readers are advised to spend the time necessary to develop a solid understanding of the research designs introduced in this chapter. Doing so will prepare the reader to select and implement appropriate research designs for addressing significant research questions. A well-informed research design choice will minimize all plausible alternative explanations for the results observed and will allow the research findings to be generalized to other participants and settings.

DISCUSSION QUESTIONS

1. If you wanted to explore whether there are discernible differences on some measure of "success" between high school students who are taking classes that are infused with technology versus those who are not, what would be your preferred *qualitative* design? What would you try to discover?

2. For Question 1, what kind of *experimental* research design would be most appropriate? What would you try to discover?

3. Assume that the results of a true experimental study found that police recruits who were randomly assigned to training that was conducted using a more innovative approach were found 10 years later to be much more effective law enforcement officers. What kind of qualitative follow-up study might you conduct?

4. If you had previously conducted several narrative studies of retired social workers and now wanted to confirm some themes among current social workers, what are some ways that you could do so using a *quantitative* design?

KEY TERMS

Between-subjects research designs: research designs in which participants may be in the treatment or control group but not in both.

Cluster randomized trial: research design in which the unit of assignment is a cluster of individuals.

Pre-experimental research design: a set of designs used to examine the impact of that intervention on some attribute but do not have a control condition.

Probabilistically equivalent groups: on average, across an infinite number of repeated random assignments to the treatment and control conditions, the groups are equivalent on all measured and unmeasured attributes. The observed differences will only differ from the population differences by chance and not in any systematic way.

Quasi-experimental research designs: a set of research designs used to examine the impact of interventions but do not use randomization to ensure group equivalence.

Randomization (aka random assignment): the process describing how individuals or clusters of individuals are assigned to treatment and control conditions, regardless of how they are sampled from the population. Random assignment creates groups that are probabilistically equivalent.

True experimental research designs: a set of research designs used to examine the impact of interventions and use randomization to ensure group equivalence.

Unit of assignment: the unit (e.g., individuals or clusters of individuals) that is assigned to the treatment and control conditions.

Within-subjects research designs: research designs in which every participant is exposed to the treatment, and individuals act as their own controls.

REVIEW OF PUBLISHED RESEARCH ARTICLES

In this section, we describe two published research articles that use experimental research designs. The full articles are available online at **www.sagepub.com/odwyer**.

Article 5 (Van Voorhis, 2011)

This study is classified as a quasi-experiment because the author's goal was to examine the effect of an intervention by comparing the outcomes in a treatment condition with the outcomes in a control condition, and individuals were not randomly assigned to the treatment and control conditions. Readers will notice that with these types of design, the research creates a condition (i.e., creates a manipulated independent variable) but does not do so using a random process.

Readers are cautioned not to confuse quasi-experimental designs with the type of design in which the researcher compares pre-existing groups (we referred to this design as causal comparative in Chapter 3). Readers should notice that in a quasi-experiment, the researcher does, in fact, create a manipulated independent variable by forming groups, but he or she does not use a random assignment process. Van Voorhis characterized her study as a quasi-experiment because she was unable to randomly assign students to classrooms. She did, however, create treatment and control conditions by assigning (randomly, in this case) some teachers to use the intervention, and others to a control condition. She stated the following:

> At each school, one teacher was randomly assigned to implement the Teachers Involve Parents in Schoolwork (TIPS) interactive math homework assignments weekly along with other homework, and the other teacher used "regular" math homework assignments in a matched Control classroom. Thus, teachers were randomly assigned to the intervention and Control conditions. Although students were not randomly assigned to classrooms, every effort was made to select similar, "average" classrooms of students in Grade 3. (p. 319)

As we first pointed out when we discussed this article in Chapter 5, the author addressed potential subject characteristics threats to the internal validity of the study by randomly assigning teachers to treatment and control conditions *within* schools. This had the effect of minimizing any systematic school-to-school differences as plausible explanations for the results observed.

Article 6 (Booksh, Pella, Singh, & Gouvier, 2010)

This study is an example of a basic true experimental between-subjects research design described in Chapter 8. Under this design, the researcher randomly assigned individuals to the treatment and control conditions (and included a retrospective clinical sample), and collected only post-implementation data. However, given that the instruments that were administered induced the treatment effect, this approach was reasonable. Overall, the authors' use of random assignment and their exclusion criteria according to the following description strengthened the internal validity of the study:

> Because it is assumed that a number of those malingering during an ADHD evaluation do not actually meet criteria for ADHD, the researchers thought it was necessary to use participants from a normative sample to obtain a more generalizable sample. So too, we elected to screen out other conditions that may otherwise account for participants' performance on the cognitive measures. Therefore, exclusion criteria were as follows: age less than 18 years, history of LD, and diagnosis of ADHD or current complaints of significant problems with ADHD-related symptoms or neurological problems. (p. 328)

9

Descriptive Analyses for Data Generated by Quantitative Research

CHAPTER OUTLINE

- Fundamentals of Descriptive Analysis
- Summarizing and Describing Univariate Distributions
- Summarizing and Describing Relationships

This chapter introduces readers to descriptive analyses as a means for analyzing data generated by research in the quantitative tradition. Descriptive analyses are used to summarize and describe data; the aim is to reveal patterns in the data that are not immediately apparent when inspecting raw data. Descriptive analyses are usually conducted first, regardless of whether the purpose of the study is descriptive, predictive, or explanatory. The reason for conducting descriptive analyses is to allow the researcher and the reader to understand the data before trying to understand what it conveys. As with the choice of research design, the choice of data analysis procedure will depend on the purpose of the research, the research questions that are posed, and the type of data collected. Furthermore, the choice of data analysis procedures should be guided by previous research in the field.

Although we use the term *analysis* for both qualitative and quantitative studies, there is no denying that we use the language of statistics when referring to the analysis of quantitative data. We remind readers that statistical techniques exist for one reason and one reason only—to help make sense out of data in relation to the research questions. Where possible, we will provide conceptual explanations and descriptions for the analysis; however, in cases where mathematical formulas are essential to our explanations, we will refer to them but in a judicious manner! For more complete coverage of the statistical analysis procedures, we refer readers to classic statistics textbooks such as Privitera (2012), Howell (2010), Glass and Hopkins (1996), and Shavelson (1996). Also note that most of the statistical analyses we describe are seldom conducted by hand. Instead, researchers use statistical software such as SPSS, Stata, Excel, or SAS to analyze their data.

❖ FUNDAMENTALS OF DESCRIPTIVE ANALYSIS

Descriptive analyses are used to summarize and describe data, and to reveal patterns in the data that are not immediately apparent through inspecting the raw data alone. Moreover, descriptive statistics can be used to summarize the distribution of scores for a single variable or can be used to summarize the relationship among variables (Figure 9.1).

Descriptive analyses play a central role in the analysis of quantitative data. In fact for non-experimental, descriptive research studies, descriptive analyses are sufficient for addressing the research questions. However, even in situations where the research objectives include prediction and explanation and the research questions require more complex forms of analysis, descriptive analyses remain essential. Before conducting the analyses for addressing the research questions, researchers are advised to conduct descriptive analyses as a way to become familiar with the data, to summarize the raw data, and to describe the sample.

When conducting descriptive analyses, researchers can use frequency distributions, visual representations, measures of central tendency and dispersion, correlations, and prediction models. In reality, researchers typically use multiple ways to summarize and present their data. In the sections that follow, we describe the most common types of descriptive analyses.

Figure 9.1   Two Branches of Descriptive Analysis

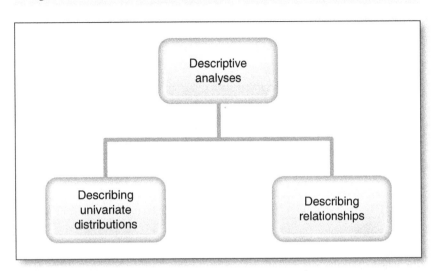

❖ SUMMARIZING AND DESCRIBING UNIVARIATE DISTRIBUTIONS

In this section, we describe the most common methods used by researchers to describe and characterize arrays of values for only one variable. Technically, the term for a distribution of scores on only one variable is a **univariate distribution**.

Frequency Distributions and Grouped Frequency Distributions

A **frequency distribution** is a tabulated summary of the frequency with which each score occurs in the distribution. A frequency distribution can be used to summarize continuous or categorical data. For example, consider the following continuous distribution of raw scores measured on at least an interval scale (see Chapter 5).

Raw score distribution: 8, 8, 8, 9, 10, 12, 12, 12, 12, 14, 15, 17, 19

For example, these could be individuals' test scores (interval) or ages (ratio). Table 9.1 presents a simple example of a frequency distribution for these raw scores.

Sometimes, the amount of information presented in the frequency distribution is too "fine-grained" to allow the patterns to emerge. For example, a frequency distribution summarizing the annual income for

Table 9.1 Hypothetical frequency distribution

Value	Frequency	Percentage
8	3	23.1
9	1	7.7
10	1	7.7
12	4	30.8
14	1	7.7
15	1	7.7
17	1	7.7
19	1	7.7
Total	13	100[a]

a. Within rounding error.

every person who lives in a town would likely provide such detailed information that patterns may be obscured. In these cases, the researcher may choose to use a **grouped frequency distribution**, a tabulated summary in which the raw scores are grouped into mutually exclusive intervals. In the case where the income level for a town is reported, the raw annual income data could be grouped into ≤$25,000, $26,000 to $50,000, and ≥$51,000 per year. However, it should be noted that as intervals become larger, more precise information is lost. Table 9.2 shows a simple example of a grouped frequency distribution for the 13 raw scores, where the intervals are 8–10, 11–13, 14–16, and 17–19.

Visual Representations

Visual displays of data are very useful for researchers and for the audiences to whom they present their findings. The old adage "a picture is worth a thousand words" is highly relevant when presenting summaries of data! Visual summaries can often simplify the complex patterns in the data for readers. In addition, visual displays can be used by researchers to identify the shape of distributions as well as extreme scores. Depending on whether the researcher is summarizing continuous or categorical variables, different representations can be used. Here, we will focus on the histogram, the frequency polygon, and the bar graph.

Table 9.2   Hypothetical grouped frequency distribution.

Frequency Distribution		
Value	Frequency	Percentage
8-10	5	38.5
11-13	4	30.8
14-16	2	15.4
17-19	2	15.4
Total	13	100[a]

a. Within rounding error.

Histograms

A **histogram** is a visual summary of the frequencies of values on a continuous variable. The possible values of the variable are placed on the horizontal x-axis, and the frequency (number or percentage) is represented by bars whose lengths are proportional to the prevalence of the value in the distribution. Since the data are continuous, the values represent differences in amount and so the bars are touching to signify that continuum. Figure 9.2 presents a histogram for the distribution of 13 continuous raw scores in the hypothetical data set.

Frequency Polygons

A **frequency polygon** is a visual summary of the data presented in a frequency distribution or grouped frequency distribution. In this type of graph, the possible raw scores or groups of raw scores are placed on the horizontal x-axis, and the frequency (usually represented as a percentage) is placed on the vertical y-axis. Figure 9.3 presents the frequency polygons for the distribution of 13 continuous raw scores in the hypothetical data set. Notice that the shapes of the polygons are quite different due to the loss of information when the data were grouped.

Bar Graphs

A **bar graph** is a visual summary of the frequencies of values on a categorical variable. In this type of graph, the possible values of the categorical variable are placed on the horizontal x-axis, and the frequency (again, usually represented as a percentage) is represented by

Figure 9.2 Example of Histogram for Continuous Data

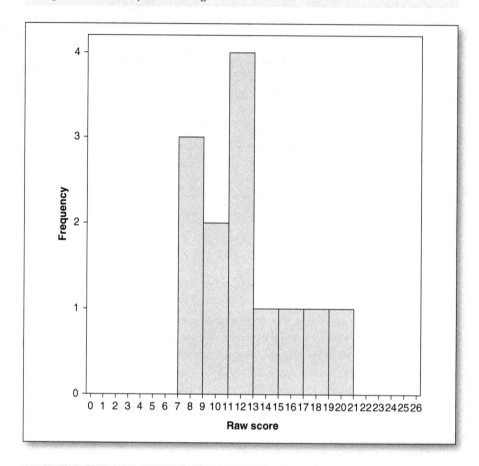

Figure 9.3 Examples of Frequency Polygons for Individual and Grouped Data

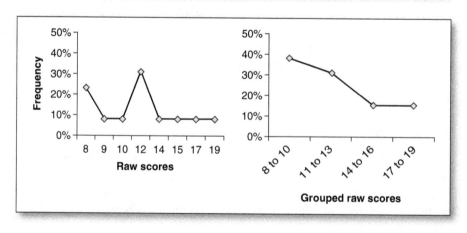

bars whose lengths are proportional to the prevalence of the value in the distribution. Since the values on a categorical variable do not represent differences in amount, the bars do not touch each other. To illustrate this, we have created a bar graph for parts of data first presented in Table 3.1 in which students' name and eye color are displayed for five students. Recall that eye color is a categorical variable in which 1 = *brown eyes*, 2 = *blue eyes*, and 3 = *green eyes*, three students have brown eyes, one has blue eyes, and one has green eyes. The simple bar graph in Figure 9.4 shows that the height of the vertical bars represents the percentage of students with each eye color.

Measures of Central Tendency

Measures of central tendency are single values used to describe the typical score in a distribution of raw scores. The most commonly reported central tendency statistics are the mode, median, and mean.

The **Mode** is the most frequently occurring value in a distribution of raw data. Moreover, the mode must be an actual value in the distribution, and distributions can have more than one mode. Consider again the frequency distribution in Table 9.1. Since the number 12 occurs most frequently (4 times, accounting for 30.77% of all scores), the mode = 12.

The **Median** is the middle value in a distribution of raw scores that is ordered from the lowest to the highest (or the highest to the lowest). This is the point in the distribution of scores where 50% of the scores are below and 50% are above; therefore, the median is equal to the 50th percentile. Unlike the mode, the median does not have to be an actual

Figure 9.4   Example of Bar Graph for Categorical Data

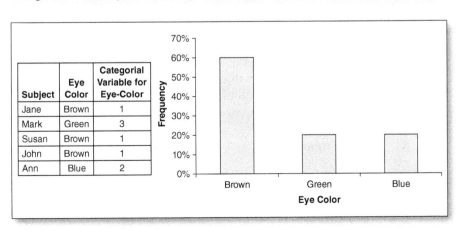

value in the distribution; if there is an even number of scores in the distribution, the median is the average of the two middle values. In the ordered distribution used in the previous example, where there is an odd number of scores, the median is the 7th number (middle number) among the 13 numbers, and so the value is 12.

Raw score distribution: 8, 8, 8, 9, 10, 12, ⌈12,⌉ 12, 12, 14, 15, 17, 19

An easy way to find the location of the median is to add 1 to the total number of data points in the distribution (13 in the case) and then to divide by 2. So, for example, the median can be found at the (13 + 1)/2 or the 7th place in the *ordered raw score distribution*.

The **Mean** is the arithmetic average of all the values in the distribution and is calculated by summing all the values in the distribution and dividing by the total number of data points. In mathematical notation, we say that the mean ($\bar{X}$, referred to as X-bar) for the raw scores represented by X_i in a distribution of sample size N is

$$\bar{X} = \frac{\sum X_i}{N}$$
(9.1)

The symbol in front of the X_i is the summation symbol (Σ), and it indicates that the value the value in the numerator is the "sum of all the values of X." The N in the denominator is the number of individual data points in the distribution. For the distribution used in the previous example, the mean is 12:

$$\frac{8+8+8+9+10+12+12+12+12+14+15+17+19}{13} = 12$$

Like the median, the mean does not have to be an actual value in the distribution. However, unlike the mode and the median, every single score in the distribution is used in the calculation of the mean. As a consequence of using every score in the distribution, the mean is most susceptible to extreme values. For example, say that an extreme value (e.g., 200) was added to the previous distribution, and the mode, median, and mean are recalculated:

Raw score distribution: 8, 8, 8, 9, 10, 12, 12, 12, 12, 14, 15, 17, 19, 200

In this case, the mode and median remain at 12, but the mean is now approximately 25. Despite being susceptible to extreme values, the mean is usually more desirable than either the mode or the median.

This is because it is more precise and contains less sample-to-sample variability than either the median or the mode. In most cases, the mean is also the most useful statistic for describing the central tendency of a distribution. However, for distributions that are *skewed*, the median is often a more appropriate choice. We will discuss this point in more detail shortly when we summarize the ways in which to describe the shape of a distribution of raw scores.

Measures of Dispersion or Spread

When describing a distribution of raw scores, it is usually not sufficient to describe the typical score using the mode, median, or mean. This is because researchers also want to know how much the values in the distribution vary from each other; that is, they want to know how much *variability* there is among the scores. As an example of why it is important for researchers to consider both measures of central tendency *and* measures of dispersion, consider the two histograms in Figure 9.5.

Simply by looking at the figure, one can see that the centers of the two distributions are at approximately the same point on the horizontal *x*-axis. As such, if one were to calculate the mean, median, or mode for each distribution, they would likely be approximately the same. However, it also appears that the distribution represented by the broken line is "skinnier" than the distribution represented by the solid line. In

Figure 9.5   Two Hypothetical Distributions

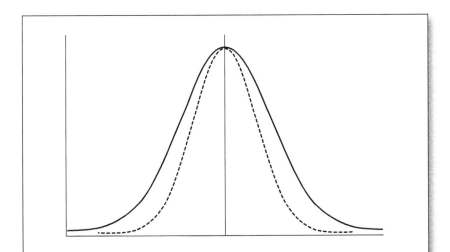

technical terms, we would conclude that the distribution represented by the broken line is *less variable* than the distribution represented by the solid line. If the researcher were only to look at the measures of central tendency, he or she would have an incomplete description of the distributions. For this reason, descriptive summaries of raw data should include measures of central tendency *and* measures of dispersion. The **measures of dispersion** are single values used to describe the amount of variability in a distribution of raw scores. The three most commonly used measures of dispersion are the range (and the interquartile range), the variance, and the standard deviation.

The **range** is the difference between the highest value and the lowest value in the distribution. This statistic is the simplest way to describe the dispersion of values in a distribution of raw data; however, it does not take every value in the distribution into account (it is based on only two data points) and is susceptible to extreme values. As such, it is rarely reported. Using the same raw score distribution as before, the range is 19 – 8 = 11:

Raw score distribution: 8, 8, 8, 9, 10, 12, 12, 12, 12, 14, 15, 17, 19

Now take the distribution where we added a value of 200; in this case, the range increases from 11 to 192 with the addition of only one data point!

The interquartile range is often used in place of the range to avoid the influence of extreme values. The **interquartile range** is the range calculated using only the middle 50% of raw scores in the distribution. However, there is some loss of information since the highest and the lowest quartiles of the raw score distribution are eliminated. When the top and bottom quartiles are removed (the grayed out values), the interquartile range is equal to 14 – 9 or 5:

Raw score distribution: 8, 8, 8, 9, 10, 12, **12**, 12, 12, 14, 15, 17, 19

In most real-life research situations, neither the range nor the interquartile range provides a satisfactory estimate of the dispersion in a distribution of raw scores.

Instead, the variance and standard deviation are the most commonly reported measures of dispersion. Unlike the range and the interquartile range, the variance and the standard deviation are calculated using every raw score in the distribution. In addition, since the variance and the standard deviation are used in more advanced statistical procedures (e.g., the analyses conducted when making inferences from a sample to a population), they are the most commonly calculated and presented measures of dispersion.

When we were describing the mean, we said that its advantage over the mode and the median is that every score in the distribution is taken into account, and it is calculated by adding up every score (ΣX) and dividing by the total number of data points (N) (Equation 9.1). It would make sense then that we would want a similar approach to calculate the amount of dispersion in a distribution; specifically, it would be helpful to know how much, on average, each data point deviates from the mean. Looking at Figure 9.5, one might speculate that, on average, the data points in the distribution represented by the solid line deviate more from the mean than those in the distribution represented by the broken line.

So as a first step and using the 13-point hypothetical distribution used in our previous examples, we can calculate how far each raw score is from the mean value of 12. To do this, we would subtract the mean $\left(\overline{X} \right)$ from every raw score (X_i) in the distribution. The technical term for the difference between the mean and a raw score $\left(X_i - \overline{X} \right)$ is called a *deviation score*. For example, for the first raw score (8), the deviation score is 8 – 12, or –4. The complete list of deviation scores are as follows:

Raw Scores	8	8	8	9	10	12	12	12	12	14	15	17	19
Deviation Scores	–4	–4	–4	–3	–2	0	0	0	0	2	3	5	7

To calculate how much, on average, each data point deviates from the mean of 12, we could calculate the average deviation score. However, this is where we run into a problem with this approach: The average deviation is zero!

$$\frac{(-4)+(-4)+(-4)+(-3)+(-2)+0+0+0+0+(2)+(3)+(5)+(7)}{13}=0$$

To avoid this problem, we square the deviation scores and then calculate the average squared deviation:

Raw Scores	8	8	8	9	10	12	12	12	12	14	15	17	19
(Deviation Score)^2	16	16	16	9	4	0	0	0	0	4	9	25	49

$$\frac{16+16+16+9+4+0+0+0+0+4+9+25+49}{13} = 11.38$$

The value 11.38 is called the *variance*, and it provides us with a single number that tells us how much, on average, each raw score value is from the mean. Formally, the **variance** is the average squared deviation of all raw scores points from the mean, and larger values indicate greater dispersion (i.e., more variability) among the raw scores in the distribution.

The variance for a distribution of scores is

$$\text{Variance} = \frac{\Sigma(\text{Raw score} - \text{Mean})^2}{\text{Sample size}} \tag{9.2}$$

However, because we squared the deviation scores, the calculated value can be difficult to relate to the original raw scores that ranged from 8 to 19. To place this average deviation score back on the original scale, we calculate the square root of the number: $\sqrt{11.38}$ or 3.37. Now, we can use this number as an estimate of how far the raw scores vary from the mean. The value 3.37 is called the standard deviation. Formally, the **standard deviation** is the square root of the variance and is an estimate of how far the raw scores vary from the mean. Again, larger values indicate more variability among the raw scores in the distribution. The standard deviation is calculated as follows:

$$\text{Standard Deviation} = \sqrt{\text{Variance}} \tag{9.3}$$

We must also note that in cases where the distribution does not include every unit (person or group) in the population, we have to make a slight adjustment to these formulas. Specifically, when using a sample to make inferences about a population, the denominator in the equations must be the sample size minus 1. In situations where the sample size is large, subtracting 1 will have only negligible effects on the values of the variance and standard deviation. Additional details about this correction can be found in more detailed statistics textbooks, such as Privitera (2012), Howell (2010), Glass and Hopkins (1996), and Shavelson (1996).

Describing the Shape of Univariate Distributions

Describing the shape of a univariate (single variable) data distribution is an important part of the analysis process. Many naturally occurring attributes are normally distributed or bell shaped. This means that there are many scores around the center of the distribution and fewer scores in the tails of the distribution. For example, the height of adult males in the United States is normally distributed—many males have heights around the typical height, and few males are extremely short or extremely tall. Technically, *the* **normal distribution** is a theoretical model for the way that many variables, including physical and behavioral variables, are distributed. The normal distribution is a unimodal (only one mode), symmetrical (both halves are symmetrical), bell-shaped histogram that shows the frequency with which values occur in the distribution. As Figure 9.6 shows, scores in the center of the distribution occur more frequently than scores in the tails of the distribution. In a perfectly normal distribution, the mean = median = mode. However, we are often faced with distributions that are not normally distributed. For example, the distribution of raw scores depicted in Figure 9.2 are not normally distributed.

One of the ways that researchers describe univariate distributions is to evaluate how *skewed* it is from the normal distribution. Compared with a normal distribution, there are more or fewer data points in one tail of a **skewed distribution**, and as a consequence of this, the mean, median, and mode are no longer equal. Moreover, since the mean is the only one in which all scores are used (see Equation 9.1), it is the one most affected by extreme scores. This is the reason why we mentioned earlier

Figure 9.6   The Normal Distribution

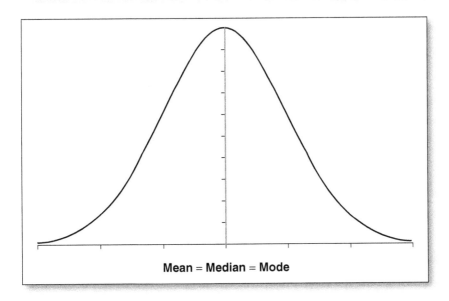

Mean = Median = Mode

that the median is a more useful estimate of central tendency when the distribution is skewed. When scores in a distribution are bunched at the lower end of the score range, the mean will be pulled toward the positive tail, and so the distribution is **positively skewed**. For example, if the majority of students had low scores on an achievement test, the distribution of scores would be positively skewed. Conversely, when scores in a distribution are bunched at the upper end of the score range, the mean will be pulled toward the negative tail, and so the distribution is **negatively skewed**. The distribution of test scores on a relatively easy test would be negatively skewed since the majority of students achieved high scores.

Figure 9.7 depicts how the mean, median, and mode are pulled away from each other when the distribution is skewed. In a positively skewed distribution, the mean is greater than the median, and the median is greater than the mode. While in a negatively skewed distribution, the mean is less than the median, and the median is less than the mode.

Positively skewed distribution: Mean > Median > Mode

Negatively skewed distribution: Mean < Median < Mode

It is important that researchers examine how the data are distributed prior to choosing a data analysis (descriptive or inferential) procedure. Most of the commonly used inferential procedures described in Chapter 10 are referred to as **parametric analyses** because they make an assumption about the shape of the data distribution (see the descriptions of t-tests and analysis of variance [ANOVA]). Conversely, inferential procedures that do not make assumptions about the shape of the data distribution are referred to as **non-parametric analyses** (see chi-square analysis, Chapter 10). We advise our readers to take the time to understand how the data they collect are distributed and to understand the consequences of violations of the data distribution assumptions for the interpretation of the results. Readers should refer to standard statistical texts, such as Privitera (2012), Howell (2010), Glass and Hopkins (1996), or Shavelson (1996), for more detailed information.

Measures of Relative Standings on the Normal Distribution

In the normal distribution depicted in Figure 9.6, we said that the mean = median = mode and that the distribution is symmetrical.

Figure 9.7 Positively and Negatively Skewed Distributions

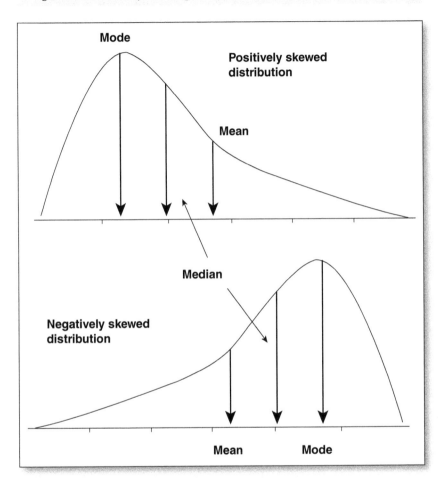

Readers will also notice that the curve is the highest closest to the mean, median, and mode (i.e., most of the scores in a normal distribution will be clustered around the center) and the lowest farther away from the center (i.e., there are fewer and fewer scores as you move away from the center of the distribution).

The median is the middle score in an ordered distribution, and since the normal distribution is symmetrical, 50% of the scores will fall below the mean, median, and mode. Moreover, since the standard deviation is the average of how the scores in a distribution deviate from the mean (also the median and mode in this case), the area under the normal curve can be divided into *standard deviation units* that contain a fixed percentage of scores. For example, when data are normally distributed, approximately 68% of scores fall between +1 and −1 standard deviations around the mean. Since the height of curve gets lower as you move away from the mean, the percentage of scores in the tails of the distribution is small; in fact, only about 0.3% of the scores in a normal distribution fall outside of ±3 standard deviation units. Figure 9.8 shows the percentage scores falling within a range of standard deviation units from the mean. It shows that in a normal distribution, approximately 68% of scores fall within ±1 standard deviation around the mean; 95% of scores fall within ±2 standard deviations from the mean; and that more than 99% of scores fall within ±3 standard deviations from the mean.

Since the proportion of scores above or below each score is known in the normal distribution, we can calculate the *relative position* of scores. For example, the percentages depicted in Figure 9.8 confirm that 50% of the scores in a normal distribution fall below the mean, median, and mode (i.e., 0.13% + 2.15% + 13.59% + 34.13% = 50%). Here, we will discuss two ways to report relative scores: z-scores and percentile ranks.

z-scores indicate how many standard deviations a raw score is away from the mean; z-scores are raw scores expressed in standard deviation units. The mean for a distribution of z-scores is 0 and the standard deviation is 1. A raw score at the mean (median and mode) of

Figure 9.8   Area Under the Curve in a Normal Distribution

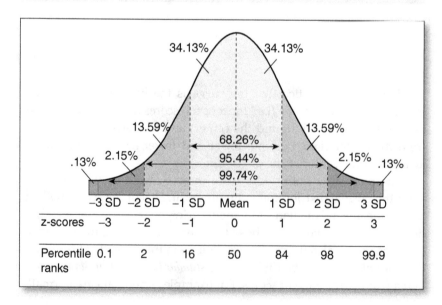

any normal distribution is 0 when expressed as a z-score. This is because a raw score at the mean (median and mode) is 0 standard deviations away from the mean. When expressed as z-scores, raw scores above the mean will be positive and raw scores below the mean will be negative. A raw score on any scale can be converted to a z-score by subtracting the mean for the distribution from it and, subsequently, dividing by the standard deviation of the distribution. The formula is as follows:

$$z\text{-score} = \frac{\text{Raw score} - \text{Mean}}{\text{Standard deviation}} \tag{9.4}$$

Consider the SAT, a standardized assessment that individuals complete when applying to undergraduate programs in the United States, which is reported on a scale ranging from 200 to 800 for each sub-test. The mean SAT score is typically 500 with a standard deviation of 100. If an individual has a scale score of 600, he or she scored above the mean, and the corresponding z-score is +1.

$$\frac{600 - 500}{100} = +1$$

If an individual has a scale score of 400, he or she scored below the mean, and so the individual's z-score will be –1.

$$\frac{400 - 500}{100} = -1$$

Percentile ranks are used to indicate the percentage of scores that fall below a particular raw score relative to a reference group. SAT scores, for example, are reported as percentile ranks in addition to scale scores. In the case of this assessment, an individual's raw score is compared with the distribution of scores in a norm group, and the relative position of the score is reported as a percentile rank. A **norm group** is a large and representative sample from the population (Chapter 5). Assuming a mean of 500 and a standard deviation of 100, an individual with an SAT score of 600 will be positioned 1 standard deviation above the mean, and his or her z-score is equal to +1. In addition, approximately 84% of scores (i.e., 0.13% + 2.15% + 13.59% + 34.13% + 34.13% ≈ 84%) fall below the individual's score; his or her percentile rank is approximately 84. An individual with an SAT score of 400 is positioned 1 standard deviation below the mean, and his or her z-score is equal to –1.

Therefore, approximately 16% of scores (i.e., 0.13% + 2.15% + 13.59% ≈ 16%) fall below the individual's score; his or her percentile rank is approximately 16. Figure 9.8 can be used to estimate the percentile rank for other scores.

❖ SUMMARIZING AND DESCRIBING RELATIONSHIPS

In the previous section, we discussed the ways that researchers summarize univariate data distributions. However, it is very often the case that researchers need to describe how the variability in one distribution is associated with the variability in another distribution. That is, they need to quantify how much and in what direction two variables vary together (i.e., covary). We first introduced the correlation coefficient in Chapters 5 and 7 as *a statistic used to quantify the relationship between two attributes,* and as we pointed out, for a relationship to exist between two variables, there must be variability in the distribution of each attribute. For example, since there is no variability on at least one attribute, it would not be possible to answer the following questions: "In a sample of students who scored 800 on the SAT Verbal test, how is college freshman GPA related to SAT Verbal scores?" or "In a sample of female college athletes, what is the relationship between gender and body image?"

In this section, we will use the hypothetical data set in Table 9.3 for 20 students who participated in a study to examine the impact of a new teaching method. As part of the study, the researcher randomly assigned students to either a treatment condition that was exposed to the new method (1) or a control condition that used the traditional teaching method (0). The condition column in Table 9.3 represents the group to which students were assigned. The researcher collected pretest scores at the start of study, and students in the treatment condition were exposed to a new teaching method. At the end of the study, the researcher collected posttest data. According to the descriptions in Chapter 8, this design is a *pretest–posttest true experimental design.* Using descriptive methods, the researcher is interested in discovering (a) whether there is a relationship between students' pre- and posttest scores and (b) whether the condition to which students were assigned is related to their posttest scores.

Using this hypothetical data set, we will present a more complete description of the types of visual representations we use to examine relationships, correlation coefficients for quantifying relationships, and simple ordinary least squares regression (i.e., prediction) models. In the descriptions that follow, we will limit our discussion to **bivariate**

Table 9.3   Hypothetical Data Set for Exploring Relationships

Person ID	Pretest Score %	Posttest Score %	Condition	Person ID	Pretest Score %	Posttest Score %	Condition
1	85	87	0	11	90	98	1
2	73	76	0	12	86	97	1
3	76	80	0	13	85	90	0
4	85	94	1	14	86	88	0
5	79	78	0	15	88	90	1
6	87	93	1	16	86	89	0
7	89	99	1	17	87	95	1
8	80	82	0	18	87	88	0
9	83	84	0	19	90	98	1
10	88	90	1	20	86	98	1

relationships (i.e., relationships between two variables) that are described and summarized. **Multivariate relationships** among more than two variables also exist but are beyond the scope of this text.

Visual Representations of Relationships

Depending on whether the data being analyzed are continuous or categorical, the researcher can use either a scatterplot or a line graph to represent relationships. Using a scatterplot as a visual representation of the relations, the researcher can examine whether there is a relationship between students' pre- and posttest scores, both continuous variables. For the second question, whether the condition to which students were assigned is related to their posttest scores, the researcher can use a line graph to look at the relationship between the continuous test score data and the categorical (dichotomous in this case) condition variable.

A **scatterplot** is a graphical representation of the strength and direction of the relationship between two continuous variables. To create a scatterplot, a pair of scores on two continuous variables must be available for each individual. In this type of graph, one continuous variable is placed on the horizontal x-axis and the other continuous variable is placed on the vertical y-axis. Each point in the scatterplot simultaneously represents the position of an individual on both the x-axis variable and the y-axis variable.

The scatterplot in Figure 9.9 representing the relationship between pre- and posttest scores from Table 9.3 shows that there appears to be a positive relationship between the two distributions of scores; students with high scores on the pretest also had high scores on the posttest. As such, the relationship would be characterized as moderately strong and positive. However, based on this information alone, the researcher cannot quantify the relationship between the two.

In addition to allowing the researcher to "eyeball" how the measures are related to each other, scatterplots allow researchers to identify non-linear relationships that do not follow a straight line, to identify restriction of range on one or both measures, and to identify extreme scores (i.e., outliers). With regard to linearity, it is important that the researcher establishes whether the relationship between the variables is linear or non-linear prior to conducting further analyses. This is because non-linear relationships are analyzed in a different and somewhat more complex way than linear relationships, and if a non-linear relationship is analyzed using procedures that assume linearity, spurious findings can result. **Restriction of range** occurs when scores on one or both of the continuous variables do not fall along the entire range of possible scores. The consequence of restriction of range is that the strength of the relationship may be underestimated. A classic example of this occurs when highly selective colleges use SAT scores to predict students' college GPA; since every student applying to a highly selective college has SAT scores in the

Figure 9.9   Scatterplot for Relationship Between Hypothetical Pre- and Posttest Scores

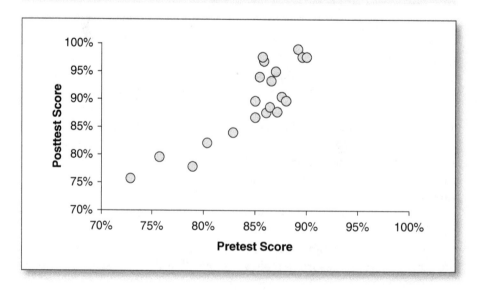

top 1% or 2%, there is no variability in the SAT measure for predicting the variability in college GPA, and the strength of the relationship is attenuated. Finally, **outliers** can have an effect on the strength and even the direction of a relationship, particularly if the sample size is small. They act like levers pulling the relationship away from the "true" relationship. For these reasons, researchers are advised to create and interpret a scatterplot of their data prior to calculating a correlation coefficient or prediction model.

A **line graph** can be used as a graphical representation of the relationship between a continuous variable and a categorical variable. To create a line graph, the averages of the continuous variable for all values of the categorical variable are calculated and subsequently plotted. The categorical variable may be represented by the lines in the graph or may be represented on the horizontal x-axis. The continuous variable will always be represented on the vertical y-axis.

For the data in Table 9.3, the mean pretest scores for the treatment and control groups, and the mean posttest scores for the treatment and control groups were calculated and plotted as lines in the graph. Figure 9.10 summarizes the pre- and posttest means by treatment and control group as a contingency table and a line graph. Looking first at the pretest scores, it appears that the treatment group students scored higher than the control group students (by 5 percentage points) prior to the implementation of the new teaching method. At the posttest, the treatment group students outperformed the control group by 11 percentage points. If all threats to the internal validity of the study were controlled, the researcher may conclude that the condition to which students were assigned is related to their posttest scores.

Correlation Coefficients for Describing Relationships

As we introduced in previous chapters, a **correlation coefficient** is a single numerical value between −1 and +1 used to indicate the strength (size) and direction (− or +) of the relationship between two variables, and provided it is calculated correctly, the information provided by the correlation coefficient will corroborate the pattern observed in the scatterplot. A negative correlation coefficient indicates that as one attribute increases, the other decreases, whereas a positive correlation indicates that as one attribute increases, so too does the other. Correlation coefficients close to zero indicate weak or no relationships. Figure 9.11 presents some simple patterns that may be observed.

As a reminder, correlation does not imply causation; attribute A could be causing attribute B, attribute B could be causing attribute A,

Figure 9.10 Line Graph for Hypothetical Pre- and Posttest Data by Group Membership

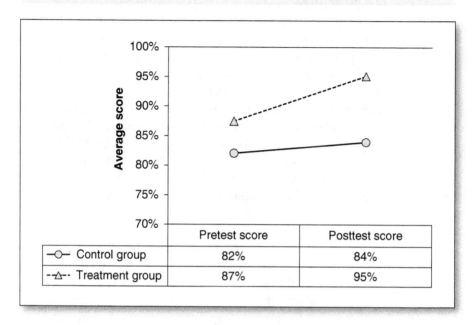

	Pretest score	Posttest score
—O— Control group	82%	84%
--△-- Treatment group	87%	95%

Figure 9.11 Hypothetical Scatterplots

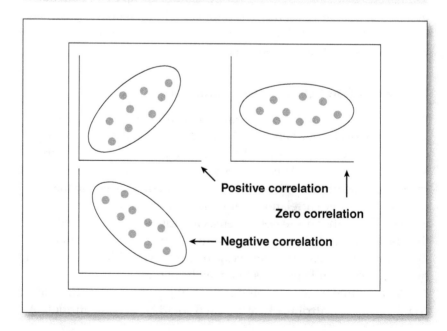

or a third attribute could be the underlying "cause" of both A and B. Various types of correlation coefficients may be calculated, depending on how the attribute is measured.

The **Pearson product–moment coefficient** is used to quantify the linear relationship between two continuous variables measured on interval or ratio scales. For example, this correlation coefficient would be used to quantify the relationship between test scores (interval-level measures) or physical measures such as height or weight (ratio-level measures). This type of correlation is commonly reported, and in a sample, it is represented by the symbol r.

Point-biserial and biserial correlation coefficients are used to quantify the relationship between a continuous variable measured on an interval or ratio scale and a dichotomous variable (i.e., one that can only have two values). The difference between two coefficients relates to what the dichotomous variable represents. A **point-biserial correlation** is used when the dichotomous variable represents a "true dichotomy," whereas a **biserial correlation** is used when the dichotomous variable is a "false dichotomy." For example, a point-biserial correlation would be used to quantify the relationship between gender (a true dichotomy where, for example, 0 = *male* and 1 = *female*) and performance on a mathematics achievement test, a continuous variable. Conversely, for example, a biserial correlation would be used to quantify the relationship between students' pass or fail status on a science course (a false dichotomy where, for example, 0 = *fail* and 1 = *pass*) and performance on a mathematics achievement test, again a continuous variable.

Phi and tetrachoric correlation coefficients are used to quantify the relationship between two dichotomous variables. If both are true dichotomies (e.g., gender and correct/incorrect), a phi correlation is used. However, if both are false dichotomies (e.g., pass/fail, minority/ non-minority status), a tetrachoric correlation is used. Finally, the **Spearman rho correlation** is used to quantify the relationship between two ordinal (ranked) variables.

The Coefficient of Determination for Describing Relationships

The coefficient of determination is calculated from the correlation between two variables and is also used to characterize bivariate and multivariate relationships. In the two-variable case, the **coefficient of determination** is the squared correlation coefficient (r^2) and indicates the proportion (or percentage if multiplied by 100) of the variability in one variable that is explained by the variability in another. If, for example, 100% of the variability in A can be explained by the variability in B, then A can be perfectly predicted from B (or vice versa). Conversely, if 0% of the variability in A can be explained by the variability in B, then A cannot be predicted from B (or vice versa). The more closely two variables are related, the closer the correlation coefficient is to −1 or +1, and the closer the coefficient of determination is to 1 or 100%. Notice that because the coefficient of determination is a squared value, it will always be positive, regardless of whether the correlation coefficient is positive or negative. Figure 9.12 presents a visual representation of how the variability in one variable may be associated with the variability in another variable. In this figure, the circles represent the variability in variables A and B, and the degree of overlap between the pairs indicates the proportion of overlap in the variance in A and B. For example, in the top left, the circles do not overlap, and so variables A and B do not share any variance. In this case, we would expect the coefficient of determination to be 0. In the bottom left example, there is a large degree of overlap between the two variables, and so the coefficient of determination would be close to 1 (or 100%). The remaining two pairs represent varying degrees of overlap between the variables.

For example, consider a correlation of +0.86 between pre and posttest scores. In this case, the value of r^2 is 0.74, and so 74% of the variability in posttest scores can be explained by the variability in pretest scores (and vice versa, although in this case, since pretest data were

Figure 9.12   Venn Diagrams Illustrating Various r^2

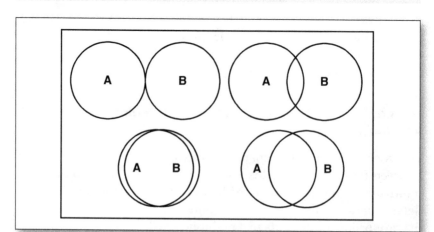

collected before posttest data, it would not be appropriate to predict pretest scores from posttest scores).

Regression Analysis for Describing Relationships and Prediction

When the scatterplot or line graph and the correlation coefficient and coefficient of determination indicate a non-zero relationship between two variables, the researcher can predict one variable from the other. If this is the case, the researcher would conduct a regression analysis. When conducting such an analysis, a mathematical model is used to predict the values of a dependent variable from the values of an independent variable. Recall from Chapter 3, that the **independent variable** is hypothesized to lead to changes in some other variable being studied, and it may be naturally occurring (e.g., pretest scores) or may be manipulated (e.g., treatment vs. control group). The **dependent variable** is hypothesized to change in response to changes in the independent variable. In regression analysis, the independent variable is sometimes called the *predictor variable*, and the dependent variable is called the *criterion variable*.

In the simplest case where a dependent variable is predicted from one independent variable, the analysis is referred to as **simple regression analysis**. When more than one independent variable is used to predict the values of the dependent variable, the analysis is referred to as **multiple regression analysis**. The independent variables may be categorical or continuous, but in the case of simple or multiple regression analysis, the dependent variable is continuous and measured on an interval or ratio scale. While it is possible to predict dichotomous outcomes using **logistic regression analysis**, our discussion here will focus on simple regression analyses used to predict a continuous dependent variable from one independent variable. We refer the reader to Privitera (2012), Howell (2010), Glass and Hopkins (1996), or Shavelson (1996) for more information about multiple regression, logistic regression, and other more advanced regression techniques.

Formally, *a regression model is a mathematical equation for the line that best describes the relationship between the dependent variable and the independent variable.* The line that best describes the relationship is placed through the scatter of data points so that the distance between each point and the line is simultaneously minimized. In statistical parlance, this type of model is referred to as an **ordinary least squares regression model** because the sum of squared deviations from each point to the line is minimized simultaneously.

Recalling your early training in high school mathematics, you may remember that the equation of a line can be written as "$Y = mx + b$"— this is in fact the mathematical form of the regression model. Equation 9.5 presents the more common form of the ordinary least squares regression model used in social science research:

$$Y = a + bX + e \quad \text{or} \quad \hat{Y} = a + bX \tag{9.5}$$

In this model, the "e" in the equation indicates that the value calculated from the equation is a predicted value that contains some amount of error but may also be indicated by placing a "hat" over the Y—that is, $\hat{Y}$. In Equation 9.5,

— $\hat{Y}$ is the predicted value of dependent variable.
— a is the intercept. This is where the regression line meets the vertical y-axis and is the predicted value of Y when X is equal to 0. Note that the intercept does not have to be a possible value in the range of Y scores.
— b is the regression coefficient or slope of the line and indicates the predicted change in the dependent variable for every one-unit change in the value of X. The larger the value of the regression coefficient, either positive or negative, the steeper the line.
— X is the value of the independent variable.

The regression equation is used to calculate the predicted values of Y; the equation is formulated based on the entire sample, and single fixed values of a and b are estimated for the entire sample. To calculate the predicted score on Y for Person A using the regression model, the researcher multiplies Person A's score on X (the independent variable) by the value of b and adds the value of a. An example using the hypothetical data in Table 9.3 follows.

Figure 9.13 recreates the scatterplot first presented in Figure 9.9 but with an added regression line that best describes the relationship between students' posttest scores (the dependent variable) and' pretest scores (the independent variables). As you can see from the plot, not all points lie on the regression line; this means that if you were to use the regression line to predict students' posttest scores from their pretest scores, some students' scores would be under-predicted, while others would be over-predicted. For this reason, there is always error in a prediction model. According to Figure 9.13, the regression equation that best describes how the pre- and posttests are related is as follows: $Y = -23.77 + 1.34X + e$. Using the legend for Equation 9.5, this equation tells us the following:

— The intercept (a) is –23.77. This is the predicted value of Y when X is equal to 0. Note that this is not a possible value in the range of Y scores (0% to 100%).

— The regression coefficient (b) is 1.34. This indicates that for every 1% increase in students' pretest scores, their posttest scores are predicted to increase by 1.34%.

By inserting values for students' pretest scores (X) into the equation, one can predict students' posttest scores (Y). For example, Student 10 has a pretest score of 88% (Table 9.3), and so his predicted posttest score ($\hat{Y}$) is –23.77+1.34(88) or 94.15%. Since Student 10's actual posttest score is only 90%, the regression model has overpredicted his score. Looking instead at Student 19 who had a pretest score of 90%, his predicted score is –23.77+1.34(90) or 96.83%. In this case, since Table 9.3 shows that Student 19 has a posttest score of 98%, the regression model under-predicted the posttest score. As

Figure 9.13   Scatterplot With Regression Line

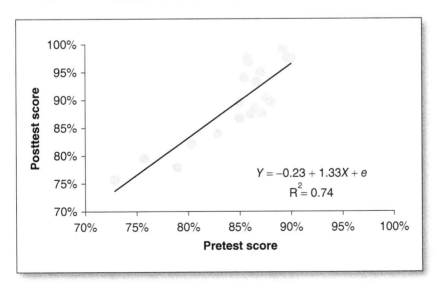

these examples illustrate, there is always error in the prediction model. On average, however, the errors in prediction will be 0. In general, the stronger the relationship between the independent and dependent variables, the less prediction error there will be in the regression equation.

When multiple regression analysis is needed because more than one independent variable is included to predict the values of the dependent variable, the regression coefficients are interpreted in the same way, with one small addition. Specifically, when there is more than one variable in the equation, the regression coefficient is the predicted change in the dependent variable (Y) for every one-unit increase in the independent variable (X_1), holding all other variables (e.g., X_2, X_3, X_4, etc.) constant.

The simple regression model we presented in Equation 9.5 is referred to as an *ordinary least squares regression model*. An assumption for using this type of regression model is that the data come from a simple random sample of individuals (see Chapter 4). When simple random sampling procedures are used, the data from one individual will not be associated with or similar to the data from any other individual; statistically, the observations are independent and each individual provides a unique piece of information. However, with other types of sampling procedures, this assumption cannot be met. In Chapter 4, we described cluster sampling as well as stratified and multistage cluster random sampling; with these types of procedures, clusters of individuals are sampled and so the assumption that the observations on individuals are independent may not be met. Specifically, individuals in a cluster (e.g., a classroom or school) will be more like other individuals in the same cluster than they are like individuals in other clusters.

Due to the lack of independence in clustered samples, ordinary least squares analysis cannot be used. Instead, more complex regression models that account for the dependence among individuals in the sample must be used. *Hierarchical linear modeling* (HLM, also referred to as multilevel modeling or linear mixed modeling) is one such analysis procedure. With this type of analysis, the clustering is accounted for in the model by a more complex error term than the one in Equation 9.5; instead of the simple "*e*" in Equation 9.5, multiple error terms are included in the model. Comprehensive coverage of HLM models is beyond the scope of this text, so we refer readers to specialized texts such as Raudenbush and Bryk (2002), Bickel (2007), and Gelman and Hill (2006).

❖ CONNECTIONS TO QUALITATIVE RESEARCH

Descriptive statistics are akin to description in the qualitative tradition. Perhaps not equivalent to "thick" description, but they serve a similar purpose by providing readers with the kind of data that allow them to visualize more clearly critical attributes of phenomena under study. Descriptive statistics can also play an important role in mixed methods studies.

Although frequency distributions are most clearly associated with the quantitative tradition, they can also help readers of qualitative or mixed methods studies get a better understanding of the nature of participants and settings. For example, while the focus of a phenomenological approach is exploring the commonalities of experiences among participants, knowing the number of participants who exhibit particular demographic characteristics (e.g., age, ethnicity, gender, etc.) may not only serve to increase understanding but also raise legitimate questions related to issues such as transferability. If multiple settings are used in a qualitative study, frequency distributions can serve to convey the range of characteristics (e.g., city, urban, and rural schools). Rather than detract from the interpretive focus of qualitative studies, the judicious use of frequency distributions can serve to support the interpretive act.

"Visual data" are a perfect way to depict qualitative data although many of us in the qualitative field focus primarily on textual data whether derived from observations or interviews. Photos, movies, and drawings can be used to describe settings in rich detail and can be perfect complements to textual data. Classic novels use not only rich verbal description but often contain drawings of scenes that further draw the reader into the story. While the visual displays described above for quantitative analysis may not have the same artistic appeal as a drawing or photograph of an audience sitting in rapt attention at a play, they serve the same purpose by allowing us to use our sensory modalities to help us understand phenomena that can be difficult to comprehend from looking at an array of numerical data even if these data are organized in a frequency distribution.

Finally, the shorthand that is used to convey important characteristics of numerical data, including Greek symbols that sometimes engender "symbol shock" to those of us who look for rich linguistic description, can become quite intelligible with just a little practice! While there is no question that the languages differ between traditions, we ask that you try to keep in mind that underlying these symbols and equations are words and sentences and that increased understanding can oftentimes accompany a translation of these symbols into sentences. For example, Equation 9.2 might be translated to the following:

> I take each raw score and subtract the mean. This gives me a set of new values. Then, I square each of these values and add them up, giving me a single number. Finally, I divide this single number by the number of participants in the study.

We make the following two observations: (1) words seem like an unwieldy way to explain this equation (which is why symbols are used) and (2) while these "words" may seem unwieldy, they do in fact correctly describe what we need to think about when we (or a computer) actually do this calculation! The point here is that no matter how esoteric an equation may seem, there are underlying concepts and processes that can be expressed in sentences to describe what is happening. By articulating these sentences, those of us who "think" qualitatively can more easily decipher seemingly opaque numerical expressions and, more important, come to understand their underlying meaning!

Correlation forms the basis for much of what we do in statistics because it indicates if variables or phenomena of interest are related in a way that goes beyond random chance. When we take the time to translate numbers and equations into words, our understanding of correlation and regression and descriptive statistics (as well as what follows regarding inferential statistics) will get a real boost! As we move to inferential statistics, it is important to remember that we are all in the business of trying to understand reality by first analyzing and then interpreting data in light of the purpose for doing a study and what we are trying to discover.

❖ CONCLUDING REMARKS

This chapter introduced readers to descriptive analyses for analyzing the data generated by quantitative research studies. Descriptive analyses are used to summarize the patterns and relationships in the raw data and are the basis for all subsequent analyses that are conducted. We want to remind readers that the data analysis phase of all research studies should begin with conducting descriptive analyses—the information provided by descriptive analyses is the starting point for all subsequent data analysis, regardless of the research objective. In Chapter 10, we describe inferential analyses and the most commonly used types of inferential tests.

DISCUSSION QUESTIONS

1. What *similarities* do you see between qualitative data analysis and the descriptive quantitative analyses described in this chapter? What about *differences*?

2. What do you find most useful about descriptive quantitative data analyses described in this chapter? What do you find limiting?

3. What do you find to be the most understandable aspects of the descriptive data analysis procedures described in this chapter? What are the most confusing?

KEY TERMS

Bar graph: a visual summary of the frequencies of values on a categorical variable. In this type of graph, the possible values of the categorical variable are placed on the horizontal x-axis, and the frequency (again, usually represented as a percentage) is represented by bars whose lengths are proportional to incidence of the value in the distribution.

Biserial correlation coefficient: a correlation coefficient used to quantify the relationship between a continuous variable measured on an interval or ratio scale and a true dichotomous variable.

Bivariate relationship: the relationship between two variables.

Coefficient of determination: is the squared correlation coefficient (r^2) and indicates the proportion (or percentage if multiplied by 100) of the variability in one variable that is explained by the variability in another.

Correlation coefficient: a single numerical value between -1 and $+1$ used to indicate the strength (size) and direction ($-$ or $+$) of the relationship between two variables. A negative correlation coefficient indicates that as one attribute increases, the other decreases, whereas a positive correlation indicates that as one attribute increases, so too does the other. Correlation coefficients close to zero indicate weak or no relationships.

Dependent variable: a variable that is hypothesized to change in response to changes in the independent variable.

Descriptive analyses: a branch of statistics in which analyses are conducted to summarize and describe data and to reveal patterns in the data that are not immediately apparent through inspecting the raw data alone.

Frequency distribution: a tabulated summary of the frequency with which each score occurs in the distribution. It can be used to summarize continuous or categorical data.

Frequency polygon: a visual summary of the data presented in a frequency distribution or grouped frequency distribution.

Grouped frequency distribution: a tabulated summary in which the raw scores are grouped into mutually exclusive intervals.

Histogram: a visual summary of the frequencies of values on a continuous variable. The possible values of the variable are placed on the horizontal x-axis, and the frequency (number or percentage) is represented by bars whose lengths are proportional to incidence of the value in the distribution.

Independent variable: a variable that is hypothesized to lead to changes in some other variable being studied. It may be naturally occurring (e.g., pretest scores) or may be manipulated (e.g., treatment vs. control group).

Interquartile range: the range calculated using only the middle 50% of raw scores in the distribution.

Line graph: a graphical representation of the relationship between a continuous variable and a categorical variable.

Logistic regression analysis: a regression analysis in which a dichotomous dependent variable is predicted from one or more independent variables.

Mean: the arithmetic average of all the values in the distribution and is calculated by summing all the values in the distribution and dividing by the total number of data points.

Measures of central tendency: single values used to describe the typical score in a distribution of raw scores. The most commonly reported central tendency statistics are the mode, the median, and the mean.

Measures of dispersion: single values used to describe the amount of variability in a distribution of raw scores. The most commonly reported measures of dispersion are the range, the interquartile range, the variance, and the standard deviation.

Median: the middle value in a distribution of raw scores that is ordered from the lowest to the highest (or the highest to the lowest).

Mode: the most frequently occurring value in a distribution of raw data.

Multiple regression analysis: a regression analysis in which a continuous dependent variable is predicted from more than one independent variable.

Multivariate relationship: the relationship between more than two variables.

Negatively skewed distribution: a distribution with more scores in the higher end of the score range. The mean will be pulled downward toward the negative tail, and so the distribution is called "negatively skewed."

Non-parametric test: types of inferential tests that do not make an assumption about the shape of the data distribution. For example, chi-square tests are non-parametric tests that make no assumption that the data are normally distributed (Chapter 10).

Norm group: a large and representative sample from the population (Chapter 5).

Normal distribution: a theoretical model for the way that many variables, including physical and behavioral variables, are distributed. It is a unimodal, symmetrical, bell-shaped histogram distribution that shows the frequency with which values occur in the distribution.

Ordinary least squares regression model: a mathematical equation for the line that best describes the relationship between the dependent variable and the independent variable(s). The line is placed through the scatter of data points so that the distance between each point and the line is simultaneously minimized.

Outliers: extreme scores or data points.

Parametric test: types of inferential tests that make an assumption about the shape of the data distribution. For example, *t*-tests and ANOVA are parametric tests that assume that the data are normally distributed (see Chapter 10).

Pearson product–moment coefficient: a correlation coefficient used to quantify the linear relationship between two continuous variables measured on interval or ratio scales.

Percentile ranks: scores used to indicate the percentage of scores that fall below a particular raw score relative to a reference group.

Phi correlation coefficient: a correlation coefficient used to quantify the relationship between two true dichotomous variables.

Point-biserial correlation coefficient: a correlation coefficient used to quantify the relationship between a continuous variable measured on an interval or ratio scale and a true dichotomous variable.

Positively skewed distribution: a distribution with more scores in the lower end of the score range. The mean will be pulled upward toward the positive tail, and so the distribution is called "positively skewed."

Range: the difference between the highest value and the lowest value in the distribution.

Restriction of range: occurs when scores on one or both of the continuous variables do not fall along the entire range of possible scores. The consequence of restriction of range is that the strength of the relationship may be underestimated.

Scatterplot: a graphical representation of the strength and direction of the relationship between two continuous variables.

Simple regression analysis: a regression analysis in which a continuous dependent variable is predicted from only one independent variable.

Skewed distribution: a distribution with more or fewer scores in the tails compared with a normal distribution.

Spearman rho correlation: a correlation coefficient used to quantify the relationship between two ordinal (ranked) variables.

Standard deviation: the square root of the variance and is an estimate of how far the raw scores vary from the mean.

Tetrachoric correlation coefficient: a correlation coefficient used to quantify the relationship between two false dichotomous variables.

Univariate distribution: a distribution of scores on one attribute or variable.

Variance: the average squared deviation of all raw scores points from the mean, and larger values indicate greater dispersion (i.e., more variability) among the raw scores in the distribution.

z-scores: scores used to indicate how many standard deviations a raw score is away from the mean. z-scores are raw scores expressed in standard deviation units and have a mean equal to 0 and a standard deviation equal to 1.

REVIEW OF PUBLISHED RESEARCH ARTICLES

In this section, we describe three published research articles that use experimental research designs. The full articles are available online at www.sagepub.com/odwyer.

Article 1 (Yang, Cho, Mathew, & Worth, 2011)

The objective of this non-experimental study was both descriptive and predictive. The authors' goals were to examine whether there were gender differences in students' effort in online versus face-to-face courses, whether team learning orientation predicted student effort in online versus face-to-face courses, and whether students' sense of classroom community predicted their effort in an online versus face-to-face class. Students' gender was used as a statistical control variable (covariate) for the second and third questions, and students' scores on the team learning orientation measure was included as an additional covariate for the third question.

Before they addressed the research questions, the authors conducted descriptive analyses and summarized the findings in Tables 1, 2, and 3 (pp. 627 and 628). Table 1 presents the sample sizes (Ns), the means, and the standard deviations for the team learning, sense of classroom community, and effort measures by gender. In addition, the descriptive results are further classified by course types—online versus face-to-face courses.

In Table 2, the Pearson correlation coefficients among the team learning, sense of classroom community, and effort measures are presented for the students in the online courses. Table 3 presents similar correlations among the variables for the students in the face-to-face courses. Beyond presenting the results from the descriptive analyses, the authors said little about the patterns in Tables 1 to 3.

Table 1 displays the means and standard deviations for each class delivery format and gender as well as the overall sample. The three measures included are student team learning orientation, five components of SOCC, and amount of effort expenditure. The descriptive statistics for the major variables for online and face-to-face courses are shown in Tables 2 and 3, along with internal consistency reliability estimates and bivariate correlations for the two subsamples. Ideally, authors should provide the audience with some interpretation of the descriptive analyses, even if the overall objective of the study is predictive or explanatory.

Article 2 (Clayton, 2011)

The purpose of this non-experimental, longitudinal trend study was both descriptive and predictive. When describing the analyses, the author stated the following:

> Quantitative methods were used and included the reporting and analysis of descriptive statistics; multiple regression analysis using SOL [the Virginia Standards of Learning test] scores as dependent variables and poverty, diversity, and teacher quality as independent variables; and correlational analysis to examine the relationship between variables. (p. 677)

Prior to addressing the research question relating to whether diversity and teacher quality predict academic performance on state-mandated tests, the author reported the racial and economic composition of the fifth graders in Virginia over time as proportions (Table 1, p. 680). Subsequently, she presented the mean ethnic diversity index over time (Table 2, p. 680). Interestingly, the author does not present any information about the variability (e.g., variance or standard deviation) of the diversity index over time. Readers are advised that it is good practice to present measures of dispersion (spread) when presenting a measure of central tendency such as the mean.

In Tables 3 and 4 (p. 681), the researcher presented the mean pass rates for reading and mathematics, respectively, for the three ethnic groups being studied by the minority and poverty status of the school. Finally, in Tables 5 and 6 (p. 682), the author presents the correlations among all the variables. According to the author, "This helped provide preliminary information about the relationships between variables prior to examining the results of the regression" (p. 681). Between pages 679 and 683, the author spent several paragraphs interpreting the results of the descriptive analyses for the reader and, therefore, provided a basis for understanding the inferential analyses that were subsequently conducted to address the central research question.

Article 3 (Porfeli, Wang, Audette, McColl, & Algozzine, 2009)

The goal of this non-experimental study was to use archival data for students in 80 elementary schools to examine the association between educational achievement and school demographics and community capital. At the start of the Results section, the authors stated the following:

> We were interested in relationships between school and student char-
> acteristics and academic achievement. We analyzed extant data from
> elementary schools in a large urban school district. We completed
> descriptive comparisons and regression analyses to illustrate and
> evaluate the extent and influence of school and student characteristics
> on academic achievement. (p. 80)

Following this statement, the authors presented the results of several descriptive analyses and dedicated several paragraphs to their
interpretation. In Table 2 (p. 81), they presented the means, standard
deviations, and range for the target variables, which were grouped
according to whether they were control variables, independent variables, or dependent variables. The authors' organization of the type
was helpful as it helped galvanize the readers' understanding of the
variables being studied.

In Table 3 (p. 82), the authors presented correlations among all the
variables included in the study and included a discussion about the
observed patterns of the relationships. Table 4 presents the comparisons of special education concentration differences for wealthy versus
poor schools with respect to community capital. Readers will notice
that the authors conducted hypothesis (significance) tests using the data
provided in Tables 3 and 4 and reported the results under the descriptive heading. Researchers will often do this in an effort to be more
concise in their presentation. We will hold off our discussion about the
results of the hypothesis tests until after Chapter 10.

Figure 1 (p. 83) is a type of descriptive graphical display called a
box-and-whisker plot. The box is the length of the interquartile range
(the middle 50% of scores in the distribution), the line inside the box
denotes the median (the point below which 50% of the scores fall), and
the length of the lines (whiskers) indicates the spread of the scores
beyond the middle 50%. Points outside the whiskers represent outliers
or extreme values in the distribution. Box-and-whisker plots are useful
for comparing the spread of scores and the symmetry of distributions
and for identifying outliers. The plots in Figure 1 indicate that poor and
wealthy differ on several characteristics.

10

Inferential Analyses for Data Generated by Quantitative Research

I n this chapter, we introduce readers to the fundamental characteristics of inferential analyses and describe the most common types of inferential analyses conducted in social science research. As with the choice of research design, the choice of data analysis procedure will depend on the purpose of the research, the research questions that are posed, and the type of data collected. Furthermore, the choice of data analysis procedures should be guided by previous research in the field. For more complete coverage of the inferential analyses described in this chapter, we refer readers to classic statistics textbooks such as

Privitera (2012), Howell (2010), Glass and Hopkins (1996), and Shavelson (1996). Also note that most of the statistical analyses we describe are seldom conducted by hand. Instead, researchers use statistical software such as SPSS, Stata, Excel, or SAS to analyze their data. Corollary software in the qualitative tradition includes NVivo, XSight, and MAXqd.

❖ FUNDAMENTALS OF INFERENTIAL STATISTICS

Inferential analyses are used by researchers to make inferences about the attributes or characteristics in a population using a sample from that population. When conducting inferential analyses, researchers use the attributes or characteristics measured in a sample (*sample statistics*) to make inferences about the attributes or characteristics in a population (*population parameters*). Moreover, inferential statistics rely on probability theory to either estimate the characteristics of the population (point or interval estimation) or test specific hypotheses about the population (hypothesis testing) using data collected in the sample.

Figure 10.1   Branches of Inferential Analyses

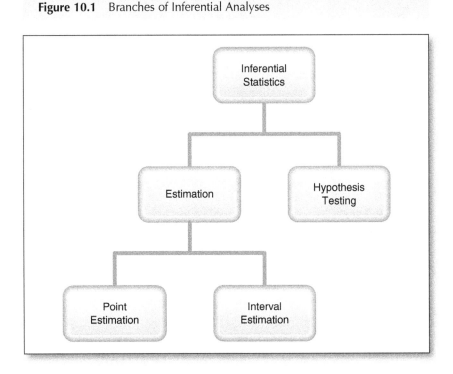

Recall from Chapter 4 that *a* **population** includes all individuals or groups that possess the characteristic that the research aims to investigate and a **sample** is a subset of units (e.g., individuals, groups of individuals) from that population. Also in Chapter 4, we described several ways in which a sample can be selected from a population; non-probability (non-random) and probability (random) sampling procedures. While non-probability sampling procedures can be useful in some situations, probability sampling procedures that provide representative samples from the population are assumed when conducting inferential analyses. Specifically, since population characteristics are generally unknown, there is always a chance that the inferences made from a single sample will be incorrect. However, without a representative sample from the population, the probability theory underlying inferential statistics will not hold, and researchers risk the possibility of making false inferences about the population.

In describing exactly *how* inferential analyses work, some fundamental concepts need to be introduced. These include sampling distributions, point and interval estimation, hypothesis testing, and statistical decisions and error. Once we have described these concepts, we will discuss their application in commonly used inferential tests (i.e., *t*-tests for comparing means and for testing correlation and regression coefficients, ANOVA, and chi-square analysis).

Sample Statistics and Population Parameters

When using inferential statistics, the aim is to make inferences from a sample to a population; data are collected from a sample, summary statistics are calculated (e.g., measures of central tendency and measures of dispersion), and these statistics are used to make inferences about unknowns in the population. Summary statistics that are calculated using sample data are referred to as **sample statistics**, and these are used to make inferences about unknown **population parameters**. Every sample statistic (e.g., mean, standard deviation, correlation coefficient, etc.) has a corresponding population parameter; by convention, sample statistics are represented using letters from the Roman alphabet, and population parameters are represented using Greek letters. For example, the sample statistic for the standard deviation is represented by the letter *s*, and its corresponding population parameter is σ (sigma). Table 10.1 summarizes the most frequently used sample statistics and corresponding population parameters.

For all but the variance and standard deviation, population parameters are calculated in the same way as the sample statistics. As we

Table 10.1   Sample Statistics and Corresponding Population Parameters

	Sample Statistic	Population Parameter
Mean	$\overline{X}$	μ (mu)
Variance	s^2	σ^2 (sigma-squared)
Standard Deviation	s	σ (sigma)
Correlation Coefficient	r	ρ (rho)
Regression Coefficient	b	β (beta)

described in Chapter 9, a slight adjustment to the variance and standard deviation formulas (Equations 9.2 and 9.3) is needed when sample data are used; the denominator in both equations is replaced by the sample size minus 1. As a reminder, the denominator in both equations should be replaced by the sample size minus 1. When the sample size is large, this will have only negligible effects.

Sampling Distributions

Sampling distributions play a central role in inferential analyses. A **sampling distribution** is a theoretical distribution of sample statistics created from an infinite number of probability samples of a particular size drawn from a single population. For example, say that the size of the population of 12th-grade students in the United States is 1,000,000 and that researchers are interested in the average SAT mathematics score in this population. Unless researchers have the resources (e.g., access, time, money) to measure every 12th grader in the population, the true population parameter (i.e., mean SAT mathematics score) cannot be known. We denote this unknown population mean as μ (mu), the population parameter. Note that we are using the mean as an example of a sample statistic here, however, we could have selected any sample statistic (e.g., the median, the correlation coefficient, or the regression coefficient) to illustrate the concept of the sampling distribution.

Now, say that the researcher selects a random sample (Sample 1) of 1,000 12th graders from the population and calculates the mean SAT mathematics score; this mean is a sample statistic, and we denote it as $\overline{X}_1$ for Sample 1. If the researcher chooses another random sample of 1,000 students (Sample 2) and calculates the mean performance, this new sample statistic will be $\overline{X}_2$. Even with random sampling, by chance $\bar{X}_2$ will not be exactly the same as $\bar{X}_1$, and neither sample statistic will be the exact same as the unknown population parameter, μ. Likewise, $\bar{X}_3$ and $\bar{X}_4$, and so on, will not be identical to each other or to μ; some sample means will be higher than the population mean, and some will be lower. In fact, even though random sampling procedures are used, the value of the sample statistic, the mean in this case, varies from sample to sample because of *random sampling error* (Chapter 4). The result is a distribution of sample statistics, and this distribution is called the *sampling distribution*.

Since we used the mean as the sample statistic in this case, the sampling distribution is referred to as the *sampling distribution of the mean*. If we had illustrated the concept using the median, the sampling distribution would be referred to as the *sampling distribution of the median*. Likewise, the sampling distributions for the correlation coefficient and regression coefficient are referred to as the *sampling distributions of the correlation coefficient* and the *sampling distributions of the regression coefficient*, respectively.

The sampling distribution is typically characterized by its mean and standard deviation. First, if a very large number of random samples of a particular size are selected from the population, the *mean of all the sample statistics* equals the population parameter. For example, if 100,000 samples of 1,000 12th graders were selected from the population, the mean of the means would equal the population mean SAT score, μ. Second, the standard deviation of the sampling distribution indicates the amount of sample-to-sample variability we can expect, and the technical term for this is the **standard error** of the sampling distribution. In the case of the mean, the standard deviation of the sampling distribution of the mean is referred to as the standard error of the mean. The larger the standard error, the more sampling error there is in the sampling distribution. Sampling distributions are used in estimation and hypothesis testing, and so we recommend that readers take some time to develop a solid understanding of this concept before moving ahead.

Point and Interval Estimation

As we mentioned at that start of this chapter, inferential statistics encompass estimation and hypothesis testing (Figure 10.1). Within the estimation branch, researchers can use either a specific number (point estimation) to estimate the population characteristics or a range of numbers (interval estimation) within which they expect the population parameter to fall.

Point estimation involves the calculation of a single number to estimate the population parameter. For example, when illustrating the concept of the sampling distribution, we used the mean of a distribution of sample statistics to estimate the population mean, μ. However, due to sampling error, we expect the sample means to vary from sample to sample, and so point estimates of population parameters can often be incorrect.

As an alternative, **interval estimation** uses a confidence interval that ranges from a lower confidence limit to an upper confidence limit around a sample statistic ($\overline{X}$, r, b, etc.) and has a known probability of including the population parameter. By convention, researchers create 95% confidence intervals, with which they are willing to be wrong 5% of the time, or 99% confidence intervals, where they are willing to be wrong 1% of the time. Although it may seem counterintuitive, the 99% confidence interval is wider than the 95% confidence interval: Because there is a lower probability of being incorrect (1% chance with a 99% confidence interval compared with a 5% chance with a 95% confidence interval), the interval must be wider. With a 95% confidence interval, over an infinite number of repeated random samples from the population, the population parameter will fall within the interval around the sample statistic 95% of the time. Likewise, for a 99% confidence interval, over an infinite number of repeated random samples from the population, the population parameter is expected to fall within the interval around the sample statistic 99% of the time.

It is important to note that a confidence interval is always placed around a sample statistic, not around a population parameter. Specifically, confidence intervals are created by subtracting and adding a specified amount of error to the value of the sample statistic: The lower confidence limit is (sample statistic − specified amount of error), and the upper confidence limit is (sample statistic + specified amount of error); together these are written as (sample statistic ± specified amount of error). Once the lower and upper confidence limits are calculated, the researcher subsequently checks whether the population parameter falls within the interval around the sample statistic:

$$\text{(Sample statistic} - \text{Error)} \leq \text{Population parameter} \leq$$
$$\text{(Sample statistic} + \text{Error)}$$

In the case where the sample mean ($\overline{X}$) is used to estimate the population parameter (μ), the confidence interval would be:

$$\bar{X} - \text{Error} \le \mu \le \bar{X} + \text{Error}$$

− Error		Is μ in		+ Error	
┠──────	$\bar{X}$	the	$\bar{X}$	──────┨	
		interval?			
Lower				Upper	
Confidence				Confidence	
Limit				Limit	

For additional details about calculating confidence intervals, see Privitera (2012), Howell (2010), Glass and Hopkins (1996), or Shavelson (1996).

Hypothesis Testing

Hypothesis testing (aka significance testing) is a branch of statistics in which the researcher states statistical hypotheses and subsequently tests whether the collected data support those hypotheses. Statistical hypotheses are central to hypothesis testing and are referred to as the *null hypothesis* and the *alternative hypothesis*. **The null hypothesis, H_0,** is a statistical statement about a population parameter that is assumed to be true. By convention, H_0 states that no difference or relationship exists in the population and this hypothesis is tested using the collected data. In fact, for this reason, many statistical texts refer to hypothesis testing as *null hypothesis significance testing*.

The alternative hypothesis, H_1, is also a statistical statement about a population parameter, but in this case, it states that the population parameter is some value other than the value stated in H_0. Also by convention, we state H_0 and H_1 together, and since they both cannot be true, the collected data can either support H_0 as being tenable or support H_1 as being tenable.

One could actually draw an analogy between null hypothesis significance testing and a criminal trial: At the start of a trial, jurors are instructed to assume that the accused party is innocent until proven guilty. In the case of hypothesis testing, we assume H_0 to be true until we have evidence to support any other conclusion.

One point to note here is that we don't ever "prove" the null hypothesis; recalling our description of the sampling distribution and sampling error, there is always a chance that we are wrong in our statistical conclusions. Instead, we estimate the probability of observing differences or relationships as large or larger by chance if the null hypothesis is true, and we subsequently make a decision as to whether we *reject* or *fail to reject* the H_0. The probability of observing differences or relationships of the size observed or larger by chance if the null hypothesis is true is referred to as the *p*-value.

To illustrate how null and alternative hypotheses are written, consider a high school administrative team that wishes to know whether the mean SAT mathematics score of 545 ($\bar{X}$) in its district is different from the national average of 500 (μ) for all SAT test-takers in the United States. In words, the null hypothesis states that there is no difference and that the mean for the high school is the same as the population mean. The alternative hypothesis states that the mean for the high school is not the same as the population mean of 500, and that the sample with a mean of 545 was drawn from a population that does not have a mean of 500. This type of inferential test is called a *one-sample t-test*, and it will be discussed in more detail in the section that describes the most commonly used inferential tests. In statistical notation, the null and alternative hypotheses are written, respectively, as follows:

$$H_0: \mu = 500$$

$$H_1: \mu \neq 500$$

Notice that H_0 and H_1 are written in population parameters and that the sample statistic ($\bar{X} = 545$) is not included in either. Under the assumption that H_0 is true, if the probability of observing a sample mean of 545 or larger by chance is small (i.e., the *p*-value is small), we conclude that it is unlikely that the sample with a mean of 545 belongs to the population with a mean of 500. Therefore, we fail to retain H_0 and conclude that there is a statistically significant difference between the sample mean of 545 and the population mean of 500. Conversely, if the probability of observing a sample mean of 545 or larger by chance is large (i.e., the *p*-value is large), we conclude that it is likely that the sample with a mean of 545 belongs to the population with a mean of 500. Therefore, we retain H_0 and conclude that there is no statistically significant difference between the sample mean of 545 and the population mean of 500.

To illustrate further, say the administrative team wanted to know whether the mean SAT mathematics scores for males ($\bar{X}_M$) is different from the mean SAT mathematics scores for females ($\bar{X}_F$). In this case, the null hypothesis states that there is no difference between the population means for males and females, $\mu_M - \mu_F = 0$; that is, the population parameter $= 0$. The null and alternative hypotheses are written, respectively, as follows:

$$H_0: \mu_M = \mu_F \quad \text{or} \quad H_0: \mu_M - \mu_F = 0$$

$$H_1: \mu_M \neq \mu_F \quad \text{or} \quad H_1: \mu_M - \mu_F \neq 0$$

This type of test is called an *independent samples t-test*, and it will be discussed in more detail in the section that describes the most commonly used inferential tests. Again, under the assumption that H_0 is true, if the probability of observing a difference of the size observed or larger between males and females by chance is small, we fail to retain H_0 and conclude that there is a statistically significant difference between the scores for males and females. If the probability of observing a difference of the size observed or larger between males and females by chance is large, we retain H_0 and conclude that there is no statistically significant difference between the scores for males and females.

Both these examples used the mean ($\overline{X}$) as the sample statistic to estimate the population parameter (μ). However, the same procedures are used with other sample statistics and population parameters, such as the correlation sample statistic, r, to estimate the population parameter ρ (rho) or the regression coefficient sample statistic, b, to estimate the population parameter β (beta). In addition, both examples are non-directional; that is, H_0 states that there is no difference and H_1 states that there is a difference, but neither states that one is less than/greater than the other. *A* **non-directional hypothesis** does not specify the direction of the difference or relationship. These are also referred to as *two-tailed hypotheses*. Conversely, directional hypotheses can be used when there is prior evidence of the directionality of the difference. Specifically, **directional hypotheses** specify the direction of the difference or relationship. These are also referred to as *one-tailed hypotheses*.

Statistical Decisions, Error, and Power

Hypothesis testing involves estimating the probability of observing the differences or relationships of the size observed or larger by chance if the null hypothesis is true and subsequently making a decision as to whether to reject or fail to reject the H_0. If the probability of is small when H_0 is true, we fail to retain H_0 and conclude that there is a statistically significant difference or relationship. If the probability is large when H_0 is true, we retain H_0 and conclude that there is no statistically significant difference or relationship. The next obvious question then is "What exactly constitutes small versus large probabilities?"

By convention, the cutoff probabilities of .05 (5%) or .01 (1%) are used to decide whether the differences or relationships observed or larger are likely or unlikely if H_0 is true. These values are referred to as the *significance* or *alpha (α) level* and, as a rule, are set before any analyses are conducted. Choosing an α level of .05 means that the sample statistic of the size observed or larger (e.g., $\bar{X}$, r, b, etc.) would be expected to occur by chance less than 5% of the time if the null hypothesis were true. An α level of .01 is more conservative since the sample statistic would be expected to occur by chance less than 1% of the time if the null hypothesis were true. Therefore, if the probability of observing a sample statistic of the size observed or larger is less than .05 (or .01), we fail to retain H_0 and conclude that there is a statistically significant difference between the sample statistic and the population parameter. Conversely, and again assuming that H_0 is true, if the probability of observing a sample statistic of the size observed or larger is greater than or equal to .05 (or .01), we retain H_0 and conclude that there is no statistically significant difference between the sample statistic and the population parameter.

Due to sampling error, there is always a possibility that the researcher will make a false-positive error (reject a true H_0) or a false-negative error (fail to reject a true H_0). We refer to these as Type I and Type II errors, respectively; Table 10.2 shows the decisions that are possible when conducting hypothesis testing. By convention, researchers are more concerned with minimizing the probability of **Type I errors** (i.e., the probability of rejecting a true H_0 when in truth there is no difference or relationship) than they are with minimizing the probability of **Type II errors** (i.e., the probability of failing to reject a true H_0 when in truth there is a difference or relationship). Therefore, the **alpha (α)** levels used as cutoff points (.05 or .01) represent the risk that the researcher is willing to take of making a Type I (false positive) error, and the choice of setting the α level to .05 or .01 will depend on the severity of the consequences of making such an error. The probability of making a Type II (false negative) error is referred to as **beta (β)**.

The probabilities of making Type I and Type II errors are related to each other in that they cannot be reduced simultaneously. Since both types of errors cannot be reduced simultaneously, researchers aim to optimize the probability of making each type of error. By convention, researchers minimize the false-positive (Type I) error rate (α) and then choose a sample size that will let them optimize their analyses. Since β is the probability of making a false-negative (Type II) error, $1 - \beta$ is the probability of correctly rejecting a false null hypothesis—this is **statistical power** (first mentioned in Chapter 4 in relation to sample size). Typically, researchers aim to optimize the size of their samples such that power is equal to .80; this means that β is .20, or four times the size of α, the Type I error rate. In Chapter 4, we said that researchers should

Table 10.2   Decisions Possible When Conducting Hypothesis Testing

		True Circumstances in the Population	
		H_0 Is True in the Population	H_0 Is False in the Population
Observed circumstances in the sample	Sample data indicates that the researcher should fail to reject H_0	Correct decision $(1-\alpha)$	Type II error (β) False-negative error
	Sample data indicates that the researcher should reject H_0	Type I error (α) False-positive error	Correct decision $(1-\beta)$

aim for sample sizes that are large enough to allow them to "see" the differences or relationships that exist, and to provide generalizable findings. However, sample sizes should not be so large that they waste resources and provide results that are not practically important. The issue with large samples is that they can produce results that are statistically significant but not practically important; that is, even very small differences or relationships may appear statistically significant when sample sizes are large. To avoid this, researchers should always conduct a statistical power analysis prior to starting their study so that their sample size can be optimized, and they should discuss the practical significance of their findings. Readers are referred to Privitera (2012), Howell (2010), Glass and Hopkins (1996), or Shavelson (1996) for more information about statistical power.

A common way in which researchers report on the practical significance of their findings is to calculate **effect size** indicators that convey the size of the difference or the magnitude of the relationship observed. Depending on whether researchers are testing differences between means or the strength of relationships, they may calculate effect sizes that are standardized differences between means (e.g., Cohen's *d*, Hedges's *g*, or Glass's Δ [delta]), or they may calculate effect sizes based on the percentage of variance explained (e.g., omega-squared [ω^2] or eta-squared [η^2]). By reporting effect size indicators in addition to statistical significance, researchers can avoid overinterpreting small but significant differences and relationships and can more easily convey the practical importance of the findings to their audience.

❖ SUMMARY OF THE STEPS FOR INTERVAL ESTIMATION AND HYPOTHESIS TESTING

The following is a summary of the steps involved in conducting hypothesis testing and interval estimation:

a. Decide whether the test will be non-directional or directional.

b. State the statistical hypotheses (H_0 and H_1) to be tested.

c. Specify the degree of risk of making a Type I error (α) you will accept—usually .05 or .01.

d. Using the data collected, calculate the sample statistic ($\bar{X}, r, b$, etc.).

e. Calculate the upper and lower confidence limits around the sample statistic:

(Sample statistic – Error) ≤ Population parameter
≤ (Sample statistic + Error).

f. Test whether the population parameter falls within the interval around the sample statistic, and draw a conclusion:

- If the population parameter falls within the interval, the researcher can conclude that over all possible randomly sampled means, the probability is .95 (or .99) that the population mean falls within the interval around the sample statistic.

- If the population parameter does not fall within the interval, the researcher can conclude that over all possible randomly sampled means, the probability is .95 (or .99) that the population mean does not falls within the interval around the sample statistic.

g. Find the probability (p-value) of obtaining the sample statistic of the size observed or larger ($\bar{X}, r, b$, etc.) if H_0 is true, and use the following decision rules:

- Fail to reject H_0 if $p \geq \alpha$, and conclude that the finding is not statistically significant.

- Reject H_0 if $p < \alpha$, and conclude that the finding is statistically significant.

h. State the statistical decision using appropriate technical language, and interpret the findings in the context within which the hypothesis was stated.

As you will see in the following section, these steps are common across many different types of inferential tests.

❖ COMMONLY USED INFERENTIAL TESTS

Depending on the research questions posed at the outset of a study, the researcher can choose from several different types of inferential tests. Here, we will discuss some of the most common tests used by linking them to the types of research questions that researchers might pose. The tests we discuss here are limited to those that are easily accessible to an audience that is new to data analysis in the quantitative tradition. For additional statistical tests, we refer readers to texts devoted to statistical analysis, such as Privitera (2012), Howell (2010), Glass and Hopkins (1996), or Shavelson (1996). Table 10.3 summarizes the number and type of dependent and independent variables required for each type of inferential test.

t-Tests for Comparing Means

t-**Tests** are types of inferential tests used to compare two means and are named for the type of sampling distribution used to estimate the probability of observing the sample statistic by chance if the null hypothesis is true. Specifically, the **t-distribution** is the sampling distribution when the null hypothesis is true, and there is one t-distribution for every sample size. When conducting a *t*-test, a *t*-value is calculated to represent the difference between the sample statistic and the population parameter in standard error of the mean units (i.e., in standard deviation units of the sampling distribution), with larger values of *t* indicating larger differences (in either the positive or the negative direction) between the two. Larger values of *t* are associated with smaller probabilities of observing the sample statistic of the size observed or larger by chance if the null hypothesis is true and, as such, result in the rejection of H_0 and the conclusion that the findings are statistically significant. In general, values of *t* larger than approximately ±2 will result in statistical significance. Various types of *t*-tests are commonly used in social science research.

Depending on the research question, researchers can choose between three different forms of the test: (1) the one-sample *t*-test, (2) the independent samples *t*-test, and (3) the paired samples *t*-test. For each type, the dependent variable should be continuous (i.e., quantitative) and should be measured on an interval or ratio scale, and in the

Table 10.3   The Number and Type of Dependent and Independent Variable for Each Type of Inferential Test

Inferential Test	Dependent Variable		Independent Variable	
	Number	Data Type	Number	Data Type
Parametric				
t-Test	1	Continuous, measured on an interval or ratio scale	1	Categorical, 2 categories
One-way ANOVA	1	Continuous, measured on an interval or ratio scale	1	Categorical, 2+ categories
Factorial ANOVA	1	Continuous, measured on an interval or ratio scale	2+	Categorical, each with 2+ categories
Pearson correlation	1	Continuous, measured on an interval or ratio scale	1	Continuous, measured on an interval or ratio scale
Ordinary least squares regression	1	Continuous, measured on an interval or ratio scale	1+	May be categorical or continuous
Non-parametric				
Chi-squared goodness of fit	1	Frequencies or percentages	1	Categorical, 2+ categories
Chi-squared test of independence	1	Frequencies or percentages	2	Categorical, 2+ categories

Note: ANOVA, analysis of variance.

case of the independent and paired samples t-tests, the independent variable should be a categorical variable with two categories.

The **one-sample t-test** is used to test the significance of the difference between a sample mean ($\bar{X}$) and a known population mean (μ). The question is "Does the sample mean differ significantly from a known population mean?" In the section "Hypothesis Testing" earlier in this chapter we used a one-sample t-test to illustrate the concept.

We said that a high school administrative team wanted to know whether the mean SAT mathematics score of 545 ($\bar{X}$) was statistically significantly different from the national average of 500 (μ) for all SAT test-takers in the United States. In this case, the dependent variable (SAT scores) is continuous and is measured on an interval scale, and the null hypotheses stated that there is no difference between the sample mean of 545 and the population mean of 500:

$$H_0: \mu = 500$$

$$H_1: \mu \neq 500$$

The more general form of the statistical hypotheses for the one-sample t-test is as follows:

$$H_0: \mu = \text{Test value}$$

$$H_1: \mu \neq \text{Test value}$$

Following the guidelines in the previous section, we calculate the confidence interval around the sample statistic and test whether the population parameter falls within the interval, and we calculate the probability of observing a sample mean as large or larger by chance if H_0 is true. Subsequently, we compare this probability with the α level set at the start of the study. Finally, the decision rules outlined in the previous section are used to decide whether the observed sample mean ($\bar{X}$) is statistically significantly different from the known population mean (μ).

The **independent samples *t-test*** is used to test the significance of the difference between the sample means for two independent groups. The question is "Does the sample mean for Group 1 ($\bar{X}_1$) differ significantly from the sample mean for Group 2 ($\bar{X}_2$)?" As the name of the test suggests, the individuals in the two groups must be independent; an individual can be in one group only. Again, in the section "Hypothesis Testing" earlier in this chapter, we used the example where a high school administrative team wants to know whether the mean SAT mathematics score for males ($\bar{X}_M$) is different from the mean SAT mathematics score for females ($\bar{X}_F$). In this case, the dependent variable (SAT scores) is continuous and is measured on an interval scale, and the independent variable (group membership) is a categorical variable with two categories (e.g., male = 0 and female = 1). For this example, the null hypothesis states that there is no difference between the population means for males and females: $\mu_M - \mu_F = 0$, and the population parameter = 0. The null and alternative hypotheses are stated, respectively, as follows:

$$H_0: \mu_M = \mu_F \quad \text{or} \quad H_0: \mu_M - \mu_F = 0$$

$$H_1: \mu_M \neq \mu_F \quad \text{or} \quad H_1: \mu_M - \mu_F \neq 0$$

The more general form of the statistical hypotheses for the independent samples t-test is as follows:

$$H_0: \mu_1 = \mu_2 \quad \text{or} \quad H_0: \mu_1 - \mu_2 = 0$$

$$H_1: \mu_1 \neq \mu_2 \quad \text{or} \quad H_1: \mu_1 - \mu_2 \neq 0$$

Again, following the guidelines in the previous section, we calculate the confidence interval around the sample mean difference $(\overline{X}_1 - \overline{X}_2)$ and test whether the population parameter under the null hypothesis $(\mu_1 - \mu_2 = 0)$ falls within the interval. We also calculate the probability of observing a sample mean difference of the size observed or larger by chance if H_0 is true and subsequently compare this probability with the α level set at the start of the study. Finally, the decision rules outlined in the previous section are used to decide whether the observed sample mean difference $(\overline{X}_1 - \overline{X}_2)$ is statistically significantly different from the population mean difference under the null hypothesis $(\mu_1 - \mu_2 = 0)$.

The **dependent samples t-test** is a special case of the t-test used to test the significance of the differences between the sample means in two groups whose members are the same or are dependent in some way. The typical situation where this type of t-test is used is when individuals are measured at two time points, and the question is "Does the sample mean for a group at Time 1 $(\overline{X}_{T1})$ differ significantly from the sample mean for the same group at Time 2 $(\overline{X}_{T2})$?" For this type of t-test, the dependent variable is continuous and is measured on an interval or ratio scale, and the independent variable is categorical, with at most two categories (e.g., Time 1 and Time 2). In addition, the relationship between the scores at Times 1 and 2 is taken into account in the calculation of the t-values and probabilities. The null hypothesis states that there is no difference between the population means for the groups at Time 1 and Time 2: $\mu_1 - \mu_2 = 0$, and the population parameter = 0. The general form of the statistical hypotheses for the dependent samples t-test is as follows:

$$H_0: \mu_{T1} = \mu_{T2} \quad \text{or} \quad H_0: \mu_{T1} - \mu_{T2} = 0$$

$$H_1: \mu_{T1} \neq \mu_{T2} \quad \text{or} \quad H_1: \mu_{T1} - \mu_{T2} \neq 0$$

Again, we calculate the confidence interval around the sample mean difference $\left(\bar{X}_{T1} - \bar{X}_{T2}\right)$ and test whether the population parameter under the null hypothesis ($\mu_{T1} - \mu_{T2} = 0$) falls within the interval. We also calculate the probability of observing a sample mean difference of the size observed or larger by chance if H_0 is true and subsequently compare this probability with the α level set at the start of the study. Finally, the decision rules outlined in the previous section are used to decide whether the observed sample mean difference $\left(\bar{X}_{T1} - \bar{X}_{T2}\right)$ is statistically significantly different from the population mean difference under the null hypothesis ($\mu_{T1} - \mu_{T2} = 0$).

t-Tests for Correlation Coefficients

t-Tests and t-distributions are also used to test the significance of correlation coefficients. The question is "Is the correlation coefficient observed in the sample significantly different from zero?" In the section "The Coefficient of Determination for Describing Relationships" (Chapter 9), we presented an example where the correlation ($r_{\text{pre-post}}$) between pre- and posttest scores was +0.86. Although this coefficient is close to the maximum possible value of 1, we would check whether it is statistically significantly different from 0. That is, we want to test whether a correlation of 0.86 or larger could have occurred by chance if the true correlation in the population was 0. As such, the null and alternative hypotheses are written, respectively, as follows:

$$H_0: \rho_{\text{pre-post}} = 0$$

$$H_1: \rho_{\text{pre-post}} \neq 0$$

The more general form of the statistical hypotheses for testing whether a correlation coefficient is statistically significantly different from 0 is as follows:

$$H_0: \rho_{xy} = 0$$

$$H_1: \rho_{xy} \neq 0$$

Again, we can follow the guidelines in the previous section to make a statistical decision as to whether the correlation is statistically significantly different from 0. We calculate the confidence interval around the sample correlation coefficient ($r_{\text{pre-post}}$) and test whether the population correlation coefficient under the null hypothesis ($\rho_{\text{pre-post}} = 0$) falls within the interval. We also calculate the probability of observing the correlation coefficient of the size observed or larger by chance if H_0 is true and subsequently compare this probability with the α level set at the start of the study. The decision rules outlined in the previous section are used to decide whether the observed correlation coefficient ($r_{\text{pre-post}}$) is statistically significantly different from the population parameter under the null hypothesis ($\rho_{\text{pre-post}} = 0$).

t-Test for Regression Coefficients

Likewise, *t*-tests and *t*-distributions are used to test the significance of regression coefficients. The question is "Is the regression coefficient observed in the sample significantly different from zero?" Recall that a simple regression model is the mathematical equation for the line that best describes the relationship between the dependent variable and the independent variable and that the the following equation (Equation 9.4) is the common form of the regression model used in social science research:

$$\hat{Y} = a + bX \text{, alternatively, } Y = a + bX + e$$

The regression equation is used to calculate the predicted values of Y; the equation is formulated based on the entire sample, and single, fixed values of a and b are estimated for the entire sample.

Once the regression model has been formulated, we typically want to know whether the regression coefficient (b) is statistically significantly different from 0. That is, we want to test whether the regression coefficient of the size observed or larger could have occurred by chance if the true coefficient in the population was 0. The null and alternative hypotheses are written, respectively, using the population regression coefficient β as follows:

$$H_0: \beta = 0$$
$$H_1: \beta \neq 0$$

As an example, we will use the regression equation we presented in the section "Regression Analysis for Describing Relationships and Prediction" (Chapter 9) for predicting students' posttest scores from their pretest scores:

$$Y = -23.77 + 1.34X + e$$

This equation tells us that the intercept ($a = -23.77$) is the predicted value of Y when the dependent variable is equal to 0, and the regression coefficient (b = 1.34) indicates that for every 1% increase in students' pretest scores, their posttest scores are predicted to increase by 1.34%. Using the guidelines in the previous section, we can make a statistical decision as to whether the regression coefficient observed in the sample (b = 1.34) is statistically significantly different from the population regression coefficient under the null hypothesis (β = 0).

To test the significance of the regression coefficient, we calculate the confidence interval around the sample regression coefficient (b) and test whether the population parameter under the null hypothesis (β = 0) falls within the interval. We also calculate the probability of observing the regression coefficient of the size observed or larger by chance if H_0 is true and subsequently compare this probability with the α level set at the start of the study. The decision rules outlined in the previous section are used to decide whether the observed regression coefficient (b) is statistically significantly different from the population parameter under the null hypothesis (β = 0).

One-Way Analysis of Variance

The one-way analysis of variance (**one-way ANOVA**) is used to test the significance of the difference between the means of two or more groups. The question is "Is there a statistically significant difference between the means of the two or more groups?" Unlike *t*-tests, which are used to test the significance of the difference between two groups using the family of *t*-distributions, one-way ANOVA uses the *F*-distribution to test the significance of the difference between two or more groups. Like the *t*-distribution, the *F*-distribution represents the sampling distribution when the null hypothesis is true. An *F*-value is calculated, and values close to 1 indicate that there is no difference between the group means. Conversely, *F*-values greater or less than 1 indicate that the observed differences between the group means are unlikely if the null hypothesis is true (i.e., that there are no differences between the group means in the population).

Like the independent samples *t*-test, one-way ANOVA requires that individuals are in one group only, that the dependent variable is continuous and is measured on at least an interval scale, and that there is one independent variable (group membership) that is categorical, with at least two or more categories. Note that it is possible to conduct an ANOVA using more than one independent variable. For example, if two categorical independent variables are analyzed, the analysis is referred to as *two-way ANOVA*. Similarly, *three-way ANOVAs* use three categorical independent variables. In general, ANOVAs in which multiple factors are considered together are referred to as **factorial ANOVAs**.

For the one-way ANOVA, the null hypothesis states that there is no difference between the population means of the i groups (e.g., $\mu_1 = \mu_2 = \mu_3 \ldots = \mu_i$). For $i \geq 2$ groups, the null and alternative hypotheses are stated, respectively, as follows:

$$H_0: \mu_1 = \mu_2 = \mu_3 \ldots = \mu_i$$

H_1: Not all the means are equal

As in the previous examples, when conducting an ANOVA, we calculate the probability of observing the sample mean differences of the size observed or larger by chance if H_0 is true (i.e., there are no differences in the population) and subsequently compare this probability with the α level set at the start of the study. Finally, the decision rules outlined in the previous section are used to decide whether the observed sample mean differences are statistically significantly different from the population mean differences under the null hypothesis ($\mu_1 = \mu_2 = \mu_3 = \ldots = \mu_i$).

You will notice that H_1 is stated in a different way from the previous tests. This is because ANOVA is an **omnibus test**, which can only specify that there are differences between the means but cannot specify which means are different from each other. For this reason, a statistically significant finding must be followed up with **post hoc tests**, which allow us to pinpoint which means are different from each other. These follow-up tests adjust the alpha (i.e., the Type I error rate) to account for the fact that multiple comparisons are being made. Commonly used post hoc tests include the Bonferroni adjustment, Tukey's range test, and the Scheffé test. For more information on these tests, we refer the reader to statistical texts such as Privitera (2012), Howell (2010), Glass and Hopkins (1996), and Shavelson (1996).

Chi-Square Analyses

Up to now we have been discussing inferential tests that make an assumption about the shape of the data distribution. Specifically, t-tests and ANOVA are *parametric tests*, which assume that the data are normally distributed. However, some types of data (e.g., counts or frequencies) are not normally distributed, and so those types of tests are not appropriate for them. In such cases, *non-parametric tests*, which do not assume normally distributed data, must be used. One of the most commonly used non-parametric tests is the chi-square test. Formally, **chi-square analyses** draw conclusions about the relative frequencies or proportions of cases in the population that fall into various categories.

While t-tests rely on the family of t-distributions and ANOVAs rely on the family of F-distributions, chi-square analyses rely on the family of χ^2 (chi-square) distributions. When conducting a chi-square analysis, the probability of observing the frequency distribution by chance if H_0 is true is calculated. Subsequently, this probability is compared with the α level set at the start of the study, and the decision rules outlined in the previous section are used to decide whether the observed frequencies are likely when the null hypothesis is true. There are two different types of chi-square tests: (1) the *goodness-of-fit* test and (2) the test of *independence*.

The **goodness-of-fit chi-square test** is used to estimate how well the observed data fit with some theory. For this type of test to be appropriate, there must be one dependent variable and one independent variable; the dependent variable represents frequencies or counts, and the independent variable must be categorical, with at least two categories. For the goodness-of-fit test, the null and alternative hypotheses are stated, respectively, as follows:

H_0: No difference in the population between the observed and expected frequencies

H_1: A difference exists in the population between the observed and expected frequencies

As an example, Table 10.4 presents hypothetical data showing the distribution of 1,000 individuals across each of four groups. If the distribution was equal across the groups, then we would expect to see 250 individuals (i.e., 25%) in each group. However, the observed values show that the individuals are not equally distributed across the groups; the question is whether the observed distribution across the groups is so different from the expected distribution (equally distributed in this

Table 10.4 Hypothetical Data for the Chi-Square Goodness-of-Fit Test

		Group 1	Group 2	Group 3	Group 4	Total
Expected value	Number	250	250	250	250	1,000
	Percentage	25	25	25	25	
Observed value	Number	300	450	150	100	1,000
	Percentage	30	45	15	10	

case) that we can conclude that a difference exists in the population between the observed and expected distributions.

The **test-of-independence chi-square test** is an extension of the goodness-of-fit test, and the goal is to test whether the patterns observed hold when data on a second independent variable are included. For this type of test to be appropriate, there must be one dependent variable and two independent variables; again, the dependent variable is frequencies or counts, and the independent variables are categorical, with at least two categories each. For the test-of-independence chi-square analysis, the null and alternative hypotheses are stated, respectively, as follows:

H_0: Variables A and B are independent in the population

H_1: Variables A and B are dependent in the population

Table 10.5 presents the same hypothetical data showing the distribution of 1,000 individuals across each of four groups, except in this case gender is added as a second categorical independent variable. In this case, the question is whether the distribution of frequencies across the levels of the variables is so different from the expected distributions that we can conclude that the variables are dependent in the population.

Table 10.5 Hypothetical Data for the Chi-Square Test of Independence

		Group 1	Group 2	Group 3	Group 4	Total
Male	Number	150	350	100	40	640
	Percentage	23	55	16	6	
Female	Number	150	100	50	60	360
	Percentage	42	28	14	17	
	Total	300	450	150	100	1,000

❖ CONNECTIONS TO QUALITATIVE RESEARCH

Now that we have finished our "treatment" of statistics (no pun intended!), we hope that you see these pages as a ready reference where you can revisit confusing concepts as you come across them in articles or when you conduct your own studies. Sampling is important in the quantitative tradition because making inferences (generalizations) beyond the particular sample used in a study to a larger population is of fundamental concern. All researchers would like others to see value in their work, including how results can be used in other contexts; however, as discussed earlier in this text, the qualitative tradition relies on rich description to convey the essential characteristics of participants and settings.

Hypothesis testing and estimation are consistent with the deductive logic underlying the quantitative tradition. Hypotheses (educated guesses) are also used in the qualitative tradition, but they are of a different nature since induction serves as the underlying logic. Rather than testing or confirming hypotheses, qualitative researchers sometimes construct "guiding hypotheses" as understanding emerges from the setting, and these are considered tentative as research questions are further refined in light of this emerging understanding. Notwithstanding the dissonance between the traditions in regard to the role of hypotheses, the connection is of a more fundamental nature. We humans seem to have a need to actively postulate what might happen and why. Although the quantitative tradition uses a more structured approach for stating and testing hypotheses, the ultimate goal under both traditions is to use our critical and creative faculties to anticipate and learn from experience.

In the most general sense, all statistical tests compare what is expected to happen by chance with what actually did happen. If the difference in this ratio is large enough, we can conclude that an intervention (whether drug therapy or an educational innovation) probably has had an impact. Deciding what has had an impact in qualitative research is not as straightforward because the data collected in qualitative studies are not reduced to the precision of numerical estimates; rather, there is still a great deal of complexity that cannot be captured and represented in such a way that comparisons can be made. However, quantitative tests can convey a unique understanding of data that can complement what has been found in qualitative studies. A perspective that is sometimes voiced is that the results of qualitative studies can serve as hypothesis generators for quantitative studies, where the hypotheses can then be tested statistically. While we agree with this contention, we also think that it can work in the reverse order, where statistical analyses can help researchers formulate both guiding hypotheses and research questions for future qualitative studies!

❖ CONCLUDING REMARKS

In this chapter, we provided readers with an introduction to inferential data analysis as a way to understand the collected data and address the research questions. The amount and complexity of the information presented may be overwhelming at first, but with practice the technical terms and procedures will become less daunting. In many ways, mastering quantitative data analysis is analogous to learning a new language or learning to swim; the most effective way to do either is to practice, practice, practice! Moreover, it is possible to practice even without analyzing actual data or conducting your own research study. For example, when reviewing empirical journal articles or research reports, take the time to review the data analysis procedures, how the results were reported, and whether they are connected to the research questions that the author(s) posed at the beginning of the piece. Over time, this type of practice will help readers become familiar with the types of analysis procedures used in the quantitative tradition. In the appendix at the end of this text, we provide a set of guidelines you can use to evaluate not only the methods and results sections but entire research reports (journal articles, dissertations, etc.).

Quality research in both the qualitative and the quantitative traditions is predicated on selecting the most appropriate data analysis procedures and presenting, interpreting, and synthesizing the findings (Questions 8 and 9 in Chapter 1). As such, we recommend that our readers spend the time necessary to cultivate their data analysis skills. In Chapter 11, we will return to how we began this text—by discussing the complementary natures of research in the qualitative and quantitative traditions.

DISCUSSION QUESTIONS

1. What *similarities* do you see between qualitative data analysis and the inferential analyses described in this chapter? What about the *differences*?

2. What do you find to be the most understandable aspects of the inferential analysis procedures we described in this chapter? What are the most confusing?

3. What do you find most useful about inferential quantitative data analyses? What do you find limiting?

KEY TERMS

Alpha (α): the Type I error rate, the probability of rejecting a true H_0 when in truth there is no effect (false-positive decision).

Alternative hypothesis, H_1: a statistical statement about a population parameter that states that the population parameter is some value other than the value stated in H_0.

Beta (β): the Type II error rate, the probability of failing to reject a true H_0 when in truth there is an effect (false-negative decision).

Chi-square analyses: inferential tests used to draw conclusions about the relative frequencies or proportions of cases in the population that fall into various categories.

Dependent samples t-test: a special case of the t-test used to test the significance of the difference between the sample means in two groups whose members are the same. The question is "Does the sample mean for a group at Time 1 ($\bar{X}_{T1}$) differ significantly from the sample mean for the same group at Time 2 ($\bar{X}_{T2}$)?"

Directional hypothesis: a statistical hypothesis that specifies the direction of the difference or relationship. This is also referred to as a one-tailed hypothesis.

Effect size: a way to convey the practical size of the difference or the magnitude of the relationship observed. Effect sizes may be reported as standardized differences between means (e.g., Cohen's d, Hedges's g, or Glass's Δ [delta]) or may be based on the percentage of variance explained (e.g., omega-squared [ω^2] or eta-squared [η^2]).

Factorial ANOVA: an ANOVA conducted with one continuous dependent variable and more than one categorical independent variable. For example, a two-way ANOVA has two categorical independent variables, and a three-way ANOVA has three categorical independent variables.

Goodness-of-fit chi-square test: a type of chi-square analysis used to estimate how well the observed data fit with some theory. For this type of test to be appropriate, there must be one dependent variable and one independent variable; the dependent variable represents frequencies or counts, and the independent variable must be categorical, with at least two levels.

Hypothesis testing (aka significance testing): a branch of statistics in which the researcher states statistical hypotheses and subsequently tests whether the collected data support those hypotheses.

Independent samples *t*-test: a type of *t*-test used to test the significance of the differences between the sample means in two independent samples. The question is "Does the sample mean for Group 1 ($\overline{X}_1$) differ significantly from the sample mean for Group 2 ($\overline{X}_2$)?"

Inferential analyses: a set of statistical procedures used by researchers to make inferences about the attributes or characteristics in a population using a sample from that population.

Interval estimation: an alternative to point estimation in which the researcher creates a confidence interval around a sample statistic ($\overline{X}$, r, b, etc.). The interval has a known probability of including the population parameter:

$$\text{(Sample statistic} - \text{Error)} \leq \text{Population parameter}$$
$$\leq \text{(Sample statistic} + \text{Error)}$$

Non-directional hypothesis: a statistical hypothesis that does not specify the direction of the difference or relationship. This is also referred to as a two-tailed hypothesis.

Null hypothesis, H_0: a statistical statement about a population parameter that is assumed to be true. By convention, H_0 states that no difference or no relationship exists in the population, and this hypothesis is tested using the collected data.

Omnibus test: a significance test that indicates whether there are differences between the means but does not specify which means are different from each other. ANOVA is an example of an omnibus test

One-sample *t*-test: a type of *t*-test used to test the significance of the difference between a sample mean ($\overline{X}$) and a known population mean (μ). The question is "Does the sample mean differ significantly from a known population mean?"

One-way ANOVA: an inferential test used to test the significance of the difference between the means of two or more groups. The question is "Is there a statistically significant difference between the means of the two or more groups?" A one-way ANOVA requires that individuals are in one group only, that the dependent variable is continuous and is measured on an interval scale, and that there is one independent variable (group membership) that is categorical, with at two or more levels.

Point estimation: the calculation of a single number to estimate the population parameter.

Population parameter: an attribute or characteristic in the population that may or may not be known. Sample statistics are used to make inferences about population parameters.

Population: all individuals or groups that possess the characteristic that the researcher aims to investigate.

Post hoc tests: significance tests that are conducted after a significant omnibus test that allow us to pinpoint which means are different from each other. Commonly used post hoc tests include the Bonferroni adjustment, Tukey's range test, and the Scheffé test.

p-Value: The probability of observing the differences or relationships of the size observed or larger by chance if the null hypothesis (H_0) is true.

Sample: a subset of units (e.g., individuals, groups of individuals) selected from the population, from whom data are collected.

Sample statistic: an attribute or characteristic measured in a sample and used to make inferences about population parameters.

Sampling distribution: a theoretical distribution of sample statistics created from an infinite number of probability samples of a particular size drawn from a single population.

Standard error: the standard deviation of the sampling distribution used in estimation and hypothesis testing. For example, the standard deviation of the sampling distribution of the mean is referred to as the standard error of the mean. The larger the standard error, the more sampling error there is in the sampling distribution.

Statistical power: the probability of correctly rejecting a false null hypothesis. It is equal to $1 - \beta$.

t-Distribution: a family of sampling distributions used when conducting t-tests. There is one t-distribution for every sample size.

Test-of-independence chi-square test: an extension of the goodness-of-fit test where the goal is to test whether the patterns observed hold when data on a second independent variable are included. For this type of test to be appropriate, there must be one dependent variable and two independent variables; again, the dependent variable is frequencies or counts, and the independent variables are categorical, with at least two levels each.

t-Tests: types of inferential test used to compare two means and named for the sampling distribution used to estimate the probability of observing the sample statistic by chance if the null hypothesis is true. *t*-Tests and *t*-distributions are also used to test the significance of correlation and regression coefficients. Respectively, the questions are "Is the correlation coefficient observed in the sample significantly different from zero?" and "Is the regression coefficient observed in the sample significantly different from zero?"

Type I error: a false-positive decision in which a true null hypothesis (H_0) is rejected.

Type II error: a false-negative decision in which a false null hypothesis (H_0) fails to be rejected.

REVIEW OF PUBLISHED RESEARCH ARTICLES

In this section, we describe four published research articles that use experimental research designs. The full articles are available online at **www.sagepub.com/odwyer.**

Article 1 (Yang, Cho, Mathew, & Worth, 2011)

Subsequent to presenting the results of the descriptive analyses, the authors presented the results of the inferential analyses. The authors broke out the results according to the research questions.

To examine whether there were gender differences in students' effort in online versus face-to-face courses, the authors conducted a two-way, between-subjects ANOVA. Recall from earlier in this chapter that a one-way ANOVA is used to test the significance of the difference between the means of two or more groups and that this type of analysis requires that the individuals are in one group only, that the dependent variable is continuous and is measured on at least one interval scale, and that there is one categorical independent variable with at least two or more levels. We went on to say in this chapter that it is also possible to conduct an ANOVA using more than one independent variable—for example, a two-way ANOVA is used to analyze two categorical independent variables simultaneously.

Since the authors had one continuous dependent variable (effort) and two categorical independent variables with at least two levels each (gender and course delivery format), they stated the following: "To address the first research question, namely, the potential effects of gender and class delivery format on effort, a two-way, between-subjects ANOVA design was used with both gender and class delivery format as between-subject factors" (p. 626).

Also on page 626, the authors reported finding statistical significance indicating that the probability of observing the result by chance was very small if the null hypothesis (H_0) was true. Recall that H_0 always states that there is no difference or no relationship. In the case of the two-way ANOVA, the null hypotheses are written as follows:

1. There is no difference in the means on factor A.

2. There is no difference in the means on factor B.

3. There is no interaction between factors A and B.

Based on the F-ratio and p-value, the authors concluded that the relationship between gender and effort was not constant across course delivery format. Technically, this is referred to as an "interaction effect." Readers who are interested in learning more about interaction effects should refer to the statistical textbooks we recommended at the outset in Chapters 9 and 10.

To address the second and third research questions, *hierarchical linear modeling* (HLM, also referred to as multilevel modeling or linear mixed modeling) was used. Recall that in Chapter 9 we described HLM as a type of regression analysis used to account for clustering effects that can occur when complex sampling designs are used (e.g., see Chapter 4 for a description of cluster sampling and two-stage cluster sampling). We referred interested readers to more specialized texts for additional information. For now, suffice it to say that the regression coefficients in HLM are interpreted in the same way as in an ordinary least squares regression analysis; the coefficient is the predicted change in the dependent variable for every one-unit change in the independent variable, holding all other variables in the model constant.

When reporting the results of the HLM regression analyses in Table 5 (p. 630), the authors reported the percentage of variance explained by the independent variables in the model (p. 627). This is analogous to the coefficient of determination, or R^2, discussed in Chapter 9. The authors also discussed the regression coefficients and their significance. For example, for the online courses, the authors stated the following:

Of the SOCC variables, the Value and Interest subscale made the sole and greatest contribution to effort, $\beta = .47$, $t = 4.76$, $p < .001$. The more engaging and meaningful the online courses were perceived to be, the more effort students reported. (pp. 627–628)

A complete interpretation of the regression could have been stated as follows: For every 1 standard deviation increase in students' Value and Interest subscale scores, Effort scores were predicted to increase by 0.47 of a standard deviation, holding all other variables in the model constant. The t-test for the regression coefficient showed that the probability of observing a coefficient this size or larger by chance if the null hypothesis is true (H_0: $\beta = 0$) is less than .001 ($p < .001$), indicating that the coefficient $\beta = .47$ was statistically significantly different from zero. Stated differently, the Value and Interest subscale was a statistically significant predictor of students' Effort scores, and in this case, the relationship is positive.

Article 2 (Clayton, 2011)

The author first reported the results of the inferential analyses when describing the correlation coefficients in Tables 5 and 6. The author concluded the following:

The strongest correlations among any variables were for poverty and the pass rates of White students ($r = -.307$, $-.214$, $-.474$, $-.170$), suggesting that White students who attend schools with higher rates of free/reduced-price lunch eligibility demonstrate lower pass rates. (p. 682)

These four correlations have two asterisks (**) next to them in Tables 5 and 6, indicating that these correlations are statistically significantly different from zero. Looking at the legends for Tables 4 and 5, the fact that there are two asterisks next to these correlations indicates that the probability of observing correlations these sizes or larger by chance if the null hypotheses are true (H_0: $\rho = 0$) is less than .01. This means that it is a rare event, and the correlation coefficient is statistically significantly different from zero.

In Tables 7 through 13, the author reported the results of multiple regression analyses that were conducted to examine whether poverty, teacher quality, and ethnic diversity predict academic performance. The author provided clear discussions and interpretations of the results. For example, when interpreting Table 8 (p. 684), she stated the following:

> The equation for the White pass rate was significant, $R^2 = .106$, $F(2, 491) = 3.296$, $p = .038$, accounting for 10.6% of the variance in pass rates. As shown in Table 8, the predictor of poverty through free/reduced-price lunch eligibility was significant with a p value of .000, a t value of −6.915, and a standardized beta of −.324. The negative beta indicated that White students attending a school with a lower rate of poverty were predicted to perform better on the English reading exam than were students at schools with high poverty rates. (pp. 683–684)

To elaborate further, for every 1 standard deviation increase in free/reduced-price lunch eligibility, White students' reading scores were predicted to decrease by 0.32 standard deviations, holding all other variables in the model constant. The t-test for the regression coefficient indicated that the probability of observing a coefficient this size or larger by chance if the null hypothesis is true (H_0: $\beta = 0$) is less than .001 ($p < .001$). Therefore, we can conclude that for White students, free/reduced-price lunch eligibility is a statistically significant predictor of achievement scores, and in this case, the relationship is negative.

Article 3 (Porfeli, Wang, Audette, McColl, & Algozzine, 2009)

The authors conducted independent samples t-tests and correlation and regression analyses to address the research questions. Recall that the results of some inferential tests were presented under the descriptive analyses heading (first discussed at the end of Chapter 9).

In Table 3 (p. 82), the authors presented the correlations among all the variables in the study and denoted statistically significant coefficients using * and **. Interestingly, on page 80, the authors did not interpret statistical significance when they discussed the strength and direction of the correlations. The significance of the correlation coefficients is interpreted as follows: A correlation coefficient with one asterisk indicates that the probability of observing a correlation that large or larger by chance if the null hypothesis is true (H_0: $\rho = 0$) is less than .05. Since this is a rare event, we can conclude that the correlation coefficient is statistically significantly different from zero.

Also in the descriptive section, the authors reported the results of independent samples t-tests in Table 4 (p. 83). Recall that this type of inferential analysis is used to test the significance of the difference between the sample means in two independent groups. They described the process of dichotomizing the community capital variables as follows:

> We employed community capital in a dichotomous fashion to assess and depict if and to what extent distributions of students with the different special education statuses varied between poorer and wealthier schools. Poor schools (n = 13) were defined as those that exhibited less than or equal to one standard deviation from the mean on the community capital variable and wealthy schools (n = 16) were defined as those that exhibited greater than or equal to one standard deviation from the mean. (p. 81)

Subsequent to dichotomizing the variable, they compared the special education concentration differences for wealthy and poor schools using an independent samples t-test. The following are examples of the authors' interpretation of the t-tests:

> We found a much higher concentration of academically gifted students (t = –11.81, p < 0.05) and students with speech impairments (t = –3.85, p < 0.05) in wealthy schools and much higher concentrations of students with behavior disabilities in poor schools (see Table 4). (p. 81)

The p-values for the two comparisons are each less than .05, indicating that the probability of observing differences this large or larger by chance if the null hypotheses are true (H_0: $\mu_1 = \mu_2$) is less than .05. Since this is a rare event, the authors concluded that there was a statistically significant difference between the means of the two groups. As an aside, we are not convinced that this was the most appropriate analysis given that the dependent variables were percentages.

Article 4 (Núñez, Sparks, & Hernández, 2011)

The inferential analyses conducted by the authors were different from the ones conducted in Articles 1 to 3. Specifically, the authors used a non-parametric chi-square analysis and a logistic, non-linear regression approach.

A non-parametric chi-square analysis was used to compare the distributions in selected variables across groups, both for students from different racial/ethnic groups attending community college and for students attending HSIs versus non-HSIs (p. 24. Recall from this chapter that chi-square analyses are used to draw conclusions about the relative frequencies or proportions of cases in the population that fall into various categories. The authors used a goodness-of-fit chi-square test to make comparisons across the observed frequencies of the five racial/ethnic groups, compared with equal distributions for all students enrolled in community colleges. Specifically, the chi-square was used to test whether the observed distribution across the five racial groups was so different from the expected distribution (equally distributed in this case) that the authors could conclude that a difference exists in the population between the observed and expected distributions.

The results of the chi-square analysis were presented in Table 1 (p. 25), and the authors reported statistically significant differences for several of the variables among the five racial/ethnic groups. For example, they reported the following:

> Across the racial/ethnic groups of community college students, particularly Latinos and Blacks (62% and 64%, respectively), female students outnumbered male students. Hispanic and Black community college students were also more likely to be of nontraditional age and to have risk factors for not completing college. More than two thirds (68%) of Asian and one third (33%) of Latino students were first generation immigrants. (p. 25)

For these examples, the probability of observing these frequency distributions by chance if H_0 is true is less than .0001. For the chi-square goodness-of-fit test, the null hypotheses are as follows:

H_0: No difference in the population between the observed and expected frequencies

H_1: A difference exists in the population between the observed and expected frequencies

Since this is a rare event, the authors correctly concluded that differences exist in the population between the observed and expected distributions.

The authors also conducted a logistic regression analysis to predict students' enrollment in an HSI or a non-HSI, a dichotomous dependent variable. As a consequence of the dependent variable being dichotomous, traditional linear regression cannot be used—the relationship between the independent variables and the dependent variable is not linear, and so all the statistical tests based on the assumption of normality of the errors are inappropriate. Instead, logistic regression predicts the probability of being in either one group or the other on the dependent variable. Tables 3 and 4 (pp. 31–33) present the results of the logistic regression models. The authors concluded the following from the model results in Table 3:

> Latino students, Black students, Asian students, and students from other or multiple race backgrounds had much higher odds than did White students of enrolling in a 2-year HSI, holding all other variables in the model constant. Students who had earned AP credit in high school had increased odds of enrolling in a 2-year HSI, as did students who expected to earn a bachelor's degree or higher and intended to transfer to another institution. Holding other variables constant, students with one or more risk factors, compared with those who had none, had much higher odds of enrolling in a 2-year HSI. (p. 28)

The authors came to these conclusions based on the odds ratio and the confidence intervals. In a logistic regression model, the regression coefficients are measures of the changes in the ratio of the probabilities— these are the odds ratios. Therefore, the odds ratio estimates the change in the odds of membership in the target group for a one-unit increase in the independent variable, holding all other variables in the model constant. In the case of this study, the odds ratios presented in Table 3 represent the odds of enrolling in a 2-year HSI, rather than a 2-year non-HSI, for each variable listed, holding all other factors constant in the model. An odds ratio equal to 1 indicates that either outcome is likely, an odds ratio greater than 1 indicates higher odds, and an odds ratio less than 1 indicates lower odds.

The confidence intervals reported in Tables 3 and 4 are estimates of the precision of the odds ratios, with wider confidence intervals indicating less precision. In the case of this type of confidence interval, the authors checked whether 1 (the null value) was in the interval. In all cases, the results from the confidence interval were aligned with the significance of the odds ratio.

SECTION IV

Reconciling the Paradigms

As we have seen throughout this book, there are pronounced as well as muted differences that exist between the quantitative and qualitative traditions in terms of design, data collection, and analysis. The educational psychologist Woolfolk (2011) point out that

> a discontinuous change (also called qualitative) would be like many of the changes in humans during puberty, such as the ability to reproduce—an entirely different ability. Qualitative changes are contrasted with purely quantitative change, such as the adolescent growing taller. (p. 32)

While we think that these definitions may be helpful from an expository standpoint, in a deeper sense, they are artificial or incomplete. For example, while "growing taller" might seem purely quantitative, at some point, observers perceive others simply as tall or short, which is a qualitative description. Even the ability to reproduce, certainly a qualitative phenomenon, has contextual quantitative elements that proceed or accompany it such as increased hormonal activity.

What we have argued throughout this book is that the distinctions that we make between quantitative and qualitative approaches and phenomena, while sometimes useful, are often artificial because the boundaries between qualitative and quantitative data are not precise.

If this is the case, why do we insist on erecting barriers between the traditions instead of recognizing that we are all in pursuit of closer approximations to reality but go about it in different ways? As such, the final chapter discusses the complementary natures of quantitative and qualitative research.

11

The Complementary Natures of Quantitative and Qualitative Research

CHAPTER OUTLINE

- Complementary Empirical Basis
- Complementary Systematic Basis
- Differences as Strengths
- Mixed Methods
- The Crystal and the Traditions
- Final Remarks

I n the final chapter in this text, we try and pull together our intentions that underlie the entire book by pointing out the common empirical and systematic focus of both traditions as well as how these differences actually result in mutual strengths. Finally, we discuss mixed methods and finish with some "closing words."

❖ COMPLEMENTARY EMPIRICAL BASIS

The quintessential difference often cited between the quantitative and qualitative traditions positions the "gold standard" of the empirical experimental design versus the "soft" observational methods used in qualitative research. However, when defining the term *empirical*, *The American Heritage Dictionary* uses as its first definition "relying upon or derived from observation *or* [italics added] experiment" while the revised version of the *Compact Oxford English Dictionary* defines the term *empirical* as meaning "based on observation or experience rather than theory or logic." In fact, when one considers the genesis of some of the most important "scientific" insights and theories such as gravitation, motion, time, and an untold number of other discoveries, one comes away with a new appreciation of the benefits of learning by observing, listening, and experiencing. It then also becomes apparent that *both* the quantitative and qualitative tradition rely on empirical data as the basis for discovering new knowledge, which can then be interpreted in relation to a larger framework or theory.

Notwithstanding the above commentary regarding a joint reliance on empirical data, there are, of course, issues that demarcate the processes used in the two traditions for obtaining these data. Perhaps most fundamental is the issue of learning in naturalistic settings and without active researcher intervention in qualitative research versus the more contrived settings sometimes used in quantitative studies where interventions are introduced. While the intent of qualitative studies is to understand phenomena from the participant's perspective, the intent in quantitative studies is oftentimes to systematically introduce change in order to quantify results. However, it should also be noted that some of the quantitative designs discussed previously do not rely on contrived settings or interventions. For example, survey, correlational, and ex post facto designs do not rely on direct active researcher manipulation in contrived settings but usually act on existing data to find out if there is any relationship or possible causal link. Regarding survey designs, the researcher typically seeks to discover what *is* and how people feel without attempting to influence behavior. However, it could be argued that the very act of asking questions (whether in quantitative *or* qualitative studies) may taint findings because of the possible impact on the way that informants may have previously thought about a phenomenon before the question was posed. This might perhaps be seen as a corollary to Heisenberg's Uncertainty Principle where the very act of trying to learn about something by introducing an external assessment may in some way alter the phenomenon.

The essential point is that while there are discernible differences in the methods and circumstances used to obtain empirical data, these differences should be viewed as shades of gray rather than black and white. The fact that both traditions rely on empirical data about individuals, contexts, and phenomena underscores our contention that these traditions metaphorically allow researchers to see different aspects of the same crystal just in different ways, from different perspectives, and often at different times. If there are no empirical data, then there is no link to the world. Even though there are various "filters" that are used to collect empirical data in the quantitative tradition (e.g., tests or questionnaires), these data originate from seeing, hearing, touching, smelling, or tasting the world and the phenomena in it. It is also clearly the case that data and facts (whether obtained via qualitative or quantitative methods) need to be interpreted in order to extract meaning from both words and numbers because without interpretation, data will simply remain data and of no more use than if we never collected it in the first place. It is, after all, the goal of all research to understand our world better, and for that to happen, we need to collect empirical data about this world and then rigorously analyze and interpret these data by exercising our creative and critical capacities.

As we have tried to make clear beginning in Chapter 1, the capacity for creativity and critical thought is the genesis of quality research whether conducted within the quantitative or qualitative traditions. It is as a consequence of the interplay between these capacities and the collection and analysis of empirical data that both traditions provide a framework that allow us to develop new insights about the world in which we live.

❖ COMPLEMENTARY SYSTEMATIC BASIS

We again begin with an accepted definition of terms. The definition that captures our use of the term *systematic* is offered by *The American Heritage Dictionary*—"characterized by *purposeful* regularity" [italics added]. Whether we are engaged in conducting quantitative or qualitative research and find ourselves in agreement with their unique ontological and epistemological bases, we must still be systematic in how we approach our study. Whether the problem and our predilections results in our choosing a survey design or a phenomenological one, we must be systematic as we seek to achieve the purpose for doing our research during the design, data collection, analysis, and interpretation stages.

While being systematic seems to fit like "hand and glove" as we design and conduct quantitative studies, it sometimes causes concern among researchers of a qualitative bent. Our position is that even though we are traditionally given more latitude to practice nonlinearity when conducting qualitative studies in relation to the literature review, data collection, analysis, and interpretation, this "latitude" does not relieve us of being able to show others that we have been rigorous in thought and action as we have conducted our studies. Researchers of every stripe must demonstrate that they planned their work and followed this plan even if the plan changed as a result of additional knowledge and insight as the study progressed.

Thoughtfully designing and systematically conducting research has no paradigmatic boundaries, and it is critical that we convey in as transparent terms as possible to our readers how we went about our work. However, we also need to be aware that being systematic cannot be divorced from purpose and ethics—there is nothing to be gained by going about our work systematically if the goals we seek and the way we treat our participants are not defensible.

❖ DIFFERENCES AS STRENGTHS

Van Kaam (1969) argues that the experimental method distorts the essence of human reality and prevents an appreciation of a full picture of the human condition if it is the sole method used. Van Kaam continues,

> Therefore the human scientist should not restrict himself to *only* [italics added] objective and detached measurement and observation. To be sure, a necessary scientific attachment should dominate the second phase of his scientific research, a phase which succeeds and presupposes his immersion in the world of experienced behavior itself, where he has already discovered the relevant questions and problems. (p. 26)

As we unpack this quote, we see that Van Kaam (who is an existentialist psychologist) believes that while an accurate understanding of the human condition should be based on lived experience or a phenomenological orientation from which good problems to solve can be found, he also endorses a belief that it is appropriate that the "second phase" of research (problem solving) should use quantitative as well as qualitative methods to solve these problems. While we obviously support this argument, we also think that this stance does an injustice to the quantitative tradition since it might be deduced that interesting and useful problems cannot emanate from it, which is certainly not the case. However, what we do glean from this discourse is that there is a clearly apparent and desirable symbiosis that exists between the two traditions that not only argues against a continuance of a "war" but on the contrary argues for a closer working partnership between the two traditions. Moustakas (1994) also reviewed Van Kaam and points out that this existentialist argues that qualitative research (especially phenomenology) can "set the stage for more accurate empirical investigations by lessening the risk of a premature selection of methods" and closes with the notion that qualitative research "does not supplant but complements the traditional methods of research available to me" (pp. 12–13). Van Kaam appears to us to be a champion of the position that we have advocated throughout this book!

Notwithstanding the "champion" accolade, some qualitative researchers might take umbrage with the "more accurate" comment because it may seem demeaning to the qualitative tradition—we choose to amplify the last comment referring to the complementary nature of the traditions. While we have pointed out the complementary nature in terms of similarities, it is also complementary in terms of differences. That is, while qualitative research might be visualized as more like the large end of a funnel that tries to catch data emanating from sight, sound, taste, smell, touch, feeling, perception, appreciation, and reflection, quantitative research might be seen as positioned at the narrow end of the funnel to contribute additional precision.

Yow (2005), while discussing the fact that qualitative researchers in various disciplines (history, anthropology, education, and sociology) may use the in-depth interview in different ways and in conjunction with other specific data collection methods, underscores the fact that there is general acceptance within qualitative research that the interview can be thought of as an almost universal glue that holds data in "suspension." Data in this suspended state can then be sympathetically analyzed and interpreted to gain a fuller understanding of the lives and intentions of participants. Yow also argues that instead of asking what methods we should use we should simply ask what we need to do to find the answer (p. 9). Although not specifically intended for this purpose, this comment also provides the "glue" for those of us who ask questions that suggest methods that cross the artificial boundaries that we have sometimes created between and within research traditions. Especially in the qualitative tradition where interpretation is perhaps its most distinctive characteristic (Erickson, 1986), there should be no reluctance to use quantitative methods since qualitative researchers center their work on the meaning or "assertions" that arise from data whether that data happen to be numerical or non-numerical. In fact, it seems that just as in the medical field, where we now have subspecialties within specialties, we sometimes seem to work harder to differentiate what we do rather than recognize that the entire person is our domain and not just the particular facet that captures our interest at a particular moment. This is not to minimize the contributions of specialization, since from a pragmatic standpoint, it seems to have "worked" whether with cars or medicine; rather, it is a plea that we recognize that while our mental apparatus seems to demand that we first analyze and dissect in order to learn, we also cannot forget that we must next synthesize and heal because it is the living entity in his or her complexity (the entire crystal) that we want to understand and appreciate. Although "research questions" much like the beam from a flashlight guides our quest, there is also a surrounding context that lies just beyond the periphery of this beam of light that may very well envelop a larger truth than that which we have thus far discovered.

❖ MIXED METHODS

Metaphors, similes, and analogies are wonderful linguistic devices and heuristics for extending understanding of what one already knows to things that may currently be beyond our reach. One caveat, however, is that at some point the congruence between the old (known) and the new (unknown) diminishes, which hampers further understanding of the new. This caveat makes eminent sense because, if the old provided a full and complete understanding of the new, there would be nothing "new" about the new; rather, it would simply be a duplicate or rehash of the old!

Keeping this caveat in mind, we would like to promote appreciation of mixed methods by using a different type of referent to highlight the unique roles that the quantitative and qualitative traditions play in knowledge production. Instead of comparing these traditions in terms of degree and quantity versus essence and quality, we would like to point out their complementary nature in mixed methods designs, especially in relation to education. While the quantitative tradition tends to focus on cognitive outcomes such as whether the use of technology results in higher levels of achievement, the qualitative tradition tends to focus on perceptions, values, and experiences such as why students may find technology useful or not useful. This juxtaposition suggests to us a connection between the taxonomy of educational objectives:

cognitive domain (Bloom, Englehart, Furst, Hill, & Krathwohl, 1956) with the quantitative tradition, taxonomy of educational objectives: affective domain (Krathwohl, Bloom, & Masia, 1964) with the qualitative tradition, as well as with the taxonomy for the technology domain (Tomei, 2005).

We think that this taxonomic analogue provides a different angle for viewing the complementary nature of the two traditions because the theorists who devised these taxonomies did not think of cognitive and attitudinal objectives as being in competition with one another but simply as two aspects of human learning and understanding. Based on this recognition, we find extrapolating to make the case for using mixed methods strategy (at least as it relates to learning) rather straightforward since each tradition can provide perspectives for understanding phenomena. Of course, our support for using mixed methods is contingent on whether the problem statement and research questions *clearly suggest* that mixed methods is an appropriate methodology to pursue rather than a purely quantitative or qualitative approach. We have also tried to underscore in this book that while it may not be considered "scientific" to formulate approaches and questions according to one's own predispositions (e.g., using ethnographic or experimental methods), every researcher has a unique perspective for viewing phenomena in the service of promoting greater understanding.

Unfortunately, both authors have independently concluded that there is sometimes almost a faddish proclivity to use mixed methods, especially in doctoral dissertations, presumably because they may be in vogue. Neither of us supports this position because we know that trying to design a quality study, conduct it properly and ethically, and draw meaning from results challenges the skills of a researcher working exclusively within one tradition, let alone both simultaneously. A high-quality mixed methods study requires that a researcher either spends adequate time becoming a journeyman of both traditions or works cooperatively with others who possess the necessary complementary skills. We hope that our book proves to be a positive influence for both options!

While we have tried to create a seamless transition between this section and the previous one, we would now like to ask our readers to think about research (whether qualitative or quantitative) as a conversation. When you think of the times when you were engaged in a good conversation, it was probably characterized by an interesting topic where the participants not only described their own unique experiences but also listened empathetically to others as they described their views and perspectives. As a consequence of this kind of conversation and empathetic listening, did you ever find your own views being validated at one time but also challenged and modified at the other times? We think that good research is much like a good conversation where the researcher is validated and changed based on "conversation" with participants, the literature base, resulting data, as well as the self-conversations that occur as he or she reflects and writes about his or her awareness of findings in relation to his or her own frameworks and paradigms. In fact, it is through one's own reflections that have been co-constructed through these type of conversations (whether of the dialogical, self-dialogical, or research type) that worthwhile and quality problems, questions, concepts, designs, analyses, and interpretations are born (see Merriam, 1998, pp. 44–50, for a related line of thought).

Now, imagine that you are in a conversation, like the one described above, with a person who shares your passion for the integration of technology in education. It soon becomes apparent that your new friend is most interested in how technology can be used to raise academic achievement in struggling schools so that these schools can achieve Adequate Yearly Progress (AYP). You readily agree with this but excitedly add that your interest is discovering why technology is effective and how it might be used in new ways not only to raise achievement but also to engender creative thinking. As you continue to converse (and perhaps munch on pretzels!), it dawns on you that although you are a "qualitative" person that if it can be shown that technology can help achieve AYP goals as well as engender creativity (and perhaps even show a link between increased creativity and improved AYP results) that this would not be a bad thing—in fact, it would be hallelujah time! This contrived scenario was craftily devised by the authors not only to show how conversation and research as ways of knowing share similar aims and processes but also to offer perhaps yet another way to think about mixed methods. We end our section on mixed methods by quoting Connolly (2007), who after describing the demeaning comments still made about both traditions as "nonsensical" goes on to say,

> It is equivalent to a builder arguing that hammers are more important than screwdrivers. It just does not make any sense. The point is that both tools are useful but for different jobs. Imagine if the builder advertised his or her services but stated that whatever the job, he or she would only ever use a hammer. How many of you would invite them into your house to re-tile your bathroom? It may sound silly but how is this any different from someone in an educational research context claiming that they only do quantitative (or qualitative) research? (p. 4)

The only implication that we disagree with is that every individual engaged in scholarly inquiry must be ready, willing, and able to use both qualitative and quantitative methods; rather, we strongly believe in researcher autonomy and value the unique approach for viewing and understanding phenomena that each of us brings to the table. However, based on what we have presented in this book, we hope that even if you choose to use an exclusive quantitative or qualitative approach that you have an enhanced appreciation for how methods and those who use them on the other side of the "divide" can help each of us arrive at a more accurate and complete picture of phenomena. Yow (2005) describes an appropriate use of mixed methods "when data from several in-depth interviews are coded and expressed mathematically" (p. 7). The point is that while research questions may point primarily to a quantitative or qualitative approach, by having an array of both quantitative and qualitative "arrows in the quiver," it provides us with a valuable repertoire of tools for both analysis and interpretation and, thus, provides valuable support for producing quality research.

Johnson and Onwuogbuzie (2004) argue that researchers should use research tools based on pragmatic grounds, which they cite as "contingency theory," because "circumstances" determine if quantitative, qualitative, or a mixed methods approach is the best one to use (pp. 22–23). These "circumstances," in our view, are primarily defined by purpose, problem statement, research questions, as well as an underlying hunch or predisposition that a researcher believes that he or she can most effectively use. Anderson and Shattuck (2012) when discussing "design-based research" that seeks to establish the validity of interventions in real-world educational contexts, says that "DBR [design-based research] is largely agnostic when it comes to epistemological challenges to the choice of methodologies used and typically involves mixed methods using a variety of research tools and techniques" (p. 17). We do not deny the deep philosophical differences between the traditions—in fact, we celebrate them because they each contribute to our understanding in unique ways!

❖ THE CRYSTAL AND THE TRADITIONS

Let us conclude by revisiting the metaphor of the crystal and the purpose of a study as the unifying themes of this book. Why researchers identify a particular problem or phenomenon as significant and compelling and consequently invest time and energy to investigate it is based on their interests, values, and worldviews. Consequently, they should be able to articulate their purpose, reasons, and goals for conducting a study. There is, of course, great variability among researchers in terms of what they find to be important problems to solve as well as the preferred ways that they choose to go about solving or learning more about these problems. This rich complexity that exists among all thoughtful persons regarding what they find interesting and how they go about investigating phenomena is consistent with a constructivist way of learning. While constructivism does not deny that there can be more and less accurate depictions of reality, it nonetheless welcomes a diversity of realities as the basis for conceiving, framing, and processing knowledge, ideas, and concepts. Embracing divergent thinking is based on the recognition that every individual person possesses unique insights and experiences that shape how each of us look at the world, reflect on our relationship to it, as well as act on it. Each of us is indeed our own best informant!

We have used the analogy of a crystal to show that a diversity of viewpoints transcends the barrier that we have artificially constructed both within and between the research traditions. While it is a natural characteristic of the formal thinking process to analyze and dissect things in order to try and understand them better, we also need to remember that human beings (who are generally the subjects of our inquiry) are living and breathing entities who continuously seek to attain their own unique identity (Marcia, 1991) and if we truly want to understand our informants better, we must work to reconstruct the whole being after we have explored its components. While qualitative research may introduce "interpretation" at a relatively early stage of the research process to make sense of the parts in light of the whole, so too does quantitative research seek to make connections in order to understand the problem in context, although this is typically done at the end of the written report. However, our advocacy of mixed methods does not at all imply that we should feel a compulsion to conduct mixed methods studies because they may currently be in vogue; rather, as we have stressed throughout, once the researcher has defined the problem in the way that accurately reflects what she or he wants to discover, the method or methods to investigate this problem should be relatively easy to discern. Even if the problem clearly suggests that a particular method in a particular tradition should be employed, we each need to consider including studies from both traditions in our review of literature, since together they can enhance both our own and our readers' understanding of the phenomenon under investigation.

A part of our diversity is that we each exhibit particular capabilities for capturing insights and an intrinsic propensity to identify with either the quantitative or the qualitative tradition. We have tried to convince readers that just as a crystal offers multiple angles and ways for appreciating and learning about its uniqueness, so too do both traditions offer this same kind of richness. Whether this is reflected in conducting mixed methods studies ourselves or simply our willingness to recognize and celebrate others' unique ways of conceptualizing and appreciating the world and those who live in it, our purpose for writing this book will have been well served.

From an educational perspective, the phrase "waves of reform" has been used to point to different foci in educational change efforts, such as the "back to basics," the "standards" movements, or current initiatives. While it is easy to be cynical about these efforts, we have come to recognize that it is due to the complexity of the educational and social science enterprise (especially the humans at the center of it) that results in researchers and policymakers with good intentions seizing on some aspect of this complexity to gain a foothold and then using this foothold as leverage with the hope of raising the entire enterprise. Unfortunately, while specific initiatives can sometimes result in educational improvement, these improvements tend to be either short-lived or for various reasons limited in wider impact. It is precisely because of the complexity of the challenge that we argue that finding effective solutions requires that we draw on the tools and methods offered by both research traditions because their diversity also defines and enlarges their potential to discover answers that currently elude us. A predisposition for *appreciating* the contributions that each tradition can make increases the probability that solutions for existing problems will be found or that potentially richer problems or better definitions of existing ones will emerge. The reason for this optimistic assessment is that we can now enter the fray with a full complement of ways of knowing and methodological tools instead of only a subset of them. Using these multiple ways of knowing and methodological tools in a complementary manner may not only help us solve challenging problems but also help us connect the dots so that perhaps for the first time we begin to see and conceptualize our educational problems or other problems in a way that more accurately portrays their actual nature, including their physical, psychological, sociological, emotional, and political characteristics.

As Stake (1995) reminds us, "Good research is not about good methods as much as it is about good thinking" (p. 19). Because of a willingness to accept the complexity of reality that is revealed by both the quantitative and qualitative traditions and to explore this reality using both perspectives and methods opens the gates to finding fuller, deeper, and more satisfying problems as well as an increased understanding of them.

❖ FINAL REMARKS

Yow (2005) writes, "Quantification has its appropriate use, as does qualitative research. The kind of question asked leads to the choice of research method" (p. 7). While this advice is at once wise, we also recognize while we adhere to this view, it can also be construed as overly simplistic. Each of us is unique in terms of our thoughts, emotions, experiences, dispositions, as well as philosophical and spiritual beliefs. We don't think that it is easy to simply flip a switch and become interested in a phenomenon from a quantitative versus a qualitative viewpoint, or vice versa, and then be willing to invest large amounts of time to investigate the phenomenon from this often uncomfortable perspective. It is also equally faulty to think that an individual can switch methodological approaches because he or she thinks that it will be easier to churn out a publication with one or the other for promotion considerations. We heartily hope that our focus on producing quality research based on the 10 questions presented in Chapter 1 has resonated with readers throughout this book. As Wolcott (1994) argues, "Research is research; those unable to make sense out of one mode of inquiry are not that likely to make sense out of another" (p. 416). Harkening again back to Chapter 1, we defined research as "a systematic process to make things known that are currently unknown by examining phenomena multiple times and in multiple ways." Whether one is drawn to the quantitative or qualitative traditions, the emphasis should be on producing quality work and the odds for accomplishing this ultimate goal are greatly enhanced when we spend adequate time examining phenomena that excite and engage us—it is our opportunity to make our own unique and lasting mark, and we encourage you to do so regardless of which "tradition" you decide to follow.

Appendix

Guidelines for Evaluating Research Summaries

S taying current with the literature in your field, being able to critically evaluate this literature, and possessing the skills to plan your own research are essential components of being a professional. Consequently, the purpose of this appendix is to provide guidelines to help readers independently evaluate research reports (journal articles, dissertations, etc.). Although these guidelines are "slanted" toward quantitative research, we show parallels with qualitative research, which is consistent with the theme of this book. These guidelines also include embedded descriptions of the sections that are linked to the content covered in Chapters 1 to 10 of the text. These guidelines have been "field tested" for several years in graduate research classes and are consistent with the 10 questions posed in Chapter 1 regarding quality research.

Although the Guidelines for Evaluating Research Summaries were designed as an aid for evaluating any research article in the social sciences, they use the formal headings often used in dissertations. Typically, these sections are as follows:

Abstract

I. Introduction

II. Review of Related Literature

III. Methods

IV. Results

V. Conclusions and Implications

References

Although many published articles do not explicitly use these headings, they are very likely to contain all of the information that is presented under these headings, even if in abbreviated form.

These guidelines are offered as a way to evaluate any research report that summarizes the findings from an empirical study (e.g., journal articles, dissertations, etc.). In preparation for reviewing or using these guidelines, it may also be helpful to refer to the quality question criteria in Chapter 1. As a first step in evaluating a research report, we suggest that you first read the article in its entirety. This will provide you with an overview of what the study is about, how it was conducted, and what was discovered. Subsequently, these evaluation guidelines can be used to evaluate the research summary. You may need to jump back and forth from the article to the guidelines in order to "fill in the blanks"!

The guidelines include numbered questions to help you evaluate any type of research report. Follow these guidelines and answer each question since they will help to focus your work. In addition, the guidelines present a model or ideal format for published articles; however, because there is variation in how research is reported both within and between traditions, not all research summaries will conform exactly to these guidelines. Nevertheless, these guidelines have been shown to offer a reasonable way to evaluate published research. Readers should feel free to modify these guidelines as circumstances and context suggest! The following is a nine-step guide for reviewing and evaluating the sections of a research summary.

❖ STEP 1: IDENTIFY THE RESEARCH SUMMARY (JOURNAL ARTICLE, DISSERTATION, ETC.)

❖ STEP 2: REVIEW, EVALUATE, AND SUMMARIZE THE ABSTRACT

The Abstract should introduce readers to the research purpose, the problem that is being addressed, the methods used, and should summarize the findings and conclusions.

Evaluation Questions:

1. Does the Abstract describe the purpose, problem, methods, results, and conclusions? Yes or No? Describe.

2. Does the Abstract encourage you to read the rest of the article? Yes or No? Describe.

❖ STEP 3: REVIEW, EVALUATE, AND SUMMARIZE THE INTRODUCTION SECTION (I)

The Introduction serves as the next deeper level of information for readers. Although the terminology we introduced in Questions 1 to 5 (see Chapter 1) is standard in social science research, the authors of your research report may not use these same terms. In this case, you must do some detective work by reading more closely to find out if they have answered these questions. There is even the possibility that the authors did not answer some of these questions. Specifically, the Introduction section should include the following:

✓ *Purpose of the Study:* Should state *why* the researchers conducted the study.

✓ *Problem Statement, Research Questions/Hypotheses:* The problem that was addressed in the study should be stated, as should research questions and hypotheses. Researchers will either develop a testable guess as to what might happen (hypothesis) or specific questions to be answered (research questions). Whereas hypotheses are usually used with experimental or retrospective designs, research questions are often used with survey designs and most qualitative designs (although questions may "emerge" as the study progresses with qualitative designs).

✓ *Significance of the Problem:* The significance of the study should be described, and it should be clear *why* solving the problem is important. Potential impacts on practice or policy may be described.

✓ *Background:* The Introduction should provide a "mini-review of the literature" to provide some context for the study. An effective Introduction will demonstrate that the researchers "have done their homework" by reviewing what others have already found, and consequently, they identified a "niche" for their own study.

Evaluation Questions:

1. Is a purpose given that describes *why* the researchers conducted the study? Yes or No? Describe.

2. Is a problem statement stated? Yes or No? Describe.

3. Is the significance of the problem stated? Yes or No? Describe.

4. Is the background of the problem described using key references? Yes or No? Describe.

5. Are the research hypotheses or research questions stated? Yes or No? Describe.

❖ STEP 4: REVIEW, EVALUATE, AND SUMMARIZE THE RELATED LITERATURE SECTION (II)

The Review of Related Literature is an extension of the Background discussion in the Introduction section. Notice the adjective "related"— this means that only those sources that shed light on the current study should be selected for review. While the Review of Literature section is typically the longest section of a thesis or dissertation, it is sometimes quite short in journal articles due to space limitations. In fact it may not be labeled as the Review of Literature section but might simply be subsumed under the Background section. The following characteristics are present in an effective Related Literature section:

✓ The purpose of the Review of Related Literature is to illuminate the study, and therefore, sources cited need to be related in more than a cursory way to the topic and purpose.

✓ The Review of Related Literature not only should relate to the study in a general way, some sources in the Review of Related Literature should show in a specific way that the problem statement, research questions, or hypothesis are important and reasonable in light of what has already been discovered by others.

✓ The Review of Related Literature should be written in a way that is not simply "He said" or "She said"; rather, it should flow, and sentences and thoughts should be connected by the researcher so that readers can learn from it—that is the beauty of reading a good study—you learn both from the researcher whose work you are currently reading as well as from researchers whose work he or she describes in the Review of Related Literature.

✓ Note that it may be difficult to assess the quality of the Review, especially for qualitative studies where it is not always given the same prominence as with quantitative studies. Also, there should be a one-to-one correspondence between sources reviewed in the Review of the Related Literature and References cited at the end of the study. As you come across sources in the Review, a good practice is to check to make sure that it is listed accurately in the References and that there are no sources listed in the References that are not cited in the text of the article.

Evaluation Questions:

1. Do the reviewed sources relate to the topic and purpose of the study? Yes or No? Describe.

2. Do the sources support the problem statement, hypothesis/research questions? Yes or No? Describe.

3. Is the Review written as a "good story" that informs the reader? Yes or No? Describe.

❖ STEP 5: REVIEW, EVALUATE, AND SUMMARIZE THE METHODS SECTION (III)

The Methods section should provide a description of the participants, the instruments used to collect data, the research design and data analysis, and the operational procedures.

✓ *Description of the Participants:* The report should describe the participants ("subjects" may be used in experimental research) in terms of characteristics that are relevant to the study. Note that in behavioral and social science research, researchers usually collect data from people, although records and artifacts are also used. Relevant characteristics sometimes include age, ethnicity, gender, years of teaching experience, and so on. You will need to decide if the author provided adequate information based on the nature of the study.

✓ *Instrumentation:* Data are the essence of research, and there must be some instrument used to collect data. Even in qualitative research where the "researcher is the primary instrument," there is usually an observation or interview protocol that is used. If there is no mention of data collection instruments, then answer "no"! Regarding validity and reliability, the authors will often indicate what kind of validity and reliability measures were used to evaluate instruments, and in the case of quantitative studies, numerical indices are often given, whereas "trustworthiness" and "triangulation" are often used in qualitative studies. If there is no mention of validity or reliability, the article is deficient in this important area!

✓ *The Research Design:* The name of the research design is often explicitly stated in the article, but sometimes it is not. If it is not identified, you will need to try and discern the design that has been used. Sometimes researchers might use elements of more than a single design, especially in mixed methods studies. The authors should provide a thorough description of what analyses were conducted to answer the research questions or test the hypotheses.

✓ *Operational Procedures:* The ideal procedures section should be written with enough clarity and detail so that other researchers (like you!) could replicate the study. If you do not think that other competent researchers could replicate the study given the information provided, then the article is deficient in this area.

Evaluation Questions:

1. Are the participants described in terms of important characteristics? Yes or No? Describe.

2. What method of sample selection was used (random, purposive, etc.)? Yes or No? NA? Describe.

3. What was the size of the sample? Yes or No? NA? Describe.

4. Are the data collection instruments identified (tests, observation protocols, etc)? Yes or No? NA? Describe.

5. What information about validity and reliability is given? Yes or No? NA? Describe.

6. Is the research design identified (e.g., survey, case study, experimental, narrative)? Yes or No? Describe.

7. If a research design is not explicitly identified, what do you think it is and why? Yes or No? Describe.

8. Are data analysis procedures adequately described? Do they allow the research questions to be answered or the research hypotheses to be tested? Yes or No? NA? Describe.

9. For quantitative research reports, were descriptive statistics (means, standard deviations, etc.) or inferential statistics (t-test, ANOVA, ANCOVA, etc.) discussed? Yes or No? NA? Describe.

10. For qualitative research reports, was textual analysis used to analyze data (segmenting, coding, themes, etc.)? Yes or No? NA? Describe.

11. Do the authors provide an adequate description of how the study was conducted? Yes or No? NA? Describe.

❖ STEP 6: REVIEW, EVALUATE, AND SUMMARIZE THE RESULTS SECTION (IV)

The Results section should provide a comprehensive summary of the findings from the study. The results should be tied back to the research questions or hypotheses. In the case of quantitative research reports, the authors should describe the empirical results in detail, including the significance levels (p-values) and the practical significance (e.g., effect sizes) of the results. For a qualitative research report, the authors should describe any textual analyses used to analyze data (segmenting, coding, themes, etc.).

Evaluation Questions:

1. If research hypotheses were stated, do the results support them? Yes or No? NA? If research hypotheses were stated, do the results support them? Describe.

2. If research questions were stated, do the results support them? Yes or No? NA? If research questions were stated, do the results support them? Describe.

3. In the case of quantitative research reports, were any descriptive statistics (means, standard deviations, etc.) reported? Yes or No? NA? Describe.

4. In the case of quantitative research reports, were any inferential statistics (t-test, ANOVA, ANCOVA, etc.) reported? Yes or No? NA? Describe.

5. In the case of quantitative research reports, were significance levels (p-values) reported? Yes or No? NA? Describe.

6. In the case of quantitative research reports, was practical significance (e.g., effect sizes) discussed? Yes or No? NA? Describe.

7. In the case of qualitative research reports, was textual analysis used to analyze data (segmenting, coding, themes, etc)? Yes or No? NA? Describe.

❖ STEP 7: REVIEW, EVALUATE, AND SUMMARIZE THE CONCLUSIONS AND IMPLICATIONS SECTION (V)

Section V is sometimes called the Discussion or Interpretation section. Whatever the title used, this section should "wrap up" the study by relating and interpreting what has been found in the Results section to themes such as those described in the bullets above. Remember—data, facts, and results do not speak entirely for themselves, they must be interpreted to "make meaning." In a quantitative study, this is the first opportunity for the researcher to speak because all the previous sections were probably written in the third person ("the researcher"). The Conclusions and Implications section give quantitative researchers "voice" or the right to now say what they think their study actually means! In a qualitative study, this section continues the opportunity for researchers to "voice" their views on what the study means, since "interpretation" is often embedded with "analysis" based on the inductive nature of qualitative research. The section should include the following:

✓ Conclude/summarize based on the problem statement, research questions or research hypotheses.

✓ Interpret the meaning of the results, the limitations of the study, and any plausible alternative explanations.

✓ Integrate the results with the background information from the Introduction and Related Literature sections.

✓ Theorize about connections between Results and existing theory. The beginnings of new theories may also be discussed.

✓ Discuss the implications or impact of the results on policy and/or practice.

✓ Suggest further research that may replicate and/or refine the theory.

✓ Discuss any unexpected findings and the limitations of the study.

Evaluation Questions:

1. Does the researcher use one or more of these themes to summarize the study? Yes or No? NA? Describe.

2. Are the authors' conclusions warranted given the participants, the instruments used to collect the data, the research design and data analysis, and the operational procedures? Yes or No? NA? Describe.

3. Are the limitations discussed complete? Yes or No? NA? Describe.

❖ STEP 8: REVIEW AND EVALUATE THE REFERENCES SECTION

Every source cited in the body of the research report (primarily in the Introduction and Related Literature sections) should be cited in proper format (e.g., American Psychological Association [APA]) in the References section. There should also be no sources in the references that are not cited in the research report. The references should be high quality (i.e., from reputable, peer-reviewed journals) and recent (older references are only acceptable when the works cited are seminal pieces). Sources should be authoritative, and there should be no sources from Wikipedia-like Internet resources.

Evaluation Questions:

1. Are the sources authoritative and relevant? Yes or No?

2. Is every source cited in text listed properly in the References? Yes or No?

3. Is every source listed in the References cited properly in the text? Yes or No?

❖ STEP 9: OVERALL EVALUATION OF THE RESEARCH REPORT

Taking all of the above criteria in mind, how would you rate this article?

___ Excellent: conforms to all or most of the criteria

___ Very Good: generally satisfies criteria but is somewhat lacking

___ Satisfactory: an acceptable article but could be improved

___ Unsatisfactory: significant shortcomings in terms of quality

Provide a short summary statement that justifies your rating.

References

Allison, P. D. (2001). *Missing data*. Thousand Oaks, CA: Sage.

Anderson, T., & Shattuck, J. (2013). Systematic review of design-based research progress: Is a little knowledge a dangerous thing? *Educational Researcher, 42,* 97–100.

Bickel, R. (2007). *Multilevel analysis for applied research: It's just regression*. New York, NY: Guilford Press.

Bloom, B., Engelhart, M., Furst, E., Hill, W., & Krathwohl, D. (1956). *Taxonomy of educational objectives: Book 1. Cognitive domain*. New York, NY: Longmans Green.

Campbell, D. T. (1957). Factors relevant to the validity of experiments in social settings. *Psychological Bulletin, 54,* 297–312.

Campbell, D. T., & Stanley, J. C. (1963). *Experimental and quasi-experimental designs for research*. Chicago, IL: Rand McNally.

Charmaz, K. (2006). *Constructing grounded theory: A practical guide through qualitative analysis*. Thousand Oaks, CA: Sage.

Clandinin, D. J., & Connelly, F. M. (2000). *Narrative inquiry*. San Francisco, CA: Jossey Bass.

Connolly, P. (2007). *Quantitative data analysis in education: A critical introduction using SPSS*. London, England: Routledge.

Cook, T. D., & Campbell, D. T. (1976). The design and conduct of quasi-experiments and true experiments in field settings. In M. Dunnette (Ed.), *Handbook of industrial and organizational psychology* (pp. 228–293). Chicago, IL: Rand McNally.

Cook, T. D., & Campbell, D. T. (1979). *Quasi-experimentation: Design & analysis issues for field settings*. Boston, MA: Houghton Mifflin.

Cook, T. D., & Shadish, W. R. (1994). Social experiments: Some developments over the past 15 years. *Annual Review of Psychology, 45,* 545–580.

Creswell, J. W. (1998). *Qualitative enquiry and research design: Choosing among five traditions*. London, England: Sage.

Creswell, J. W. (2007). *Qualitative inquiry & research design* (2nd ed.). Thousand Oaks, CA: Sage.

Creswell, J. W. (2008). *Educational research: Planning, conducting, and evaluating quantitative and qualitative research*. Upper Saddle River, NJ: Pearson.

DeMars, C. (2010). *Item response theory*. New York, NY: Oxford University Press.

DeVellis, R. F. (2011). *Scale development: Theory and applications* (3rd ed.). Thousand Oaks, CA: Sage.

Dillman, D., Smyth, J., & Christian, L. (2008). *Internet, mail, and mixed-mode surveys: The tailored design method* (3rd ed.). Hoboken, NJ: Wiley.

Enders, C. K. (2010). *Applied missing data analysis*. New York, NY: Guilford Press.

Erickson, F. (1986). Qualitative methods in research on teaching. In M. Wittrock (Ed.), *Handbook of research on teaching* (pp. 119–161). New York, NY: Macmillan.

Fabrigar, L. R., & Wegener, D. T. (2011). *Understanding statistics: Exploratory factor analysis*. New York, NY: Oxford University Press.

Fink, A. (2012). *How to conduct surveys: A step-by-step guide* (5th ed.). Thousand Oaks, CA: Sage.

Fowler, F. J. (2008). *Survey research methods* (4th ed.). Thousand Oaks, CA: Sage.

Fraenkel, J. R., & Wallen, N. E. (2011). *How to design and evaluate research in education* (6th ed.). Boston, MA: McGraw-Hill.

Gage, N. L. (1989). The paradigm wars and their aftermath. *Educational Researcher, 18*(7), 4–10.

Gall, M. D., Borg, W. R., & Gall, J. P. (2003). *Educational research: An introduction* (7th ed.). White Plains, NY: Longman.

Gardner, H. (1983). *Frames of mind: The theory of multiple intelligences*. New York, NY: Basic Books.

Gay, L. R., & Airasian, P. (2003). *Educational research: Competencies for analysis and application* (7th ed.). Upper Saddle River, NJ: Pearson.

Gay, L. R., Mills, G. E., & Airasian, P. (2009). *Educational research: Competencies for analysis and applications* (9th ed.). Upper Saddle River, NJ: Pearson.

Geertz, C. (2003). Thick description: Toward an interpretive theory of culture. In Y. S. Lincoln & N. K. Denzin (Eds.), *Turning points in qualitative research: Tying knots in a handkerchief* (pp. 143–168). Walnut Creek, CA: AltaMira Press.

Gelman, A., & Hill, J. (2006). *Data analysis using regression and multilevel/hierarchical models*. Cambridge, England: Cambridge University Press.

Gibbs, G. R. (2007). *Analyzing qualitative data*. Thousand Oaks, CA: Sage.

Glaser, B., & Strauss, A. (1967). *The discovery of grounded theory*. Chicago, IL: Aldine.

Glass, G. V., & Hopkins, K. D. (1996). *Statistical methods in psychology and education* (3rd ed.). Needham Heights, MA: Allyn & Bacon.

Groves, R. M., Fowler, F. J., Couper, M. P., & Lepkowski, J. M. (2009). *Survey methodology* (Wiley Series in Survey Methodology). New York, NY: Wiley.

Guba, E. G. (1981). Criteria for assessing the trustworthiness of naturalistic inquiries. *Educational Communications and Technology Journal, 29*(1), 75–91.

Hambleton, R. K., & Swaminathan, H. (2010). *Item response theory: Principles and applications*. New York, NY: Springer.

Heeringa, S. G., West, B. T., & Berglund, P. A. (2010). *Applied survey data analysis.* Boca Raton, FL: Chapman & Hall/CRC Press.

Hogarth, R. B. (2005). The challenge of representativeness design in psychology and economics. *Journal of Economic Methodology, 12,* 253–263.

Howell, D. C. (2007). *The analysis of missing data.* In W. Outhwaite & S. Turner (Eds.), *Handbook of social science methodology* (pp. 87–114). Thousand Oaks, CA: Sage.

Howell, D. C. (2010). *Fundamental statistics for the behavioral sciences* (7th ed.). Belmont CA: Wadsworth Cengage Learning.

Johnson, R. B., & Christensen, L. B. (2000). *Educational research: Quantitative and qualitative approaches.* Boston, MA: Allyn & Bacon.

Johnson, R. B., & Onwuogbuzie, A. J. (2004). Mixed method research: A research paradigm whose time has come. *Education Researcher, 33*(7), 14–26.

Karpov, Y. V., & Haywood, H. C. (1998). Two ways to elaborate Vygotsky's concept of mediation implications for instruction. *American Psychologist, 53,* 27–36.

Keppel, G., & Wickens, T. D. (2004). *Design and analysis: A researcher's handbook* (4th ed.). Prentice Hall.

Kerlinger, F. N. (1973). *Foundations of behavioral research* (2nd ed.). New York, NY: Holt, Rinehart & Winston.

Kirk, R. E. (2012). *Experimental design: Procedures for the behavioral sciences* (4th ed.). Thousand Oaks, CA: Sage.

Krathwohl, D., Bloom, B., & Masia, B. (1964). *Taxonomy of educational objectives: Handbook 2. Affective domain.* New York, NY: David McKay.

Lageman, E. (2000). *An elusive science: The troubling history of education research.* Chicago, IL: University of Chicago Press.

Lichtman, M. (2013). *Qualitative research in education: A user's guide* (3rd ed.). Thousand Oaks, CA: Sage.

Marcia, J. E. (1991). Identity and self development. In R. Lerner, A. Peterson, & J. Brooks-Gunn (Eds.), *Encyclopedia of adolescence* (Vol. 1). New York, NY: Garland Press.

Maxwell, J. A. (1992). Understanding and validity in qualitative research. *Harvard Educational Review, 62*(3), 279–300.

McMillan, J. H., & Schumacher, S. (2006). *Research in education: Evidence-based inquiry* (6th ed.). Boston, MA: Pearson.

Merriam, S. B. (1998). *Qualitative research and case study applications in education.* San Francisco, CA: Jossey-Bass.

Mertler, C. A., & Charles, C. M. (2010). *Introduction to educational research* (7th ed.). Boston, MA: Pearson.

Messick, S. (1989). Validity. In R. L. Linn (Ed.), *Educational measurement* (3rd ed., pp. 13–103). New York, NY: Macmillan.

Messick, S. (1996a). Standards-based score interpretation: Establishing valid grounds for valid inferences. In *Proceedings of the joint conference on standard setting for large scale assessments* (Sponsored by National Assessment Governing Board and The National Center for Education Statistics). Washington, DC: Government Printing Office.

Messick, S. (1996b). *Validity of performance assessment*. In G. Philips (Ed.), *Technical issues in large-scale performance assessment* (pp. 1–18). Washington, DC: National Center for Educational Statistics.

Miles, M. B., & Huberman, A. M. (1994). *Qualitative data analysis* (2nd ed.). Thousand Oaks, CA: Sage.

Moss, P. A., Phillips, D. C., Erickson, F. D., Floden, R. E., Lather, P. A., & Scheider, B. L. (2009). Learning from our differences: A dialogue across perspectives on quality in education research. *Educational Researcher, 38*(7), 501–517.

Moustakas, C. (1994). *Phenomenological research methods*. Thousand Oaks, CA: Sage.

Mulaik, S. A. (2009). *Foundations of factor analysis* (2nd ed.). Boca Raton, FL: CRC Press.

Netemeyer, R. G., Bearden, W. O., & Sharma, S. (2003). *Scale development in the social sciences: Issues and applications*. Thousand Oaks, CA: Sage.

Parlett, M., & Hamilton, D. (1976). Evaluation as illumination: A new approach to the study of innovatory programs. In G. Glass (Ed.), *Evaluation studies review annual* (Vol. 1, pp. 140–157). Beverly Hills, CA: Sage.

Polanyi, M. (1958). *Personal knowledge*. New York, NY: Harper & Row.

Privitera, G. J. (2012). *Statistics for the behavioral sciences*. Thousand Oaks, CA: Sage.

Raudenbush, S. W., & Bryk, A. S. (2002). *Hierarchical linear models: Applications and data analysis methods* (2nd ed.). Newbury Park, CA: Sage.

Rea, L. M., & Parker, R. A. (2005). *Designing and conducting survey research: A comprehensive guide* (3rd ed.). San Francisco, CA: Jossey-Bass.

Saldana, J. (2009). *The coding manual for qualitative researchers*. Thousand Oaks, CA: Sage.

Shadish, W. R., Cook, T. D., & Campbell, D. T. (2002). *Experimental and quasi-experimental designs for generalized causal inference*. Boston, MA: Houghton Mifflin.

Shavelson, R. J. (1996). *Statistical reasoning for the behavioral sciences* (3rd ed.). Boston, MA: Allyn & Bacon.

Shavelson, R. J., & Towne, L. (2002). *Scientific research in education*. Washington, DC: National Academies Press.

Springer, K. (2010). *Educational research: A contextual approach*. Hoboken, NJ: Wiley.

Stake, R. E. (1995). *The art of case study research*. Thousand Oaks, CA: Sage.

Stevens, S. S. (1951). Mathematics, measurement and psychophysics. In S. S. Stevens (Ed.), *Handbook of experimental psychology* (pp. 1–49). New York, NY: Wiley.

Stevens, S. S. (1975). *Psychophysics*. New York, NY: Wiley.

Strauss, A. L. (1987). *Qualitative data analysis for social scientists*. Cambridge, England: Cambridge University Press.

Strauss, A. L., & Corbin, J. (1990). *Basics of qualitative research: Grounded theory procedures and techniques* (2nd ed.). Newbury Park, CA: Sage.

Taylor, F. W. (1947). *Scientific management*. New York, NY: Harper & Row.

Thomas, D. R. (2006). A general inductive approach for analyzing qualitative evaluation data, 27(2), 237–246. doi:10.1177/1098214005283748

Thompson, B. (2004). *Exploratory and confirmatory factor analysis: Understanding concepts and applications*. Washington, DC: American Psychological Association.

Tomei, L. A. (2005). *Taxonomy for the technology domain*. Hershey, PA: Information Science.

Tukey, J. (1977). *Exploratory data analysis*. Reading, MA: Addison-Wesley.

van Buuren, S. (2012). *Flexible imputation of missing data*. Boca Raton, FL: Chapman & Hall/CRC Press.

van der Linden, W. J., & Hambleton, R. K. (Eds.). (1997). *Handbook of modern item response theory*. New York, NY: Springer.

Van Kaam, A. (1969). *Existential foundations of psychology*. Pittsburgh, PA: Image Books and Duquesne University Press.

Walkey, F. H., & Welch, G. (2010). *Demystifying factor analysis: How it works and how to use it*. Bloomington, IN: Xlibris.

Wiersma, W., & Jurs, S. (2009). Research design in quantitative research. In *Research methods in education: An introduction*. Boston, MA: Pearson.

Wolcott, H. F. (1988). Ethnographic research in education. In R. M. Jaeger (Ed.), *Complementary methods for research in education* (pp. 187–212). Washington, DC: American Educational Research Association.

Wolcott, H. F. (1994). *Transforming qualitative data*. Thousand Oaks, CA: Sage.

Woolfolk, A. (2011). *Educational psychology* (11th ed.). Boston, MA: Pearson.

Wright, P. V., & Marsden, J. D. (Eds.). (2010). *Handbook of survey research*. Bingley, England: Emerald.

Yin, R. K. (2012). *Case study research: Design and methods* (3rd ed.). Thousand Oaks, CA: Sage.

Yow, V. R. (2005). *Recording oral history*. Walnut Creek, CA: AltaMira Press.

Index

About the Authors

Laura M. O'Dwyer, PhD is an Associate Professor in the Department of Educational Research, Measurement and Evaluation in the Lynch School of Education at Boston College. She teaches quantitative research methods, introductory statistics, hierarchical linear modeling, survey research methods, and experimental design.

James A. Bernauer, EdD is an Associate Professor in the School of Education and Social Sciences at Robert Morris University in Pittsburgh. He teaches qualitative research, educational psychology, and research methods.

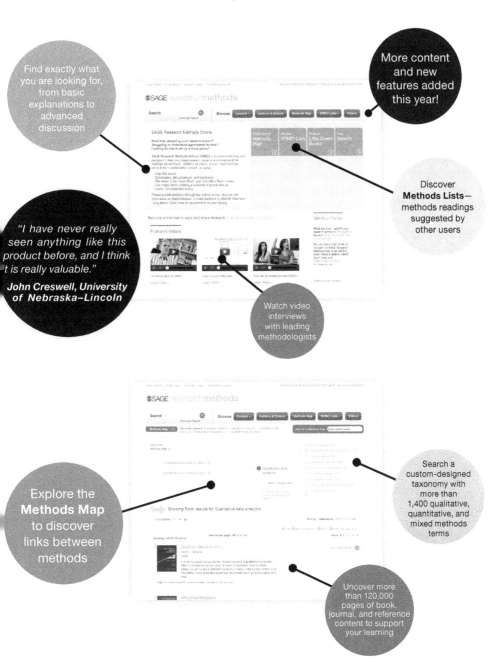

⚛SAGE research**methods**

The essential online tool for researchers from the world's leading methods publisher

Find exactly what you are looking for, from basic explanations to advanced discussion

More content and new features added this year!

Discover Methods Lists— methods readings suggested by other users

"I have never really seen anything like this product before, and I think it is really valuable."
John Creswell, University of Nebraska–Lincoln

Watch video interviews with leading methodologists

Search a custom-designed taxonomy with more than 1,400 qualitative, quantitative, and mixed methods terms

Explore the Methods Map to discover links between methods

Uncover more than 120,000 pages of book, journal, and reference content to support your learning

Find out more at
www.sageresearchmethods.com

Printed in the USA
CPSIA information can be obtained
at www.ICGtesting.com
CBHW061429050524
7985CB00009B/306